The Mary Magdalene Tradition

The Mary Magdalene Tradition

Witness and Counter-Witness in Early Christian Communities

Holly E. Hearon

A Michael Glazier Book

LITURGICAL PRESS
Collegeville, Minnesota

www.litpress.org

A Michael Glazier Book published by the Liturgical Press

Cover design by Ann Blattner. Illustration © The Crosiers/Gene Plaisted, O.S.C.

1 2 3 4 5 6 7 8 9

Library of Congress Control Number: 2004103786

To the memory of

Sarah Ellen Snyder, O.P.

Contents

Acknowledgments

This book is a revision of my doctoral dissertation, completed in 1998 at the Graduate Theological Union, under the direction of Antoinette Clark Wire. While it is substantively the same, significant portions of that document have been reworked and, in some cases, conclusions modified. There are many people to whom I am indebted for their assistance in bringing both the dissertation and this book to conclusion. In particular I am grateful to my dissertation committee for their insights, critical assessment, and unfailing support: Anne Wire, Joel Green, Robert Smith, Polly Coote, and Dan Melia. Linda Maloney also deserves special mention for her encouragement at the outset of my doctoral program, her mentoring during that process, and her continued support as I have sought to transform the dissertation into a readable book. In addition I extend my appreciation to Bill Countryman, Joanna Dewey, Mary Ann Tolbert, Anitra Kolenkow, and Jane Schaberg, each of whom took an interest in my work and helped me to shape the ideas that eventually brought it to fruition. I am grateful to Ron Allen, Marti Steussy, Felicity Kelcourse, and Newell Williams for their timely feedback at significant points in the process. My heartfelt thanks go to Sterling Rainey and Kentner Scott, Jane Grovijahn, Jann Weaver, Ann Winsor, Grete Stenersen, Marna MacKenzie, Glenda Hope, Bob Fletcher, Leigh Hearon, and Mont and Barbara Hearon for being there when it counted most. Finally, my gratitude and thanks to Lorna Shoemaker who has lived every moment of this process with me and willingly taken on every thankless task.

Chapter One

Introduction

> Composing a life involves a continual reimagining of the future and reinterpretation of the past to give meaning to the present, remembering best those events that prefigured what followed, forgetting those that proved to have no meaning within the narrative.[1]

The canonical gospels record eight stories of appearances by the risen Jesus to his followers.[2] In six of these stories Jesus appears to one or more male disciples.[3] In two of the stories he appears to Mary Magdalene: alone in John 20:1-18 and together with Mary, the mother of James and Joseph, in Matt 28:9-10. These stories of the appearances to the women delightfully confound our expectations. They disrupt the male hegemony that dominates the appearance stories and give voice to our

[1] Mary Catherine Bateson, *Composing a Life* (New York: Penguin, 1990) 29–30.

[2] Matt 28:9-10; Matt 28:16-20; Luke 24:13-35; Luke 24:36-53; John 20:1-18; John 20:19-23; John 20:26-29; John 21:1-23. Luke 24:34 refers to an additional appearance to Simon [Peter], although this appearance is never described in the narrative. The appearances recorded in Mark 16:9-20 are thought to be later additions to the text (see discussion of Mark 16:9-11 in Chapter Three).

[3] In some of the stories it is clear that the disciples are male (Matt 28:9-10; John 21:1-23). In the remaining stories the gender of the disciples is not specified and it is possible that women should be numbered among them. However, because the women, if present, play a silent role (i.e., they are never explicitly identified, nor do they speak), most readers tend to assume that the "disciples" consist entirely of men. The issue of gender in relation to the "disciples" in Matthew and John will be taken up in subsequent chapters.

suspicion that at least one woman, Mary Magdalene, figured prominently among the earliest followers of Jesus. For many, these appearance stories have invited questions concerning the historical person of Mary Magdalene and her role as a witness to the resurrection.[4] In this study I propose a different set of questions: who told the stories of the appearances to the women, and why did they tell them? The assumption underlying these questions is that people and communities tell stories for reasons. As Mary Catherine Bateson observes in the quotation at the head of this chapter, stories are told because they "give meaning to the present, remembering best those events that prefigured what followed. . . ."[5] It is the contention of this study that the stories of the post-resurrection appearance to Mary Magdalene were told and recorded because they remembered best those events that prefigured what followed and gave shape to the identities and lives of early Christian communities in distinct and crucial ways.[6]

Previous Studies of the Magdalene Tradition[7]

The roots of this study can be traced to an article published by Martin Hengel in 1963, "Maria Magdalena und die Frauen als Zeugen."[8]

[4] E.g., Susanne Heine, "Eine Person von Rang und Namen: Historische Konturen der Magdalenerin," in Dietrich-Alex Koch, Gerhard Sellin, and Andreas Lindemann, eds., *Jesu Rede von Gott und ihre Nachgeschichte im frühen Christentum* (Gütersloh: Gerd Mohn, 1989) 179–94; Martin Hengel, "Maria Magdalena und die Frauen als Zeugen," in Otto Betz, Martin Hengel, and Peter Schmidt, eds., *Abraham unser Vater: Juden und Christen im Gespräch über die Bibel* (Leiden: Brill, 1963) 243–45; Gerald O'Collins, "Mary Magdalene as Major Witness to Jesus' Resurrection," *TS* 48 (1987) 631–46; Pheme Perkins, "'I Have Seen the Lord' (John 20:18): Women Witnesses to the Resurrection," *Int* 46 (1992) 31–41; Luise Schottroff, "Maria Magdalena und die Frauen am Grabe Jesu," *EvTh* 42 (1983) 3–25; Mary R. Thompson, *Mary of Magdala: Apostle and Leader* (Mahwah, N.J.: Paulist, 1995).

[5] Bateson, *Composing a Life,* 29–30. See also Elizabeth Tonkin, *Narrating our Pasts: The Social Construction of Oral History* (Cambridge: Cambridge University Press, 1992) 12; John Miles Foley, *Traditional Oral Epic* (Berkeley: University of California Press, 1990) 10; Walter Ong, *Interfaces of the Word* (Ithaca, N.Y.: Cornell University Press, 1977) 104.

[6] I acknowledge the expression "Christian communities" as an anachronism since the Jesus movement continued to be embedded in Judaism until at least the end of the first century C.E.

[7] The literature devoted to Mary Magdalene is immense and varied. It can be divided roughly into six categories: (1) "Mary Magdalene, the Penitent Sinner"

(studies that identify Mary Magdalene as the woman who anointed Jesus' feet in Luke 7:36-50, or Mary of Bethany, or both; the most persistent feature of the studies in this category is the description of Mary Magdalene as a former prostitute): see, for example, Pierre de Bérulle, *Elévation sur sainte Madeleine: élévation à Jésus-Christ notre seigneur sur la conduite de son esprit et de sa grâce vers sainte Madeleine, l'une des principales de sa suite, et des plus signalées en sa faveur et en son évangile* (Paris, 1627); Thomas Faucillon, *Sainte Marie-Madeleine et la vie Chrétienne* (Paris: L'année Dominicaine, 1981); André Feuillet, "Les deux onctions faites sur Jésus, et Marie-Madeleine," *RevThom* 75 (1975) 357–94; Henri-Dominique Lacordaire, *Sainte Marie-Madeleine* (Paris: Poussielque-Rusand, 1860); Vincent McNabb, *St Mary Magdalen* (London: Burns Oates and Washbourne, 1942); (2) "Mary Magdalene, Not a Sinner" (studies devoted to refuting those in category 1 by demonstrating that Mary Magdalene is not the woman of Luke 7:36-50 or Mary of Bethany): Augustin Calmet, "Dissertation sur les trois Maries," *Sainte Bible en latin et en français* (Paris, 1726) 13:403–10; Jacques Lefèvre d'Étaples, *De Maria Magdalena et triduo Christi disceptatis* (Paris, 1518); Edith Deen, *All of the Women of the Bible* (New York: Harper, 1955) 200–205; Alicia Craig Faxon, *Women and Jesus* (Philadelphia: United Church Press, 1973); Webb Black Garrision, *Women in the Life of Jesus* (Indianapolis: Bobbs-Merrill, 1962); Peter Ketter, *The Magdalene Question* (Milwaukee: Bruce, 1935); Marie-Joseph Lagrange, "Jésus a-t-il été oint plusiers fois et par plusiers femmes?" *RB* 9 (1912) 504–32; Alfred Marshall, "Case of Mary Magdalene," *EvQ* 28 (1956) 43–45; Elisabeth Moltmann-Wendel, *The Women around Jesus* (London: S.C.M., 1982); Emmanuel Parvez, "Mary Magdalene: Sinner or Saint?" *TBT* 23 (1985) 122–24; Victor Saxer, "Marie-Madeleine dans les évangiles, 'La femme coupée en morceaux'?" *RevThom* 92 (1992) 673–701; Lisa Sergio, *Jesus and Woman* (McLean, Va.: EPM Publications, 1975); Joseph Sickenberger, "Ist die Magdalenen-Frage wirklich unlösbar?" *BZ* 16 (1925) 63–71; Elizabeth Tetlow, *Women and Ministry in the New Testament* (Lanham, Md.: University Press of America, 1985); (3) "The Legend(s) of Mary Magdalene" (studies in which the varied legends and traditions that have arisen in connection with Mary Magdalene are identified, traced, and analyzed): Helen M. Garth, *Saint Mary Magdalene in Mediaeval Literature* (Baltimore: Johns Hopkins Press, 1950); Hans Hansel, *Die Maria-Magdalena-Legende. Eine Quellen-Untersuchung* (Greifswald: Hans Dallmeyer, 1937); Susan Haskins, *Mary Magdalen: Myth and Metaphor* (New York: Harcourt, Brace, 1993); Urban Holzmeister, "Die Magdalenenfrage in der Kirchlichen Überlieferung," *ZKTh* 46 (1922) 402–22, 556–84; Marie-Joseph Lagrange, "Jésus a-t-il été oint plusieurs fois"; Marjorie M. Malvern, *Venus in Sackcloth: the Magdalen's Origins and Metamorphoses* (Carbondale: Southern Illinois University Press, 1975); Victor Saxer, *Le culte de Marie-Madeleine en occident des origines à la fin du Moyen Age*, Cahiers d'archéologie et d'histoire 3 (Paris: Clavreuil, 1959); Jane Schaberg, *The Resurrection of Mary Magdalene* (New York: Continuum, 2002); (4) "Mary Magdalene, Faithful Follower of Jesus" (devotional literature of all types in which Mary Magdalene is held up as a model of faith for believers): Mary Ellen Ashcroft, *The Magdalene Gospel* (New York: Doubleday, 1995); Author of the Way, *St. Mary Magdalene at the Sepulchre: A Retreat for Private Use* (New York: Morehouse-Gorham, 1956); Joseph Grassi and Carolyn Grassi, *Mary Magdalene and the Women in Jesus' Life* (Kansas City: Sheed & Ward, 1986); Rose Sallberg Kam, *Their Stories, Our Stories: Women of the Bible* (New York: Continuum, 1995); Denise Lardner Carmody,

Hengel's article represents an important shift in studies of the Magdalene.[9] Earlier studies tended to do little more than restate what could be

---

Biblical Woman: Contemporary Reflections on Scripture Texts (New York: Crossroad, 1988); Lloyd Moyer, *Holy Rosary of Mary, the Beloved: A Devotional of Mary Magdalene* (Boston: Sophia Press, 1992); Paul Sicard, *Mois de Sainte Marie-Madeleine d'après la Liturgie, les pères de l'Eglise, les Saints, les Docteurs, etc.* (Paris: P. Lethielleux, 1913); Adrienne von Speyr, *Three Women and the Lord* (San Francisco: Ignatius Press, 1986); (5) "Mary Magdalene, Witness to the Resurrection" (studies that attempt to identify the significance of Mary Magdalene for early Christian communities): Richard Atwood, *Mary Magdalene in the New Testament Gospels and Early Tradition* (New York: Peter Lang, 1993); François Bovon, "Le privilège pascal de Marie-Madeleine," *NTS* 30 (1984) 50–62; Lorraine Caza, "Disciple et apôtre à la manière de Marie de Magdala," in Michel Gourgues and Gilles-D. Mailhiot, eds., *L'Altérité, vivre ensemble différents: approches pluridisciplinaires* (Montréal: Bellarmin; Paris: Cerf, 1986) 235–55; Mary Rose D'Angelo, "Reconstructing 'Real' Women in Gospel Literature: The Case of Mary Magdalene, in Ross S. Kraemer and Mary Rose D'Angelo, eds., *Women & Christian Origins* (New York: Oxford University Press, 1999); Esther De Boer, *Mary Magdalene: Beyond the Myth* (Harrisburg: Trinity Press International, 1997); Susanne Heine, "Eine Person von Rang und Namen"; Martin Hengel, "Maria Magdalena und die Frauen als Zeugen"; Gerald O'Collins, "Mary Magdalene as Major Witness to Jesus' Resurrection"; Pheme Perkins, "'I Have Seen the Lord'"; Luise Schottroff, "Maria Magdalena und die Frauen am Grabe Jesu"; Mary R. Thompson, *Mary of Magdala;* and (6) "Romantic Fiction" (novels which invariably return to the theme of "the penitent sinner" accompanied by varying degrees of lurid detail: Marlee Alex, *Mary Magdalene: A Woman Who Showed Her Gratitude* (Grand Rapids: Eerdmans, 1988); Raymond-Léopold Bruckberger, *Mary Magdalene* (New York: Pantheon, 1953); Edward F. Murphy, *The Scarlet Lily* (Milwaukee: Bruce, 1944); Edith Oliver, *Mary Magdalene* (New York: Appelton-Century, 1935); Frank G. Slaughter, *The Galileans: A Novel of Mary Magdalene* (Garden City, N.Y.: Doubleday, 1953); Ellen G. Traylor, *Mary Magdalene* (Wheaton, Ill.: Tyndale House, 1985).

[8] See n. 4 above.

[9] Prior to that year studies on Mary Magdalene had focused on the question of whether Mary Magdalene was the same woman as Mary of Bethany and/or the sinner woman (Luke 7:36-50) who anointed Jesus (categories [1] and [2] in n. 7 above). The possibility that these women might be one and the same began to be discussed as early as the fourth century C.E., when various Church fathers speculated on the relationship of Mary Magdalene to one or the other woman. The matter was settled in the sixth century by Gregory the Great (540–604), when, in a series of homilies on Mary Magdalene, he declared that the three women were, indeed, one (*XL Homilariarum in Evangelia,* II.25 [*MPL* 76:1188–96]). This declaration would not be challenged for another ten centuries. As recently as 1975 arguments were presented in its support (André Feuillet, "Les deux onctions faites sur Jésus," 357–94). It continues to persist within popular literature on Mary Magdalene. For a brief overview of this discussion see Susan Haskins, *Mary Magdalen,* 90–95; Urban Holzmeister, "Die Magdalenenfrage," 204–22, 556–84; Peter Ketter, *The Magdalene Question,* 66–88; Marie-Joseph Lagrange, "Jésus a-t-il été oint plusier fois," 504–32.

observed by reading the text: i.e., Mary Magdalene's name is prominent within the gospel tradition and in two of the gospels she is recorded as the first person to see the resurrected Jesus. Hengel took this same evidence and pushed it a step further by observing that lists of names that appear in Second Testament documents serve a rhetorical function as indicators of status.[10] Those granted the highest esteem or authority are named first. Since Mary Magdalene's name consistently appears first in the lists of women's names, as Peter's does in those of the twelve, Hengel proposed that she, like Peter, held a place of status in early Christian communities.[11] Hengel went on to assert that since Peter's priority was based on the claim that he was the first to see the resurrected Jesus (Luke 24:34; 1 Cor 15:3-7) the priority of Mary Magdalene must be grounded in the same claim (Matt 28:9-10 and John 20:11-18).[12] Hengel attributed the absence of Mary Magdalene from the list of witnesses in 1 Cor 15:3-7 to the influence of Jewish Law on Paul (which Hengel maintained would not recognize the testimony of women in this matter), while associating the lack of an appearance to the women in Luke 24 with the apologetic purposes of the author of that gospel.[13]

What sets Hengel's work apart from earlier studies is his methodology, specifically his attention to the rhetorical strategies employed by the authors of the texts. This is most evident in his investigation of lists of names in the Second Testament and in his discussion of Luke 24. However, he stopped short of examining what interests may have prompted the inclusion of the Magdalene stories in the gospels of Matthew and John. Rather, Hengel took these reports as trace evidence of an historical event.

The next major article to examine the rhetorical function of the Magdalene stories would not appear for over twenty years. During the interim Elisabeth Schüssler Fiorenza, in three separate works, called attention to the challenge presented by the Magdalene tradition to the primacy of the Petrine tradition.[14] She observed that, despite attempts

[10] Hengel, "Maria Magdalena und die Frauen als Zeugen," 248–50.

[11] Ibid. 251, 256.

[12] Ibid. 251. Hengel went on to propose that the various names that appeared with that of Mary Magdalene pointed to a competition existing among groups of women in the early Church for the position of witness to the resurrection (ibid. 248–50). Although the same phenomenon occurs with males, Hengel omits any suggestion of a similar competition among the male followers of Jesus.

[13] Ibid. 246, 251.

[14] Elisabeth Schüssler Fiorenza, "Mary Magdalene: Apostle to the Apostles," *UTS Journal* April (1975) 22–24; "Word, Spirit, and Power: Women in the Early Christian

by some authors to diminish the role of Mary Magdalene, her primacy persisted in the gospels of Matthew and John and was clearly evident in apocryphal writings of the second century.[15] According to Schüssler Fiorenza the tenacity of the Mary Magdalene tradition reflected an ongoing debate over apostolic primacy.[16] In these studies, then, Schüssler Fiorenza continued the trajectory begun by Hengel by proposing that the Magdalene stories reflected a debate within the early Church over status and leadership. Although historical in orientation, her articles point to the rhetorical impact of the stories.

In 1984 François Bovon published his article "Le privilège pascal de Marie-Madeleine." Bovon asserted that since the legitimacy of the Church's ministry derived from the confession that "Jesus is risen," the appearance traditions reflected an ecclesiastical claim to authority and were employed by communities to authenticate leaders.[17] Bovon saw in 1 Cor 15:3-8 a negotiated settlement between two powerful groups—the Jerusalem community, represented by James and Peter, and the emerging Hellenistic communities, represented by Paul—in which each group agreed to recognize the other's leaders.[18] However, this

Communities," in Rosemary R. Ruether and Eleanor McLaughlin, eds., *Women of Spirit* (New York: Simon & Schuster, 1979) 51–56; *In Memory of Her* (New York: Crossroad, 1984) 304–309, 332, 334.

[15] *In Memory of Her,* 309, 332. A 1990 dissertation by Mary Catherine Carson offers an investigation into how the role of the women is diminished as the gospel tradition develops ("And They Said Nothing to Anyone: A Redaction-Critical Study of the Role and Status of Women in the Crucifixion, Burial and Resurrection Stories of the Canonical and Apocryphal Gospels" [Ph.D. diss., University of Newcastle upon Tyne, 1990]).

[16] Gerald O'Collins challenges Schüssler Fiorenza on several points, observing: (1) common exegetical practice distinguishes post-resurrection events by geography (Galilee and Jerusalem) rather than gender; (2) early Church writers are silent about any debate on whether women can serve as apostolic witnesses; (3) Mark 16:9 identifies Mary Magdalene as the first post-resurrection witness, yet in the verses that follow nothing is said of a conflict with Peter ("Mary Magdalene as Major Witness to Jesus' Resurrection," 641). Schüssler Fiorenza responds: (1) systems of classification reflect preconstructed typologies; it is important to examine the construction embedded in the system that classifies the appearances according to geography, yet distinguishes the empty tomb from 1 Corinthians 15 on the basis of gender; (2) O'Collins discredits her argument in part because he ascribes greater authority to the "Fathers" than to extracanonical writings, thereby revealing his rhetorical interests (*Jesus: Miriam's Child, Sophia's Prophet* [New York: Continuum, 1995] 124).

[17] Bovon, "Le privilège pascal de Marie-Madeleine," 51.

[18] Ibid. 52.

settlement was achieved at the expense of other groups, specifically the Johannine group, which, according to Bovon, favored the witness and leadership of Mary Magdalene. Bovon viewed the absence of Mary Magdalene from the list of witnesses in 1 Corinthians 15 as a reflection of the growing dominance of men in the early communities and an increasing hostility toward prophecy, with which women were associated.[19]

This line of argument was continued by Susanne Heine in her article "Eine Person von Rang und Namen: Historische Konturen der Magdalenerin," published in 1989. She asserted that 1 Cor 15:3-8 reflects an attempt by Paul to legitimate his apostolic authority by linking his vision of the risen Jesus with that of Peter and James.[20] Each of these three witnesses, Heine noted, was associated with a specific community. The only witness not so associated is Mary Magdalene (contra Bovon), who, as a result, lacked institutional support when struggles for power and authority erupted in the early Church.[21] Heine suggested that the authority of Mary Magdalene was a spiritual authority, linked to the pneumatic life of early Christian communities. As this pneumatic life was increasingly rejected in favor of institutionalization by the dominant Church the authority of women generally, and Mary Magdalene specifically, also was rejected.[22] Despite the suppression of her role, Heine viewed the tenacity of Mary Magdalene's name within the tradition as a sign of her importance among Jesus' followers.[23]

The most recent article to undertake a specifically rhetorical approach to the post-resurrection narratives is Claudia Setzer's "Excellent Women: Female Witnesses to the Resurrection," published in 1997.[24] Setzer's focus differs from the preceding studies by concentrating on mixed attitudes toward women's roles in the resurrection narratives and the roles of women in each gospel. Noting the presence of Mary Magdalene in all four gospels, her constancy as a witness to the crucifixion and burial, and her role as the first to see the risen Jesus in two of the

[19] Ibid.

[20] Heine, "Eine Person von Rang und Namen" (see n. 4 above), 187.

[21] Ibid. 188.

[22] Ibid. 191.

[23] Ibid. 185, 194. Heine cautions, however (p. 194), that within the written text Mary Magdalene serves a theological-symbolic meaning. The texts cannot be read as a strictly historical record.

[24] Claudia Setzer, "Excellent Women: Female Witnesses to the Resurrection," *JBL* 116 (1997) 259–72.

gospels (as well as the longer ending of Mark), Setzer concludes that the memory of Mary Magdalene and the women was firmly lodged in the tradition of the resurrection and indispensable to certain apologetic concerns.[25] She goes on to note that, despite the tenacity of these traditions, the evangelists underplay the role of the women so that their effectiveness as witnesses is diminished.[26] Observing a tension between how women are portrayed in each gospel and their role in the resurrection narratives, she concludes that the authors of the gospels were not content with the tradition as they had received it. Setzer identifies as possible sources of this tension discomfort both within and without the Christian community with regard to the role of women, and conflict with Jews over the identity of Jesus and the reality of the resurrection.[27]

While Setzer continues the trajectory of studies on the rhetorical function of the Magdalene stories pursued by Hengel, Schüssler Fiorenza, Bovon, and Heine, she turns attention to how the women are portrayed within the gospel narratives. However, in her search for reasons why the authors of the four gospels diminish the role of the women she looks to the general context of the world of antiquity rather than the literary and social setting of each gospel. Setzer also does not explore why the authors of the gospels of Matthew and John might choose to include the post-resurrection appearance to Mary Magdalene in their narratives. Thus Setzer's article opens the way for further exploration.[28]

[25] Ibid. 260–64.

[26] Ibid. 264–68.

[27] Ibid. 269–71.

[28] Two studies published since 1990 attempt to describe the person and role of Mary Magdalene as revealed in the canonical gospels and writings of the second century: Richard Atwood's *Mary Magdalene in the New Testament Gospels and Early Tradition* and Mary R. Thompson's *Mary of Magdala: Apostle and Leader.* These studies by Atwood and Thompson reveal the strengths and weaknesses of a redactional and historical approach. Atwood's redactional study highlights the differences between the gospel narratives but stops short of using these differences as a means to reconstruct the literary and rhetorical strategies of each narrative. Thompson does identify some of the literary strategies employed in each narrative but, because her interest is primarily historical, she is more interested in demonstrating that Mary of Magdala was a disciple and apostle. Both Atwood and Thompson are more successful when it comes to historical criticism. The excursus on the town of Magdala and demon possession by Atwood, and Thompson's overview of women as leaders in the ancient world help to contextualize the Magdalene narratives. However, what is missing in these two studies is an examination of the rhetorical interests that appear to be informing the construction of the Magdalene in each of the gospels.

Aims of This Study

The present study continues the trajectory outlined above by addressing questions surrounding the rhetorical function of the Magdalene post-resurrection stories. However, where previous studies have tended to focus on the function of the stories in relation to the Petrine tradition, pneumatic communities, or the role of women generally in early Christian communities, I will examine the function of the stories in three specific rhetorical contexts: the Gospel of Matthew, the Gospel of John, and the oral storytelling environment that thrived before and simultaneously with the period in which the gospel narratives were put into writing. I have chosen these particular contexts for three reasons: First, I am interested in digging down to the early layers of the Magdalene tradition and examining the potential impact of the tradition on shaping the identity and lives of Christian communities in their formative stages, before the turn of the first century C.E. Second, by examining the Magdalene stories in the literary and historical contexts of the gospels in which they are recorded I hope to uncover some of the specific issues that storytellers sought to engage by the telling of these stories. Third, by examining the Magdalene stories in relation to contexts rather than issues (such as competition with Peter or the role of women) I seek to gain insight into ways in which the Magdalene stories were integral to the narratives of early Christian communities.

I begin in Chapter Two by undertaking a reconstruction of the oral storytelling environment of the ancient world. This chapter establishes the larger context for my study of the Magdalene stories. It is estimated that no more than five to ten percent of the population in the world of antiquity was literate.[29] This figure includes persons who could read but not necessarily write, or who could write well enough to conduct simple business transactions but could not read beyond what they had

[29] Harry Y. Gamble, *Books and Readers in the Early Church* (New Haven: Yale University Press, 1995) 10; William V. Harris, *Ancient Literacy* (Cambridge, Mass.: Harvard University Press, 1989) 272. Richard Horsley believes that estimates of high levels of literacy among Jews are probably inaccurate ("The Oral Communication Environment of Q," in Richard Horsley with Jonathan A. Draper, *Whoever Hears You Hears Me: Prophets, Performance and Tradition in Q* [Harrisburg: Trinity Press International, 1999] 127). Meir Bar-Ilan, in a study that examines various factors related to literacy, concludes that during the first century C.E. the literacy rate for Judea was less than three percent ("Illiteracy in the Land of Israel in the First Century C.E." in Simcha Fishbane and Jack N. Lightstone, with Victor Levin, eds., *Essays in the Social Scientific Study of Judaism and Jewish Society* [Hoboken, N.J.: Ktav, 1992] 55).

written.[30] The vast majority of people functioned in an oral/aural world. These persons would have turned not to a written text to learn of the post-resurrection appearance to Mary Magdalene, but to a neighbor or an elder of the community who had a reputation for telling stories that could speak to the struggles of life while entertaining her audience.[31] In this chapter I describe who told stories to whom, what kind of stories they told and under what circumstances, giving attention to similarities and differences between storytelling in Greco-Roman, Christian, and Jewish settings.

In Chapter Three I consider the origin of the Magdalene post-resurrection stories. While some maintain that the author of the Gospel of Matthew invented the story which was subsequently borrowed from that gospel by the author of John,[32] others maintain that both authors drew on a common oral tradition.[33] Through a close examination of Matt 28:1-10, John 20:1-18, and Mark 16:9-11, I offer support for the origin of the Magdalene stories in oral tradition and for their circulation as oral text within early Christian communities. This circulation would have continued even after the stories were written down.[34] This

[30] Harris, *Ancient Literacy,* 5–7.

[31] Since all manuscripts were handwritten, the production of a literary work such as a gospel would have been expensive and time-consuming (Joanna Dewey, "From Storytelling to Written Text," *BTB* 26 [1996] 73; Harris, *Ancient Literacy,* 194–95). Once it was produced, the number of people who would have had access to or been able to read such a text would have been relatively small (Gamble, *Books and Readers in the Early Church,* 205; Harris, *Ancient Literacy,* 232).

[32] E.g., K. Peter G. Curtis, "Three Points of Contact between Matthew and John in the Burial and Resurrection Narratives," *JThS* 23 (1972) 442; Frans Neirynck, "Les femmes au tombeau: Étude de la redaction Matthéenne (Matt. XXVIII.1-10)," *NTS* 15 (1969) 168–90.

[33] E.g., Peder Borgen, "John and the Synoptics in the Passion Narrative," *NTS* 5 (1958–59) 247; Nils A. Dahl, "The Passion Narrative in Matthew," in Graham Stanton, ed., *The Interpretation of Matthew* (Philadelphia: Fortress, 1995) 46; Percival Gardner-Smith, *Saint John and the Synoptic Gospels* (Cambridge: Cambridge University Press, 1938) viii.

[34] Charles Harold Dodd, "Thirty Years of New Testament Study," *Religion in Life* 47 (1978) 324; John Miles Foley, *Traditional Oral Epic,* 5; Robin Lane Fox, "Literacy and Power in Early Christianity," in Alan K. Bowman and Greg Woolf, eds., *Literacy and Power in the Ancient World* (Cambridge: Cambridge University Press, 1994) 127; Jack Goody, *The Interface between the Written and the Oral* (New York: Cambridge University Press, 1987) 106; Eduard Nielsen, *Oral Tradition Studies in Biblical Theology* (London: S.C.M., 1954) 34–35; Bruce Rosenberg, "The Complexity of Oral Tradition," *Oral Tradition* 2 (1987) 77.

is due in part to the nature of the written documents themselves. An examination of the earliest manuscripts of the Second Testament reveals that these texts were not intended to be read such as we might read a book today. They included no punctuation, and no separation of words, sentences or paragraphs, much less numbers for chapter and verse. Nothing in the construction of the page lent itself to ease of reading, or facilitated its use as a reference.[35] This suggests that these manuscripts were intended to serve primarily as mnemonic aids to assist a speaker.[36] In the ancient world greater value was placed on memory, "the word written in the mind," than on the written text.[37] Thus the gospels, though written, were texts intended to be heard.[38] Each time one of the gospels was recited aloud, bits and pieces would leave the preserve of the written text and begin to circulate as independent oral texts.[39] This occurred as members of the audience recalled some part of the gospel narrative and told it to others. Each time an episode was

[35] Paul J. Achtemeier, "*Omne Verbum Sonat:* The New Testament and the Oral Environment of Late Western Antiquity," *JBL* 109 (1990) 10; Ruth H. Finnegan, *Oral Poetry: Its Nature, Significance, and Social Context* (Cambridge: Cambridge University Press, 1982) 161; William A. Graham, *Beyond the Written Word: Oral Aspects of Scripture in the History of Religion* (Cambridge: Cambridge University Press, 1987) 34; Eduard Nielsen, *Oral Tradition Studies,* 34–35. Walter Ong notes that only in the middle of the second century C.E. do verbatim citations from the synoptic gospels begin to supercede oral forms ("Text as Interpretation: Mark and After," *Semeia* 39 [1987] 18).

[36] Achtemeier, "*Omne Verbum Sonat,*" 10; Mary J. Carruthers, *The Book of Memory: A Study of Memory in Medieval Culture* (Cambridge: Cambridge University Press, 1990) 16.

[37] Plato, *Phaedrus,* 276a.6-10. See also Cicero, *Oratories* 2.ixxxvi, 351–60; Quintilian, *Institutes* 11.24; Papias in Eusebius, *Hist. Eccl.* 3.39.2-4. In addition, David Aune, "Prolegomena to the Study of Oral Tradition in the Hellenistic World," in Henry Wansbrough, ed., *Jesus and the Oral Gospel Tradition* (Sheffield: JSOT Press, 1991) 97; Carruthers, *The Book of Memory,* 9, 16, 83; Graham, *Beyond the Written Word,* 35; Werner Kelber, "Language, Memory, and Sense Perception in the Religious and Technological Culture of Antiquity and the Middle Ages," *Oral Tradition* 10/2 (1995) 47; Walter Ong, *Orality and Literacy* (London: Methuen, 1982) 36.

[38] Achtemeier, "*Omne Verbum Sonat,*" 15; Pieter Botha, "Living Voice and Lifeless Letters: Reserve towards Writing in the Graeco-Roman World," *HTS* 49/4 (1993) 745; Thomas E. Boomershine, "Peter's Denial as Polemic or Confession," *Semeia* 39 (1987) 52; Carruthers, *The Book of Memory,* 170–71; Gamble, *Books and Readers in the Early Church,* 203–205; Graham, *Beyond the Written Word,* 34.

[39] Werner Kelber, "Jesus and Tradition: Words in Time, Words in Space," *Semeia* 65 (1994) 162.

retold it would be modified and adapted as the occasion—and the interests of the teller—warranted.[40] In this way sayings and episodes moved freely from oral tradition to written text, and from written text to oral tradition. Oral and written existed not just side by side, but in a dynamic, interactive relationship.[41]

In Chapter Four I undertake a heuristic task: the re-oralization of the Magdalene post-resurrection stories in a first-century storytelling context. My re-oralization focuses on how the story would be shaped through the intersection of storyteller, audience, and context in performance. This reconstruction demonstrates some of the different rhetorical functions the Magdalene stories could serve in response to different circumstances.[42]

In Chapters Five and Seven I examine how the authors of the gospels of Matthew and John, respectively, have integrated the story of a post-resurrection appearance to Mary Magdalene into their gospel narratives. I consider not only how the Magdalene story fits within the narrative sequence of the gospel, but also how it is employed to develop narrative themes within the gospel. Through this analysis it becomes evident that each author has adapted the Magdalene story for specific and distinctive purposes. I also note how, in each gospel, the Magdalene story comes into tension with other narrative elements. This tension, I propose, offers evidence of historical circumstances which the author of each gospel is attempting to address through the narration of the Magdalene story.

In Chapters Six and Eight I attempt to reconstruct the historical situations the authors of Matthew and John, respectively, are addressing. The author of the Gospel of Matthew, I argue, is responding to emerging conflicts over who has the authority to speak for the risen Jesus within Matthean communities. In contrast, I propose that the author of the Gospel of John is responding to conflicts between emerging leaders and their supporters within Johannine communities. In the course of

[40] Gilbert L. Bartholomew, "Feed My Lambs: John 21:15-19 as Oral Gospel," *Semeia* 39 (1987) 74; Boomershine, "Peter's Denial as Polemic or Confession," 74; Nielsen, *Oral Tradition Studies*, 34–35.

[41] Ibid. See Dodd, "Thirty Years of New Testament Study," 324–25.

[42] My approach differs from traditional form criticism in that I do not attempt to identify a single *Sitz im Leben* for the tradition of the post-resurrection appearance to Mary Magdalene. Instead I assume that the tradition may have been told in a variety of contexts.

each chapter I examine the role of women within the gospels in order to determine the degree to which gender may or may not play a role in the conflict.

Throughout this study my work is informed by three assumptions. First, I assume that the gospels were addressed to particular communities within the early Church.[43] These communities were not necessarily confined to a small geographic region, nor did they necessarily form a self-identified group; rather, their unity was derived from shared interests and experiences as perceived by the author of each gospel.[44] The communities addressed by the gospels, therefore, are specific, not general. Second, I assume that there is a relationship between the world of the text and the historical, cultural, and social context in

[43] The word "communities" is used advisedly. Some prefer the word "group" (Dennis Duling, "'Egalitarian' Ideology, Leadership, and Factional Conflict within the Matthean Group," *BTB* 27 [1997] 125; Anthony Saldarini, *Matthew's Christian-Jewish Community* [Chicago: University of Chicago Press, 1994] 85–86). However, "group" tends to be used in reference to small gatherings of persons who know one another and interact closely (Saldarini, *Matthew's Christian-Jewish Community,* 85). Such a definition is too narrow for what I envision, since it implies persons who live within a small geographic setting. Another option is "audience" (Richard Burridge, "About People, by People, for People: Gospel Genre and Audiences," in Richard Bauckham, ed., *The Gospels for All Christians* [Grand Rapids: Eerdmans, 1998] 115). This proves unsatisfactory for the present study because it is a term that is employed expressly when speaking of performance in relation to oral narrative where "audience" means "a small group of persons who can communicate face-to-face" (George Homans, quoted in Dan Ben-Amos in *Folklore in Context* [New Delhi: South Asian Publishers, 1982] 13; see also Ben-Amos, "Toward a Definition of Folklore in Context," in Américo Paredes and Richard Bauman, eds., *Toward New Perspectives in Folklore* [Austin: University of Texas Press, 1972] 12). Still another option is "readers" (Burridge, "About People, by People, for People," 115). This is unsatisfactory because it focuses on the relationship between the individual and the text and suppresses the potential interaction between multiple readers. For these reasons I have elected to use the term "communities," where communities represent a cluster of persons who share a common sense of identity and common values (Saldarini, *Matthew's Christian-Jewish Community,* 86–87, but without Saldarini's assumption that this includes "supportive, loving contact").

[44] Here I follow the suggestion of Graham Stanton that the gospels address "a loosely linked set of communities over a wide geographical area" ("Revisiting Matthew's Communities," *Society of Biblical Literature Seminar Papers,* ed. Eugene H. Lovering [Atlanta: Scholars Press, 1994] 12). Loveday Alexander describes this in terms of a network model: "a multiplicity of intersecting lines of communication" ("Ancient Book Production and the Gospels," in Bauckham, ed., *The Gospels for All Christians,* 104).

which the text was written and to which the text is responding.[45] Unquestionably this information will be filtered through both the author's and the interpreter's (re)construction of and response to this setting. Nonetheless, it is possible to derive information from the written text about the historical situation of the communities addressed by the text. Finally, I assume that there was no single, uniform experience within the early Church. While the resurrection was a central defining event for the life of the early Church, the reports concerning the resurrection were multiple and varied. These reports not only take on different forms but reflect a variety of interests and concerns.[46] The stories of a post-resurrection appearance to Mary Magdalene represent some of these interests and concerns.

Method

There has been, in recent years, a move toward describing the world of antiquity as a rhetorical culture, as opposed to an oral or written culture.[47] This move is a response to the growing awareness of the interplay between oral and written forms of expression. Since both oral and written communication employ the tools of rhetoric (i.e., forms of social and cultural argumentation), drawing a sharp distinction between them creates a false dichotomy. Proponents of the ascription "rhetorical culture" maintain that it is more profitable to focus on the rhetorical argument of a text than to attempt to distinguish between its oral and written elements.

In this study I both draw on and diverge from this perspective. I draw on it by focusing on the rhetorical argument of the text, whether written or oral. I diverge from it to the degree that I continue to make a

[45] Duling, "'Egalitarian' Ideology, Leadership," 125; Bernard C. Lategan, "Reference: Reception, Redescription, and Reality," in idem and Willem S. Vorster, eds., *Text and Reality* (Atlanta: Scholars, 1985) 75; Elisabeth Schüssler Fiorenza, "Mary of Magdala—Re-membering the Past," in eadem, *But She Said* (Boston: Beacon, 1992) 92–96.

[46] Two studies that examine these differences are Ahn Byung-Mu, "The Transmitters of the Jesus-event," *CTC Bul* (Dec. 1984–April 1985) 26–39; Gregory Riley, *Resurrection Reconsidered: Thomas and John in Controversy* (Minneapolis: Fortress, 1995).

[47] E.g., Vernon K. Robbins, "Progymnastic Rhetorical Composition and Pre-Gospel Traditions: A New Approach," in Camille Focant, ed., *The Synoptic Gospels* (Leuven: University Press, 1993) 113–16.

distinction between oral and written text. This distinction is not so much one of form or function as it is of actualization. When a speaker verbalizes the text of the Gospel of Matthew, for example, small details may change, asides may be introduced, but the ordering of the text will remain the same, as will the overall rhetorical structure of the text. The performance of the text is, effectively, a recitation. This is not necessarily true of oral text. In oral text, critical revisions may be introduced into the narrative or an episode framed in different ways that produce significantly different rhetorical effects. This is because oral text tends to be extemporaneous: a response to a particular situation or an interjection into normal conversation.[48] As A. N. Doane observes, the "paramount difference between written and oral text is that oral text cannot be viewed as a fixed object."[49]

Each kind of text, therefore, oral or written, requires a different methodological approach.[50] In order to gain insight into the rhetorical impact of a written text it is necessary to consider the whole text: i.e., the entire Gospel of Matthew and the entire Gospel of John. The larger text provides a frame that interprets individual episodes. In the case of oral text, the text may be framed by a variety of other episodes at the discretion of the storyteller. This string of episodes will be determined by the intersection of the storyteller, the audience, and the circumstances of the storytelling event. As these elements shift, the rhetorical effect of the oral text will shift. A study that undertakes an examination of both oral and written text, therefore, must employ an eclectic approach. This is the case in the present study. Nonetheless, a unity is provided by my focus, in each case, on the structure of the text, how this structure reveals rhetorical strategies, and the relation of these strategies to historical contexts.

The chapters that focus on oral text (Chapters 2–4) address the following sub-topics, respectively: storytelling, detection of oral text in written manuscripts, and performance. Because each chapter includes

[48] Kenneth E. Bailey, "Informal Controlled Oral Tradition and the Synoptic Gospels," *Asia Journal of Theology* 5 (1991) 34–54; Barbara Kirschenblatt-Gimblett, "A Parable in Context: A Social Interactional Analysis of Storytelling Performance," in Dan Ben-Amos and Kenneth S. Goldstein, eds., *Folklore: Performance and Communication* (The Hague, Netherlands: Mouton, 1975) 105–30.

[49] A. N. Doane, "Oral Texts, Intertexts, and Intratexts," in Jay Clayton and Eric Rothstein, eds., *Influence and Intertextuality in Literary History* (Madison: University of Wisconsin Press, 1991) 78.

[50] Foley, *Traditional Oral Epic*, 5.

a discussion of method, I will provide only a brief overview here. In Chapter Two I reconstruct the storytelling environment of the world of antiquity from references to stories and storytelling in Greco-Roman, Jewish, and Christian texts. This data is supplemented by cross-references to contemporary studies of storytelling in the Middle East and North America. In Chapter Three I draw on the insights of studies in orality and oral text to establish four criteria for identifying traces of oral composition and performance in written texts. The tools of source criticism, redaction criticism, and tradition criticism are employed in measuring the written texts against the four established criteria. In Chapter Four I examine the Magdalene stories in relation to performer, audience, and context, drawing on the tools of performance analysis as described in the work of Richard Bauman, Dan Ben-Amos and Roger Abrahams.[51] An analysis of genre identifies the expectations that would accompany the stories, while a comparative analysis of Greco-Roman, Christian, and Semitic post-death appearance stories assists in identifying which elements in the stories are likely to have remained stable and which elements might be altered and adapted by the storyteller.

In my analysis of written texts (Chapters 5–8) I draw heavily on the work of Vernon K. Robbins, in addition to that of Seymour Chatman and Mark Alan Powell, each of whom focuses on the narrative structure of the text.[52] Employing the tools of socio-rhetorical analysis developed by Robbins, I consider the narrative in relation to repetitive and progressive textures, narrational texture, and argumentative texture.[53] Repetitive texture refers to the pattern of words and phrases that occur more than once in a narrative unit, while progressive texture represents sequences (progressions) of words and phrases throughout the unit.[54] Narrational texture refers to the voices in the text, whether the voice of

[51] Roger D. Abrahams, "Introductory Remarks to a Rhetorical Theory of Folklore," *JAF* 81 (1968) 143–58; Richard Bauman, *Story, Performance, Event* (Cambridge: Cambridge University Press, 1986); Ben-Amos, *Folklore in Context*; Ben-Amos and Goldstein, eds., *Folklore: Performance and Communication*; Paredes and Bauman, eds., *New Perspectives in Folklore.*

[52] Seymour B. Chatman, *Story and Discourse* (Ithaca: Cornell University Press, 1978); Mark Alan Powell, *What is Narrative Criticism?* (Minneapolis: Fortress, 1990); Vernon K. Robbins, *Exploring the Texture of Texts* (Valley Forge, Pa.: Trinity Press International, 1996); idem, *The Tapestry of Early Christian Discourse: Rhetoric, Society, and Ideology* (London: Routledge, 1996).

[53] Although I employ the language of Vernon K. Robbins, in exploring these textures I am informed, as is he, by the work of Chatman and Powell.

[54] Robbins, *Exploring the Texture of Texts,* 8, 9.

a character or of the narrator.[55] Here the rhetoric of the narrative is revealed through events (incidents or happenings), character, setting, and discourse.[56] Argumentative texture examines the inner reasoning within the narrative that may be revealed through causal relationships, logical progressions, comparisons, contrasts, and irony, among other elements of discourse.[57] Analysis of these various textures reveals how the implied author has structured the narrative and offers insight into the overall rhetorical movements within the narrative.[58] In the movement from literary text to historical context I examine rhetorical strategies within the larger context of each gospel, again focusing on patterns of repetition in terms of characterization, and comparisons and contrasts between characters and character groups. In addition, I identify points in the narrative where the text appears to be in tension with itself. On the basis of this analysis I propose social and historical conditions to which the author might have been responding through the narrative.

Context and Commitments

Every text is situated within a particular context, and this study is no exception. I approach this study of the stories of the post-resurrection appearance to Mary Magdalene from within the Church—not only within the Church, but from a position of power and status within the Church: I teach in a theological seminary and am a minister of word and sacrament. From this location I claim the stories for the life of the Church, both past and present, and, most especially, for women who are engaged in all manner of ministry in response to the gospel. While some might place the Magdalene stories at the margins of the tradition, I place them at the center because of my commitment to bringing to light what I believe to be the central and critical role of women in early Christian communities, even as they continued to function within the limitations imposed by the male-centered environment of the first-century world. To the degree that I am able, I use my position of power and status to accomplish this task.

[55] Ibid. 15.

[56] Chatman, *Story and Discourse,* 19; Powell, *What is Narrative Criticism,* 35.

[57] Robbins, *Exploring the Texture of Texts,* 21. See also Powell, *What is Narrative Criticism,* 23–34.

[58] Ibid. 8.

At the same time that I acknowledge my position of power within the Church, I also recognize that I often find myself marginalized on issues of gender equality, theology, and social justice. The Church has never been, for me, a place devoid of conflict. Rather, it is a place of struggle. One of the several reasons the Magdalene stories are of interest to me is because they represent an intersection of gender, power and status, and conflict. I resist attempts to construct histories of the early Church that cover over conflicts and tensions, believing that we may learn more from these conflicts and tensions, and how those within the early Church did or did not address them, than from histories whose harmonious visage is predicated on forced silence.

It is my hope that this study of the Magdalene stories will offer insight into how the Church, past and present, develops, shapes, preserves, and transforms its inherited traditions as it engages in polemics surrounding life and faith. The stories and traditions of the Church are not static. To the contrary, the Church in every age is engaged in a process that requires "continual reimagining of the future and reinterpretation of the past to give meaning to the present, remembering best those events that prefigured what followed. . . ."[59] This study is dedicated to the task of demonstrating how the Magdalene stories represent some of the ways in which the Church has remembered best the events that have prefigured what followed, in order that these stories might continue to offer meaning for the present day and assist the Church in reimagining the future.

[59] Bateson, *Composing a Life,* 29–30.

Chapter Two

Storytelling in the World of Antiquity

Storytelling is the oral rendering of a narrative by one person to another. For a storytelling event to take place all that is required is a storyteller and an audience, gathered together in the same place, and a story.[1] The story may be represented as traditional or new, as the personal experience of the storyteller or someone else, as true or fabulous. It will tend to conform to a formalized pattern of narrative recognizable to the audience. Although storytelling may vary in form and presentation from place to place, it is thought to occur in every culture of the world.

The prevalence of stories in Greco-Roman, Jewish, and Christian literature indicates that storytelling was everywhere present in this corner of the world of antiquity. In a time when oral speech was the primary mode of communication, stories provided a means of passing the time, passing on news, providing entertainment, instilling values and norms of behavior, and legitimating and critiquing the social life of individuals and communities. Storytelling was a form of communication in which everyone participated, either as a storyteller or as a member of the audience.

Ironically, our access to storytelling in the world of antiquity is almost exclusively through literary texts.[2] These "literary remains" of storytelling offer glimpses of storytelling events, render opinions on storytellers, and, of course, tell stories. Yet the remains amount to only a

[1] Dan Ben-Amos, *Folklore in Context* (New Delhi: South Asian Publishers, 1982) 13; Burke O. Long, "Recent Field Studies in Oral Literature and Their Bearing on Old Testament Criticism," *VT* 26 (1976) 189.

[2] There is also some pictorial evidence found on vases.

handful. Authors in the world of antiquity showed little critical interest in who told stories, to whom they were told, and under what circumstances. On the contrary, literary authors tended to view storytellers, and those who listened to their stories, with suspicion.[3] Storytelling, as a topic of discussion, was dismissed rather than explored. Nonetheless, the few references that survive contain a surprising amount of information and from them it is possible to begin reconstructing a picture of storytelling in the Mediterranean world of antiquity. This reconstruction will set the context for the origin and circulation of the Magdalene post-resurrection traditions, taken up in the next chapter.

Method

The sources employed in this reconstructive task include Greco-Roman, Jewish, and Christian texts that date from 100 B.C.E. to 200 C.E.[4] Because these writings vary widely in terms of the amount and kind of information they provide with respect to story and storytelling, a word about each is in order.

Comparatively speaking, Greco-Roman texts offer a wealth of information about storytelling in the world of antiquity. Narrative works such as the romances, Ovid's *Metamorphoses,* and the *Metamorphosis* by Apuleius contain descriptions of storytelling events, while literary discourses such as those by Plato, Quintilian, and Strabo contain passing references to storytellers as well as opinions about storytellers, their stories, and their audiences.[5] Throughout both types of literature are found the remains of oral-derived stories. From these remains it is possible to reconstruct a fairly detailed picture of storytelling in the ancient world.

[3] Plato, *Republic* III.397E; Philostratus, *Life of Apollonius* 5.14; Quintilian, *Institutes* 5.11.19; Strabo, *Geography* 1.2.8. See also Alexander Scobie, "Storytellers, Storytelling, and the Novel in Graeco-Roman Antiquity," *Rheinisches Museum für Philologie* 122 (1979) 236.

[4] I have made one exception to this rule by including Plato, because of the considerable attention he gives to storytelling. Further, his opinions continued to influence authors well into the early centuries C.E., as evidenced by Plutarch, who quotes Plato in support of his own views (Plutarch, *On Educating Children* 5).

[5] The other Greco-Roman texts included in this study are by Achilles Tatius, Apuleius, Chariton, Dio Chrysostom, Longus, Ovid, Philostratus, Plutarch, Quintilian, Strabo, Suetonius, Virgil, and Xenophon.

Literary remains of storytelling in Jewish texts from this period are found primarily in the "deeds of the sages," which are recorded in the Talmud. (See Appendix C.)[6] While the Greco-Roman sources offer specific references to narrators, audiences, and settings, the Jewish sources primarily offer allusions. This is due in large part to the nature of the Talmud. A collection of traditions, it strings together individual stories like pearls on a thread. There is no larger narrative context to suggest a setting, audience, or, in many cases, a storyteller. In a few instances a Rabbi is said to have been noted for having studied all manner of things, including parables and fables, and on several occasions a particular Rabbi is cited as the source of a story.[7] Yet for the most part the "to whom, by whom, and where" must be derived from inferences within the stories themselves. This makes it difficult to gain a comprehensive picture of storytelling within specifically Jewish communities.

The writings of the Second Testament also contain few specific references to storytelling. There is one explicit reference to storytellers in 1 Tim 5:13, where they are described as "gossips" and "busybodies." In addition, the gospels describe a few storytelling events, but for the most part very little is said about who tells stories, to whom, and where.[8] At the same time it is everywhere implied within the narrative worlds of the gospels that stories are being told about the deeds and teachings of Jesus. Since it is obvious that these stories cannot have circulated

[6] The dates of these remains are difficult to determine. The text of the Jerusalem Talmud was edited up until the fourth or fifth century C.E. and the Babylonian Talmud until the eleventh century C.E. However, the narratives recording the deeds of the sages refer to individuals who lived during the first century B.C.E. and first, second, and third centuries C.E. Thus narratives about these individuals may well date from the first centuries of the Common Era (Dan Ben-Amos, "Narrative Forms in the Haggadah: Structural Analysis" [Ph.D. diss., Indiana University, 1967] 6). It is on the strength of this potential that I include the narratives in this study. A problem, of course, arises in depending to such a large degree on the Talmudic writings. However, a review of Jewish narrative texts dating from the first centuries B.C.E./C.E. reveals that while these texts may record oral-derived narratives, they do not describe storytelling events or reflect on the process of storytelling (see, for example, Judith, *Joseph and Aseneth, The Martyrdom and Ascension of Isaiah, The Lives of the Prophets,* and 3 Maccabees). Two references do occur in 4 Macc 16:18-24 and 18:6-19. In addition, a few references appear in the writings of Josephus, but these do little more than confirm that stories about the Jews were in circulation.

[7] *b. Sukk.* 28a; *b. Šabb.* 134a; *y. Soṭah* 1:4, 16b; *b. Taʿan.* 23a; *b. Taʿan.* 25a; *b. Ber.* 48a; *b. Taʿan.* 25b.

[8] The gospels in the New Testament Apocrypha prove even less helpful in this regard.

without the aid of a storyteller and audience, storytelling events may be reconstructed from implied contexts—e.g., when someone acts upon a story she has heard. Similarly, when Paul speaks of hearing reports from various people, or tells a community that their faith has been made known to others, it is implied that stories are being passed along. Nonetheless, as with the Jewish texts, it is difficult to construct from these few references a comprehensive picture of storytelling within specifically Christian communities.

Because of these differences it is difficult to engage in any kind of comparative study between the primary source materials. The Jewish and Christian sources, considered on their own, are inadequate for reconstructing a picture of storytelling in the world of antiquity. Only the Greco-Roman materials provide sufficient information to accomplish this task. Secondarily, the Jewish and Christian sources can be employed to enlarge and particularize this picture. In addition I have found it useful to draw on folkloric studies of storytelling in the Middle East, Turkey, and rural North America. I recognize that such cross-cultural comparisons are fraught with hazards, especially when they involve great distances in time or culture. However, if employed judiciously they can be used to corroborate patterns of storytelling found in the primary source materials. While the studies of storytelling in rural North American communities may seem particularly far removed in time and place, they offer insight into settings where there are strong divisions between the social spheres of men and women. Although these divisions do not necessarily translate from one culture and time to another, certain patterns that appear in both the primary source materials and the folkloric studies suggest that some similarities between the two do exist.

Literary Remains of Storytelling in Greco-Roman Texts

In Greco-Roman texts reference is made to two kinds of storytellers: professional and informal. Professional storytellers inhabit the court of the emperor as well as the marketplace. According to Suetonius, the emperor Augustus employed professional storytellers at his feasts and would call them to his bedside when he had difficulty sleeping.[9] Dio Chrysostom, strolling in the less rarified atmosphere of the Hippo-

[9] Suetonius, *Augustus* 74, 78. See also Scobie, "Storytellers, Storytelling, and the Novel in Graeco-Roman Antiquity," 238–39.

drome, describes storytellers hawking their tales.[10] Among "professional storytellers" may also be included those who were responsible for telling stories as a function of their role within a religious cult.[11]

The primary distinction between professional and informal storytellers was one of remuneration: professional storytellers were paid for the stories they told, while informal storytellers were not. The only "pay" informal storytellers received was recognition of their skill at weaving a tale. Examples of informal storytellers also are found in Greco-Roman literature. A dinner guest is invited to tell a story in the *Metamorphosis* of Apuleius.[12] In Ovid's *Metamorphoses* a group of sisters tell stories to one another to pass the time as they work,[13] while in Xenophon's *An Ephesian Tale* an old woman at an inn offers a story to a drinking party of men.[14]

While one was paid and the other was not, professional and informal storytellers shared, in many cases, the same repertoire of stories.[15] Plato and Plutarch, for example, complain that adults are drawn to worship of the gods because they first heard the stories of these gods in the home when they were children.[16] These stories, then, were told both by those officiating at cultic festivals and by mothers and nurses in the home. Thus many stories were common property and could be told in a variety of settings.[17]

In the context of informal storytelling events anyone could, ostensibly, assume the role of storyteller. A study of storytelling in Middle Eastern villages indicates that in such settings the role of storyteller is fluid, shifting from occasion to occasion depending on who is present. In a mixed group consisting of men, women, and children it will generally fall to older, more gifted male storytellers or socially prominent

[10] Dio Chrysostom, *Orations* 20.10. Pliny the elder opens one of his letters with a story vendor's cry: "Have your copper ready and hear a first-rate tale" (Pliny, *Letters* 2.20.1).

[11] Scobie, "Storytellers, Storytelling, and the Novel in Graeco-Roman Antiquity," 241.

[12] Apuleius, *Metamorphosis* II.22.

[13] Ovid, *Metamorphoses* IV.32-42.

[14] Xenophon, *An Ephesian Tale* 3.9, trans. G. Anderson, in B. P. Reardon, ed., *Collected Ancient Greek Novels* (Berkeley: University of California Press, 1989).

[15] Plato, *Laws* X.887.D; Plutarch, *Theseus* 23.3. See also Scobie, "Storytellers, Storytelling, and the Novel in Graeco-Roman Antiquity," 243.

[16] Plato, *Laws* X.887D; Plutarch, *Theseus* 23.3.

[17] Exceptions would include some of the stories belonging to the mystery religions.

men. Among women and children it will generally fall to more gifted female storytellers or socially prominent women.[18] However, these divisions are not absolute.

Consistent with this study, both men and women are identified as storytellers in the source materials.[19] Both tell stories related to their experiences, the experiences of others, or about the gods.[20] It is only upon examining to whom the stories are told, and where they are told, that we discover evidence of "gender spheres" in storytelling. (See Appendices A and B.) Men are described telling stories to men or to mixed audiences of men and women. Women are described telling stories to women and young children. Men are depicted, most often, telling stories at banquets or while traveling—that is, in the public realm. Women are depicted, most often, telling stories at home—that is, in the private realm. Although this division along gender lines is consistent with the patriarchal social structure characteristic of the ancient Mediterranean world, it is well to keep in mind that the sources present an idealized or, at the least, a stereotypical picture.[21] It is likely that this ideal was compromised in everyday life.

In the Greco-Roman texts women as storytellers typically fall into three groups. (See Appendix A.) The first group consists of mothers and nurses who tell stories to their children. Considerable influence is ascribed to this group, if one may judge by the censure lobbed against them. Because children receive their first instruction from mothers and nurses Plato cautions that "we should do our utmost that the first stories that they [the children] hear should be so composed as to bring the fairest lessons of virtue to their ears."[22] Mothers and nurses also are credited—or discredited—with introducing children, through these stories, to the gods.[23] Thus women played at least an informal role in

[18] Kenneth E. Bailey, "Informal Controlled Oral Tradition and the Synoptic Gospels," *Asia Journal of Theology* 5 (1991) 34–54, at 40.

[19] The references to professional storytellers are not gender specific.

[20] Linda Dégh observes that it is not a preference for certain tales that describes women's folklore, but rather the manner in which the story is told, what is stressed, and what point of view is presented (*Narratives in Society: A Performer-Centered Study of Narration* [Helsinki: Suomalainen Tiedeakatemia, 1995] 69).

[21] Bruce J. Malina, *The New Testament World: Insights from Cultural Anthropology* (rev. ed. Louisville: Westminster John Knox, 1993) 28–62, 117–48.

[22] Plato, *Republic* II.378E. See also Plutarch, *On Educating Children* 5.

[23] Plato, *Laws* X.887D; Plutarch, *Theseus* 23.3. Neither writer considers this a good thing, since they believe that the stories women tell breed superstition rather than rational belief.

the religious instruction of their children. They may also have played a more formal role, since women held offices in some pagan cults.[24]

The second group consists of old women or women past the age of childbearing. The ubiquity of the expression "old wives' tales" points to the belief in the world of antiquity that old women, in particular, had a propensity to tell fabulous stories. However, this distinction did not belong to old women alone. Longus observes that old men also, "when they've had a few drinks . . . talked a lot to each other saying how they used to graze when they were young and how many pirates' raids they had escaped from."[25]

The old women who are depicted telling stories tend to be of dubious character. One serves a band of thieves;[26] another is found at an inn passing time with a drinking party of men;[27] a third is reputed "an old gossip."[28] These women move in circles and behave in ways that would threaten the honor of most women. This freedom is probably due to the women being past the age of menses and thus no longer thought to be in danger of bringing shame through sexual violation. This assertion is supported by studies of storytelling in conservative Muslim societies where, in stories told by men, it is older women who initiate action and serve as intermediaries between the sexes.[29]

A third group is suggested by a passage in Ovid's *Metamorphoses.* This passage describes how "the daughters of Minyas . . . ply their household tasks, spinning wool, thumbing the turning threads, or keep close to the loom, and press their maidens' work. Then one of them, drawing the thread the while with deft thumb, says: '. . . to beguile the tedious hours, let us take turns in telling stories while all the others listen.'"[30] These are young women, not yet married. While mothers tell stories to their children, and old women find their audiences wherever

[24] Ross S. Kraemer, *Her Share of the Blessings* (Oxford: Oxford University Press, 1992) 84.

[25] Longus, *Daphnis and Chloe* 2.32, trans. C. Gill, in B. P. Reardon, ed., *Collected Ancient Greek Novels.*

[26] Apuleius, *Metamorphosis* IV.27.

[27] Xenophon, *An Ephesian Tale* 3.9.

[28] Apuleius, *Metamorphosis* IX.17. See also 1 Tim 5:13.

[29] Margaret Mills, "Sex Role Reversals, Sex Changes, and Transvestite Disguise in the Oral Tradition of a Conservative Muslim in Afghanistan," in Rosan A. Jordan and Susan J. Kalčik, eds., *Women's Folklore, Women's Culture* (Philadelphia: University of Pennsylvania Press, 1985) 195.

[30] Ovid, *Metamorphoses* IV.32-42.

they can, young women entertain one another as they work. These passages reveal that storytelling entered into every phase of women's lives and into every ordinary setting.

The men in Greco-Roman texts are less easily categorized as storytellers. Both old men and young are described telling stories but, in contrast to women, age or marital status has little relationship to the setting or context of the storytelling event. (See Appendix B.) Notably, no men are described telling stories to young children or while they work (with the exception of professional storytellers). The latter may reflect a status bias in the literary remains. The men who tell stories in the Greco-Roman sources do represent a range of types: some are noted citizens, some are tradesmen, some are thieves, and one is a priest.[31] In this respect storytelling appears to be an activity common to all men.

The venue in which men tell their stories is typically a public forum and the stories they tell concern their own adventures or misadventures. If the story is told at a banquet or meal the audience is sometimes mixed, with both men and women present; if it is told while traveling, the audience consists of other men. In both cases the storytelling is often described as reciprocal, that is, with first one and then another individual telling a story.[32] On some occasions this exchange of stories appears to be for the purposes of entertainment or as a demonstration of mutual support. On other occasions it appears to have an agonistic quality to it, in which each storyteller attempts to best the other. Since patterns of challenge and response are characteristic of societies governed by the values of honor and shame, this seems plausible.[33] In addition, studies of contemporary storytelling in rural North American communities indicate that among men successive storytellers engage in informal competitions in which each storyteller attempts to top the one who went before.[34]

[31] Ovid, *Metamorphoses* IV.787, XII.576-579; Apuleius, *Metamorphosis* X.24, IV.9; Achilles Tatius, *Leucippe and Clitophon* 8.15, trans. J. J. Winkler, in B. P. Reardon, ed., *Collected Ancient Greek Novels.*

[32] Achilles Tatius, *Leucippe and Clitophon* 8.15; Longus, *Daphnis and Chloe* 2.32, 3.9; Xenophon, *An Ephesian Tale* 5.1.

[33] Malina, *The New Testament World,* 28–62; Pierre Bourdieu, "The Sentiment of Honour in Kabyle Society," in John G. Peristiany, ed., *Honour and Shame: The Values of Mediterranean Society* (Chicago: University of Chicago Press, 1966) 202–203; Ahmed S. Abou-Zeid, "Honour and Shame among the Bedoins of Egypt," ibid. 258.

[34] Richard Bauman, *Story, Performance and Event: Contextual Studies of Oral Narrative* (Cambridge: Cambridge University Press, 1986) 14; Margaret Yacom, "Woman

Whereas men are frequently described telling stories about their own adventures, women are rarely described as doing so.[35] More often they are shown telling stories about the gods, or love stories, or "gossiping" about other people (although the baker in Apuleius' *Metamorphosis* [X.34] provides at least one example of a male gossip).[36] The absence of women's stories about their own lives is noteworthy. It is possible that it was not considered appropriate for women, "the embodiment of shame," to publish their lives in this public fashion.[37] Yet recent studies in women's folklore indicate that personal narrative is a significant component in women's storytelling.[38] Since this sharing of personal narrative tends to occur only in the company of other women it seems likely that women told stories about their own lives more often than is indicated in these texts written by men. These studies in contemporary folklore further reveal that when women engage in storytelling events where the focus is on personal narratives, rather than try to top one another (as the men do), the women use the stories to form a supportive bond with one another.[39] In the agonistic setting of the Mediterranean world such bonding was probably reserved for members of the same kin, or fictive-kin, group. In gatherings across kin groups storytelling

to Woman: Fieldwork and the Private Sphere," in Jordan and Kalčik, eds., *Women's Folklore, Women's Culture,* 47.

[35] I found only four examples of women telling a "personal narrative" (Achilles Tatius, *Leucippe and Clitophon* 8.15; Ovid, *Metamorphoses* IX.325-391; XIII.738-898). In each case the storytellers are in the company of other women. One possible exception is found in Ovid, *Metamorphoses,* XIV.130-154. Here a sibyl tells a man a story of how she was denied eternal life because she spurned Phoebus' love.

[36] Men also tell love stories and stories about the gods, but in proportionately far fewer numbers.

[37] Julian Pitt-River, "Honour and Social Status," in Peristiany, ed., *Honour and Shame,* 43–45; John K. Campbell, "Honour and the Devil," ibid. 146.

[38] Dégh, *Narratives in Society,* 66; Susan Kalčik, ". . . like Ann's gynecologist or the time I was almost raped," in Claire R. Farrer, ed., *Women and Folklore* (Austin: University of Texas Press, 1975) 8; Yacom, "Woman to Woman: Fieldwork and the Private Sphere," 47. A study by Langellier and Peterson notes that when sharing personal narratives women will often place themselves in a minor or prototypical role in order to deflect focus from themselves (Kristin M. Langellier and Eric E. Peterson, "Spinstorying: An Analysis of Women's Storytelling," in Elizabeth C. Fine and Jean Haskell Speer, eds., *Performance, Culture and Identity* (Westport, Conn.: Praeger, 1992) 157–79.

[39] Kalčik, ". . . like Ann's gynecologist or the time I was almost raped," 8; Yacom, "Woman to Woman: Fieldwork and the Private Sphere," 49–50.

may have taken on an agonistic quality, with the women of one kin group attempting to "best" those of another kin group.

Contemporary folkloric studies may provide an additional insight into the differences between stories told by men and women. These studies observe that the difference is not in the stories themselves but in how the stories are told. Specifically, stories told by women stress the woman's point of view.[40] This can be demonstrated in the handful of samples drawn from Greco-Roman texts. For example, in Ovid's *Metamorphoses* each daughter of Minyas tells a story that revolves around the thoughts and actions of the female characters. (See Appendix A.)[41] In contrast, when the story told by a man is included in the Greco-Roman texts the story revolves around a male character—often the storyteller himself. (See Appendix B.) This is not to suggest that men never tell stories in which a woman is a primary character. Rather, when they do so, the story will be narrated in such a way that the perspective of the man dominates.[42] This is the case, for example, in Xenophon's *An Ephesian Tale* (5.1), where Aegialeus tells a story about his deceased lover, and in Ovid's *Metamorphoses* (XIII.635-674), where Anius tells how his daughters were turned into doves by Bacchus. Nonetheless, contemporary studies of oral narrative observe that the number of stories told by men that feature main characters who are female will be, overall, significantly fewer than those told by women.[43] Among the thirty-one stories told by men that I collected, women play a central role in two stories, while in the stories told by women, women are the focus of each story. (See Appendices A and B.)

The women described in the Greco-Roman texts tend to represent either an ideal type or, in the case of old women, the stereotypical. According to the ideal type, women tell stories only to other women and within the private sphere of the home. According to the stereotypical,

[40] Dégh, *Narratives in Society*, 69, 151; Rosan A. Jordan, "The Vaginal Serpent and Other Themes from Mexican-American Women's Lore," in Jordan and Kalčik, eds., *Women's Folklore, Women's Culture*, 33; Janet L. Langlois, "Belle Gunness, the Lady Bluebeard: Narrative Use of a Deviant Woman," ibid. 113–14.

[41] Ovid, *Metamorphoses* IV.32-167, IV.168-273, 274-388. See also IX.285-325; X.559-736; Apuleius, *Metamorphosis* IV.27–VI.24; Xenophon, *An Ephesian Tale* 3.9. Since these texts are authored by men it is possible that the stories are told as men envisioned a woman would tell them. However, this does not necessarily mean that the depiction is inaccurate, although it may be stereotypical.

[42] Langlois, "Belle Gunness, the Lady Bluebeard," 113–14.

[43] Mills, "Sex Role Reversals, Sex Changes, and Transvestite Disguise," 187.

the stories they relate are fantastical and do more to breed superstition than character. There are at least three notable exceptions that deserve mention.

One is the heroine Leucippe in Achilles Tatius' novel *Leucippe and Clitophon*. She, her father, and her beloved have been given shelter by a priest in the temple. Each evening, while dining, they share stories with one another and at one point Leucippe is encouraged to relate her adventures.[44] It is worth noting that she does not initiate the story herself but, once invited, she does not hold back or demur. Here, then, is at least one example of a woman telling a personal narrative to a mixed audience. However, the setting is an intimate one, among men with whom she has a specific relationship (father, beloved, priest/protector), and the storytelling event takes place in what has become, at least temporarily, home for the heroine and those with her. Thus Leucippe is speaking within the private realm, not the public. To this degree she does not violate the protocol established for the behavior of men and women.[45]

Another exception is found in *Daphnis and Chloe* by Longus. Here a similar storytelling event is described in which a mother, father, daughter, and her beloved tell stories to one another over the evening meal at home.[46] Again the women have a specific relationship to the men present and the setting is a private rather than a public one. These two examples indicate that within an intimate setting, where a known relationship existed between the men and women, women did tell stories to mixed audiences. This is consistent with a contemporary folkloric study by K. Baldwin in which she observes that in private settings of this sort men and women often collaborate in the telling of stories, with the women framing and correcting the men's tales.[47] Yacom, in a study of the relationship between women and the "private sphere," suggests that the "private sphere" is not necessarily defined by location. Rather

[44] Achilles Tatius, *Leucippe and Clitophon* 8.15.

[45] Kathleen Corley in *Private Women, Public Meals* ([Peabody, Mass.: Hendrickson, 1993] 31) observes that primary texts indicate that during the Greco-Roman period it became more common for Roman women to participate in private meals with their husbands and to attend public banquets. Unmarried daughters also may have been present at private meals. See also Carolyn Osiek and David Balch, *Families in the New Testament World* (Louisville: Westminster John Knox, 1997) 59–60.

[46] Longus, *Daphnis and Chloe* 3.9.

[47] Karen Baldwin, "Woof! A Word on Women's Roles in Family Storytelling," in Jordan and Kalčik, eds., *Women's Folklore, Women's Culture,* 155.

it may be a created sphere, such as the one formed when women gather together in a group.[48] It also includes those spheres that are under women's control.[49] In the world of antiquity this would have included the communal living quarters, sleeping quarters, and those areas devoted to the preparation of food. The latter may have included space shared by several families.[50] Hence our definition of "private space" should not be restricted to specific locations, but expanded to include spheres created by a gathering of women or members of a kinship group.

A third exception is found in the tale of an old woman at an inn in Xenophon's *An Ephesian Tale.* The obvious question is: what is this woman doing at an inn? One possibility is that she is a prostitute or, since she is an old woman, that she has prostitutes in her employ for whom she is soliciting business. Another possibility is that she is a barmaid.[51] It also is possible that she is the owner of the inn.[52] In any of these occupations she would have had considerable contact with men and, as the narrative shows, it is likely that stories would have passed between them. The old woman in *An Ephesian Tale* challenges another stereotype since the story she relates is not only true, but critical for the resolution of the central drama.[53]

Other examples exist of women being employed in occupations that would place them in frequent contact with men: There is a slave girl, Thermuthian, who is apprenticed to a man in order to learn the weaver's trade,[54] Valeria Maxima, who owns a farm,[55] Aurelius Nais, a

[48] Yacom, "Woman to Woman: Fieldwork and the Private Sphere," 48.

[49] Ibid. Carolyn Osiek and David Balch caution against describing men's and women's spheres in the world of antiquity in terms of an absolute spatial division (*Families in the New Testament World*, 10).

[50] Ramsay MacMullen, *Roman Social Relations, 50 B.C. to A.D. 284* (New Haven: Yale University Press, 1974) 16.

[51] *CIL* XIV.3709 (= *ILS* 7477.L), cited in Mary R. Lefkowitz and Maureen B. Fant, eds., *Women's Life in Greece and Rome* (Baltimore: Johns Hopkins University Press, 1992) 220.

[52] *Constantius*, cited in Lefkowitz and Fant, *Women's Life in Greece and Rome*, 117; See also *m. Yebam.* 16.7 and *m. Dem.* 3.5.

[53] Xenophon, *An Ephesian Tale* 3.9.

[54] Oxyrhynchus papyrus 1647.G, cited in Lefkowitz and Fant, *Women's Life in Greece and Rome*, 208.

[55] *CIL* VI.3482 (= *ILS* 7459.L), cited in Lefkowitz and Fant, *Women's Life in Greece and Rome*, 209.

fishmonger,[56] and Abudia Megiste, a "dealer in grains and vegetables from the middle staircase."[57] In addition, female slaves served as messengers between men and women. Moreover, those who did not belong to the infrastructure of society but lived on the margins as beggars and squatters would not have been in a position to maintain the social boundaries that prescribed separate space for men and women. Thus it seems likely that some degree of social interchange, including storytelling, did occur between men and women who came into regular contact in the public sphere.[58]

This brief picture of storytelling drawn from Greco-Roman texts of the first centuries B.C.E./C.E. highlights the extent to which storytelling occupied the lives of people in the world of antiquity. Storytelling was not an activity limited to certain individuals but was engaged in by

[56] *CIL* VI.9801 (= *ILS* 7500), cited in Lefkowitz and Fant, *Women's Life in Greece and Rome*, 223.

[57] *CIL* VI.9683 (= *ILS* 7488), cited in Lefkowitz and Fant, *Women's Life in Greece and Rome*, 224.

[58] Joanna Dewey, "From Storytelling to Written Text," *BTB* 26 (1996) 73; Osiek and Balch, *Families in the New Testament World*, 27–28. It is possible that the interaction between men and women may have been influenced by whether the setting was urban or rural. In the small rural villages of the world of antiquity, where everyone would not only know everyone else but would likely be related by marriage, it seems probable that the line between private and public space would have been less clearly defined. Tony Horwitz (in *Baghdad without a Map* [New York: Penguin, 1992] 33) records his astonishment while traveling in North Yemen at observing how many of the women walked around the villages unveiled. He was told that the village is not like the city; here everyone knows everyone else so there is no need for the women to hide. Yet the studies of public and private space cited above all focus on rural environments, suggesting that the public nature of rural life was somewhat constrained by conservative attitudes and behaviors. In contrast, urban environments tend to be less bound by the conservative attitudes and behaviors associated with rural environments. However, it is the wealthy who most enjoy the benefit of the more open atmosphere. Riet Van Bremen suggests that wealthy women moved into the public realm as a means of distinguishing themselves from less-well-off women (Van Bremen, "Women and Wealth," in Averil Cameron and Amélie Kuhrt, eds., *Images of Women in Antiquity* [Detroit: Wayne State University Press, 1993] 236). For other women the foray into the public realm of the urban world would have been necessary for economic survival. In antiquity these women would have constituted the majority. Thus it is difficult to determine the extent to which a differentiation should be made between storytelling in urban and rural environments. No clear distinction can be drawn on the basis of the primary source materials cited and a thorough investigation goes beyond the scope of this study.

young and old, men and women, cultic leaders, professional entertainers, and the public at large. To a certain degree storytelling occurred within gender-specific spheres. Women were more likely to tell stories to other women. However, older women, as well as women who enjoyed status within the local community, may have had more freedom in this regard. The evidence indicates that gender spheres, while operative, were not absolute.

The settings in which storytelling events are described as taking place represent the scope of human activity: over meals, at work, within households, at inns, while traveling.[59] Indeed, this survey supports the view that it is dubious to search for an original *Sitz im Leben* for individual stories. Rather, any one story could be told in a plurality of settings.[60] The defining parameter for a storytelling event appears to have been a small group drawn together by circumstance, either formal or informal, and/or relationship.

Literary Remains of Storytelling in Jewish Texts

The literary remains of storytelling in Jewish texts offer more examples of stories than do Greco-Roman texts, but less evidence of who told the stories, to whom, and where. In most instances a story will begin with an indirect statement such as "a story is told," or "it is said." These statements suggest that the stories were common property and circulated freely. One particular story offers a glimpse of how stories passed from one person to another. The story concludes: "Pelimo said: 'I saw that house and its beams projected about a cubit on each side'; and I was told: 'This is the house that through his prayer, R. Hanina ben Dosa framed with beams.'"[61] Here two storytellers are identified: Pelimo and the individual who told the story to Pelimo. Pelimo does not identify his source, but simply states, "I was told." This same passive construction is found in many of the stories.

Who, specifically, told stories to whom is difficult to say. One story, however, serves as a particularly rich source because it identifies not only the narrator but the audience and setting as well. In this story,

[59] So also Ben-Amos, "Narrative Forms in the Haggadah," 26–29.

[60] Long, "Recent Field Studies in Oral Literature and their Bearing on Old Testament Criticism," 255.

[61] *b. Taʿan.* 25a.

R. Simeon ben Shetach is said to have entertained the court of King Yannai with words of wisdom during banquets.[62] Among those present at the banquet is the Queen of King Yannai. Thus at least one example exists of a man addressing a mixed audience during a meal, although the woman is the wife of the host and a person of considerable status in her own right.[63]

By observing the interaction between characters in other stories it is possible to conjecture that storytelling occurred between husband and wife,[64] father and child,[65] mother and child,[66] neighbors,[67] rabbis and their students.[68] This would be consistent with the pattern of storytelling suggested by the Greco-Roman texts, with two exceptions: the interaction between father and child and between rabbis and their students. The latter is distinctive to Jewish communities; the former may be characteristic of both, although evidence for such an exchange is found in only one text.[69] Even in societies that are divided into distinct gender spheres, recent folkloric studies show that in rural communities women identify male relatives as sources for their stories.[70] Thus it seems likely that fathers, in addition to mothers, told stories to both male and female children.

In a very few texts interaction is recorded between men and women who are not related, but who appear to be known to each other.[71] Whether or not these individuals would have engaged in telling stories to one another is difficult to determine. However, there is evidence that Jewish women, too, were not always confined to the private sphere but were employed as shopkeepers and innkeepers, or acted on their own

[62] *b. Ber.* 48a (= *y. Ber.* 7:2, 11b).

[63] Sirach 9:9 also indicates that men did encounter women at banquets; men and women also dined together in the community called the *Therapeutae* (Corley, *Private Women, Public Meals*, 70).

[64] *b. Ber.* 27a-28a; *y. Giṭ.* 1:2, 43c; *y. Šabb.* 6:1, 4d; *y. Soṭah* 1:4, 16b; *b. Taʿan.* 23a-b; *b. Taʿan.* 24b-25a; *b. Taʿan.* 25a.

[65] *b. Pesaḥ.* 112a; *b. Sanh.* 24b; *b. Taʿan.* 25a; *b. Yebam.* 121b; 4 Macc 18:6-19.

[66] 4 Macc 16:18-24; 18:6-19.

[67] *b. Ber.* 33a; *y. Peʾah* 1:1, 15c; *b. Taʿan.* 25a; *b. Yebam.* 121b.

[68] *b. B. Batra* 133a-134b; *b. Bek.* 36a; *b. Ber.* 28b; *b. ʿErub.* 64b; *b. Ḥag.* 14b; *b. Hor.* 10a-b; *b. Ned.* 5:7, 39b; *b. Pesaḥ.* 72b-73a; *b. Qidd.* 32b; *b. Sanh.* 24b.

[69] Longus, *Daphnis and Chloe* 3.9.

[70] Dégh, *Narratives in Society*, 67.

[71] *y. Peʾah* 1:1, 15c; *y. Soṭah* 1:4, 16b; *b. Taʿan.* 25a.

behalf in transacting business.[72] This seems to suggest a storytelling environment similar to that represented in the Greco-Roman texts.[73]

While none of the Jewish literary remains specifically identify women as storytellers, this is of indeterminate significance since the storyteller is rarely identified in any of the texts. It may as readily be observed that few examples of men as storytellers are found. There are a number of stories in which women not only play a major role but are held up as exemplary.[74] It is possible that these were stories told by women, based on the evidence cited earlier in the discussion of storytelling in Greco-Roman texts.[75]

It also is possible that women told stories in their capacity as religious leaders within the community. Although rabbinical texts offer no evidence that women served as religious leaders, epigraphic remains do.[76] Bernadette Brooten suggests that women who served as *archisynagogoi* were responsible for the spiritual direction of the synagogue's congregation.[77] It is possible that in this capacity they may also have engaged in storytelling as they carried out this role. While their audience, on some occasions, may have consisted solely of women, it cannot be assumed that this was always the case.[78] With respect to storytelling in general, the role of these women in the synagogue would have given them a position of status within the local community. As a result they would likely be deferred to in an informal setting where storytelling took place.

[72] Tal Ilan, *Jewish Women in Greco-Roman Palestine* (Peabody, Mass.: Hendrickson, 1995) 184–90; Jewish women may also be included among the women mentioned in the Greco-Roman inscriptions, but unless they are specifically identified as Jewish it is impossible to know.

[73] It is recognized that the degree to which women interacted with men would have varied from community to community. Judith Wegner demonstrates that the world described by the rabbis in the Talmud significantly restricts the activity of women (Judith Romney Wegner, *Chattel or Person? The Status of Women in the Mishnah* [Oxford: Oxford University Press, 1988]).

[74] *b. Ḥag* 15b; *b. Ned.* 50a; *y. Šabb.* 6:1, 4d; *y. Soṭah* 1:4, 16b; *b. Taʿan.* 24b-25a.

[75] On this basis female authorship has been proposed for *The Conversion and Marriage of Aseneth* (Kraemer, *Her Share of the Blessings*, 112).

[76] Bernadette J. Brooten, *Women Leaders in the Ancient Synagogue* (Atlanta: Scholars, 1982) 28.

[77] Ibid.

[78] Ibid. 32.

The settings in which stories were told are rarely specified in these texts. However, the settings in which the action of each story takes place suggests settings similar to those identified in the Greco-Roman texts: the home,[79] banquets,[80] and journeys.[81] Three additional settings are identified in the Jewish texts that are not named in the Greco-Roman texts: the synagogue, the house of study, and an upper room.[82] All three settings are specifically associated with the rabbis. Although women are never identified as present in a house of study or an upper room, they are in the synagogue.[83] Thus the rabbis, at least on some occasions, addressed mixed audiences.

This brief overview of storytelling drawn from Jewish literary remains highlights the degree to which the pattern of storytelling in Jewish communities seems, in many ways, to have conformed to that described by Greco-Roman texts. Nonetheless, one aspect of storytelling in Jewish communities is distinctive. This is the extent to which the narratives reflect the concerns and interests of the Jewish community. (See Appendix C.) These are not stories that would interest people outside. They involve individuals, events, and occasions that belong to the Jewish community. Even when the stories involve persons going on a journey, they do not travel to exotic places, but to other Jewish communities. Nor do they encounter strangers on their journeys; they travel with persons who are known to them.[84] When outsiders do appear in the stories they are a foil and serve to highlight the wisdom of the Jews.[85] This is not to say that stories about the larger Greco-Roman world were never told among Jews, but it does demonstrate that subgroups within the Roman empire possessed distinctive stories told by and about them. The Gentiles of the empire, in turn, had their own set of stories they told about the Jews. It is precisely this that concerns Josephus. He criticizes those who, in attempting to recount the history

[79] *b. ʿErub.* 64b; *b. Ḥag.* 14b; *b. Hor.* 10a-b; *b. Ber.* 16a-b; *b. Ber.* 28b; *b. Ned.* 5:7, 39b; *y. Peʾah* 1:1, 15c; *b. Sanh.* 101a-b; *y. Soṭah* 1:4, 16d; *b. Taʿan.* 24b-25a.

[80] *b. Ber.* 48a; (= *y. Ber.* 7:2, 11b). *b. Qidd.* 32a; *b. Sanh.* 11a.

[81] *b. ʿErub.* 64b; *b. Ḥag.* 14b; *b. Hor.* 10a-b.

[82] *y. Soṭah* 1:4, 16b; *b. Bek.* 36a; *b. Sukk.* 28a; *b. Yebam.* 121b; *b. Yoma* 35b; *b. Sanh.* 11a.

[83] *y. Soṭah* 1:4, 16b. See also Ben-Amos, "Narrative Forms in the Haggadah," 27; Brooten, *Women Leaders in the Ancient Synagogue*, 139–41.

[84] An exception is recorded in *b. ʿErub.* 64b where R. Gamaliel and R. Ilai meet a Gentile. However, the force of this encounter is to reinforce the boundary between Jews and Gentiles; it does not abrogate it.

[85] *b. Ḥul.* 60a; *b. Ned.* 50b; *b. Taʾan.* 7a-b; *b. Yoma* 66b (= *y. Soṭah* 3:4).

of the Jews, draw on what he calls fictions and unauthenticated legends.[86] Folklorists describe this phenomenon as the esoteric factor in storytelling: i.e., "what one group thinks about itself and what it supposes others think of it."[87] The esoteric quality of the Jewish stories is evidence of their function in establishing and defending a sense of group identity.[88] This use of story would be particularly important for a group that experienced isolation within the dominant culture due to a distinctive set of customs and beliefs, as the Jews did within the Greco-Roman world.[89]

Literary Remains of Storytelling in Christian Texts

The texts of the Second Testament, like the Jewish texts, offer only a faint outline of storytelling in the world of antiquity. (See Appendix D.) In these texts the storytellers are mostly unknown. However, the numbers of people who are said to seek out Jesus suggest that stories about his powers as a healer and teacher are circulating freely at all levels of society. Not only do outcasts seek him—lepers, tax collectors, the demon-possessed—but also rulers and religious leaders.[90] Sometimes the same individuals who have sought out Jesus because of the stories they have heard become storytellers themselves as they report on their encounter with Jesus.[91]

A glimpse of how these stories circulated may be gleaned from a narrative recorded in the Gospel of John 1:40-46. Here Andrew has been introduced to Jesus by John the Baptist. Andrew, in turn, goes and tells his brother Simon. The next day Jesus encounters Philip who is from the same village as Simon and Andrew. (One wonders whether Philip has heard about Jesus from them.) Philip then goes and finds Nathaniel (also, perhaps, from the same village) and introduces him to Jesus. This passage is illuminating because it illustrates how stories were passed

[86] Josephus, *Antiquities* 16. 349; *Against Apion* 1.229; 1.304; 3.420.

[87] W. Jansen, "The Esoteric-Exoteric Factor in Folklore," in Alan Dundes, ed., *The Study of Folklore* (Englewood Cliffs, N.J.: Prentice-Hall, 1965) 46.

[88] Ibid. James Scott describes a similar phenomenon from a sociological perspective (*Domination and the Arts of Resistance* [New Haven: Yale University Press, 1990] 160–62).

[89] Jansen, "The Esoteric-Exoteric Factor in Folklore," 47, 49; Scott, *Domination and the Arts of Resistance,* xi.

[90] Mark 1:40; 2:15; 5:22; 6:14; Matt 9:32; 22:34; John 3:1-2.

[91] Mark 1:45; John 4:39; 5:10-15; 9:1-34.

from one person to another and also suggests the social web a story might travel: first from relative to relative, then to someone from the same region or town, who tells it to a relative or acquaintance or even a tradesman from yet another town.

The audiences suggested by these texts highlight the degree to which storytelling belongs to the local community: People gathered in a synagogue in Jesus' home town compare stories about him (Mark 6:2-3); neighbors and kinsfolk of Elizabeth and Zechariah wonder at the stories they hear about the birth of John (Luke 1:65); the Samaritan woman amazes the people of her village with the story of her encounter with Jesus (John 4:39); two followers of Jesus share stories about his last days (Luke 24:13-14). These are people who live in close proximity to one another, who meet on a day-to-day basis, and who are familiar with the intimate details of each other's lives. Storytelling is not reserved for particular times and places, although particular stories may be; it is the thread that weaves together the individuals of a community into a whole cloth.

In these texts both men and women tell stories. Since the audiences are often simply described as a crowd, it is difficult to discern the degree to which gender spheres are determinative of storyteller and audience. However, a number of stories feature women in prominent roles, suggesting that women were active storytellers.[92] While the author of 1 Tim 5:13 describes women going from house to house to tell their stories to other women, there are at least two examples of a woman addressing an audience inclusive of men: the Samaritan woman in John 4, through whom many come to believe in Jesus, and the women who tell the disciples what they have seen at the tomb in Matthew 28, Luke 24, and John 20.[93] The first example probably represents a rural town setting, the second a setting in which the women are related by voluntary association to the men.

Women also form an audience alongside men. In Luke 10:38-42 Mary and Martha host a meal at which Mary insinuates herself into the audience addressed by Jesus.[94] The complaint here is not that Mary is mingling with the men, but that she is neglecting her domestic duties.

[92] See especially Mark 5:25-34; 7:24-30; 14:3-9 (and parallel texts in Matthew and Luke); Luke 10:38-42; John 4:7-42.

[93] The line between "telling stories" and "telling the news" may, at times, be so thin as to be imperceptible. The distinction will more likely be in form than in content.

[94] The audience is implied in the text rather than explicit. One could conclude that the audience was composed entirely of women.

A parallel version found in John 12:1-8 has Mary anointing Jesus' feet. Again the complaint is not over her presence at the table but over her action. Since women participated in synagogue gatherings, it is fair to assume that women were among those listening to Jesus in Mark 6:2-3 (*parr.* Matt 13:54-56; Luke 4:22). These few examples suggest a picture similar to that described by the Greco-Roman texts in which there is some division along gender lines, but these lines are not absolute.

In the Greco-Roman texts two situations presented themselves in which women were more likely to address a mixed audience. One was indicated by women's employment in the public sphere. The Second Testament contains several examples of women who would have had occasion to conduct business in public: Lydia, who is described as a seller of purple (Acts 16:14), Prisca, who is said to be a tentmaker (Acts 18:2-3), and Mary and Martha, who appear to be householders (Luke 10:38-42; see also Col 4:15), as is Chloe (1 Cor 1:11). In addition there are the women who follow Jesus and his disciples in Galilee and are said to support them from their own means (Luke 8:2-3). In order for them to have done so, these women must either have been in trade or possessed independent wealth. All these women would have interacted with both men and women and engaged in the storytelling that seems to have been characteristic of social interaction in the world of antiquity.

The second situation in which women tell stories to a mixed audience arises when women are in the company of men with whom they have a recognized relationship. The women and men who were followers of Jesus appear to have entered into a fictive-kin relationship in which they assumed an identity as brothers and sisters in the Lord.[95] This relationship may have given women greater freedom to address gatherings of the community that included both men and women. This is at least suggested by the command of the risen Jesus to the women to "go, tell my brothers . . ." recorded in Matt 28:10 and John 20:17. What is not known is whether particular individuals within Christian communities were deferred to as storytellers. It is possible that elders and apostles served in this capacity. Paul speaks of handing on the traditions that were handed on to him (1 Cor 15:3), but he refers here to summary lists of witnesses, not narrative material.[96] Whether elders,

[95] E.g., Mark 3:31-35 (*parr.* Matt 12:46-50; Luke 8:19-21).

[96] There is a striking lack of stories about Jesus in Paul's letters. This raises the possibility that stories were only told to and by those resident within local commu-

who were associated with local communities, were deferred to as storytellers remains unknown. However, there is nothing in the little that is said about elders in the texts of the Second Testament to suggest that this office was not held by both men and women. Thus if elders were accorded status as storytellers it is a role that would have fallen to both men and women.[97]

The primary setting in which storytelling takes place in the texts of the Second Testament is loosely identified as the local community, since the setting is rarely specified beyond the name of a region or town. In the few instances in which a more specific setting is identified it conforms to those found in the Greco-Roman and Jewish texts: i.e., a banquet or meal, a journey, or a home. (See Appendix D.) It may be that the synagogue should be included in this list. Both Jesus and the apostles are described as teaching in the synagogue, and it is known that Christians continued to participate in the synagogue through much of the first century C.E.

Two of these settings are of particular interest. One is the home, since the earliest gatherings of Christians are believed to have been in house churches.[98] Because these gatherings took place in what was commonly viewed as private space they offered women an opportunity to assume leadership in a way that would have been restricted in a more public setting.[99] Further, since women have always been storytellers in the home, there may have been less censure against their assuming this role in that setting. The second setting of interest is the banquet or meal, since Paul's correspondence with the Corinthians indicates that, very early in the life of the Church, Christians celebrated cultic meals

---

nities. Kenneth Bailey has observed in his studies of storytelling in Middle Eastern villages that only those within the community who have grown up hearing the stories may recite them in public gatherings (Bailey, "Informal Controlled Oral Tradition and the Synoptic Gospels," 40). In this case Paul, as an itinerant and, consequently, an outsider, may not have had authority to tell stories about Jesus in these local contexts (ibid. 51).

[97] The title "elder" was borrowed from the synagogue where it was an office in which both men and women served (Karen Jo Torjesen, *When Women Were Priests* [San Francisco: HarperSan Francisco, 1993] 5). In the synagogue the elders appear to have served an administrative function (Brooten, *Women Leaders in the Ancient Synagogue*, 53–54). Whether this function was altered when taken over by the Christian communities is not known.

[98] Elisabeth Schüssler Fiorenza, *In Memory of Her* (New York: Crossroad, 1984) 175–84.

[99] Ibid. 176.

together. According to the evidence of Greco-Roman and Jewish texts, meals were a common setting for storytelling events. This also was a setting in which a woman might address an audience of both men and women, particularly if she was in some way related to the men who were present. This would have been the case for women in these early Christian communities, since they entered into a fictive-kinship relationship with other members of the community.[100]

The stories told by early Christians also are characterized by the esoteric factor in storytelling: they are stories that involve individuals, events, and occasions that belong to the Christian community and would have been of limited interest to those outside the community. This underlines the role of storytelling in the formation and maintenance of group boundaries for early Christians. The various versions that exist of some of these stories suggest that they also may have been told to defend or distinguish the identity of group against group within the larger Christian community.[101]

As in early Jewish communities, storytelling in early Christian communities mirrored the patterns of storytelling revealed by Greco-Roman texts. What may be distinctive to these Christian communities is the fictive-kinship relationship between men and women and the location of churches within the home, which may have offered women a greater opportunity to address audiences of both men and women in cultic as well as informal settings. It may also be that older women and women who enjoyed status because of their service as benefactors, elders, or widows were deferred to as storytellers in both formal and informal settings. Further, it is likely that women, by telling stories to children, were instrumental in the religious formation of children within the community. Since women tend to tell stories from the perspective of their gender, this suggests that women may have exercised considerable influence in the community through storytelling. This would be particularly so in communities, such as those of the early Christians, that represented subgroups within the dominant culture and for whom stories played a significant role in the formation of their identity.[102]

[100] E.g., Mark 3:31-35 (*parr.* Matt 12:46-50; Luke 8:19-21).

[101] Werner Kelber, "Jesus and Tradition," *Semeia* 65 (1994) 161.

[102] Bauman, *Story, Performance and Event*, 113; Alan Dundes, "Defining Identity through Folklore," in Anita Jacobson-Widding, ed., *Identity: Personal and Socio-Cultural* (Atlantic Highlands, N.J.: Humanities, 1983) 239, 250.

Conclusion

This reconstruction of storytelling in the world of antiquity begins to give body and voice to the nameless faces that are the sources, shapers, and bearers of the "oral tradition" preserved in literary texts as story. Storytelling in the world of antiquity was a communal activity in which everyone participated. While a few earned their living as professional storytellers, the vast majority of storytellers were women and men who entertained, educated, encouraged, remonstrated, and challenged one another with their stories. Audiences consisted of whomever was near at hand. Yet audiences were far from passive. It is likely that the audience participated in determining who would assume the role of storyteller in any particular setting while audience, setting, and context influenced the choice of story told. The skilled storyteller would, in turn, shape her story to the setting and interests of her audience. The available evidence gives no clear indication that women and men told different stories; however, the stories they told tended to emphasize the perspective and experience of their gender. Similarly, while men told stories in both public and private settings, the evidence suggests that women tended to limit their storytelling to settings that could be defined as "private," either because of the physical setting or the social makeup of the group. However, this boundary was not absolute and depended to a certain degree on the social status and occupation of the women involved. Although stories were shared across genders, they were not necessarily shared across groups. Romans, Jews, and Christians each told stories that reinforced particular aspects of their religious and cultural identity. Yet, on the basis of the extant evidence, the pattern of storytelling seems to have varied little from group to group.

This reconstruction of storytelling also becomes the backdrop against which to consider the origin and circulation of the Mary Magdalene tradition. Although the tradition has descended to us as a written text, the storytelling environment of the world of antiquity argues strongly for its circulation orally as story. As story, the tradition would have been shaped and reshaped as it was given voice by different storytellers to different audiences, each framed by its own particular set of circumstances. No less a process of "shaping" the tradition would have been at work when certain storytellers incorporated the tradition into their written narratives. In each case the Magdalene tradition was told by believers to believers in order to provide courage as well as encouragement, and to give definition to the identity of the gathered community. In the next chapter I will begin exploring the impact of the Mary Magdalene traditions on early Christian communities by first considering questions surrounding their origin and circulation.

Chapter Three

The Written and the Oral Text

The stories we have inherited of a post-resurrection appearance to Mary Magdalene have come down to us in the form of written texts (Matt 28:9-10, John 20:1-18, and Mark 16:9-11).[1] Some scholars maintain that these stories originated as written texts. According to this scenario Matthew invented the appearance narrative (28:9-10), modeling it on the appearance by the angel to the women (28:1-8).[2] John, drawing on

[1] An account of a post-resurrection appearance to Mary Magdalene also is recorded in the *Epistola Apostolorum* and in a Gnostic text, the Coptic *Gospel of Bartholomew.* In addition, Mary Magdalene enters into dialogue with the risen Jesus in other Gnostic texts: Dialog of the Savior, Sophia of Jesus Christ, Pistis Sophia, Questions of Mary, and *Gospel of Mary*. Although this literature has much to contribute to our understanding of how Mary Magdalene traditions continued to function within the early Church, it is beyond the scope of this project to engage this material.

[2] A number of scholars consider the narrative the invention of the author: John E. Alsup, *The Post-Resurrection Appearance Stories of the Gospel Tradition* (Stuttgart: Calwer, 1975) 110; Edward L. Bode asks: why would the Lord appear to women? (*The First Easter Morning. The Gospel Accounts of the Women's Visit to the Tomb of Jesus* [Rome: Biblical Institute Press, 1970] 56); Lyder Brun, *Die Auferstehung Christi in der Urchristlichen Überlieferung* (Oslo: H. Aschehoug and Co., 1925) 54; Rudolf Bultmann, *History of the Synoptic Tradition,* trans. John Marsh (New York: Harper & Row, 1963) 288; K. Peter G. Curtis, "Three Points of Contact between Matthew and John in the Burial and Resurrection Narratives," *JTS* 23 (1972) 442; David Hill, *The Gospel of Matthew* (Grand Rapids: Eerdmans, 1972) 359; Hans Grass discounts the appearance to the women since Luke knows of no appearance at the grave (*Ostergeschehen und Osterberichte* [Göttingen: Vandenhoeck and Ruprecht, 1962] 28); Frans Neirynck,

the text of Matthew, then enlarged and adapted the Magdalene story, weaving into it the story of Peter and the beloved disciple at the tomb.[3] Subsequently the author of the Longer Ending of Mark created a summary account of the appearance stories recorded in the canonical gospels.[4] The impression left by this scenario is that the post-resurrection appearance to Mary Magdalene is a literary fiction that plays a role in the narrative structure of the written text but had no apparent function as a living tradition in early Christian communities.

Although this scenario does not preclude oral circulation of the Magdalene stories, it does imply that their existence and influence apart from the written text is in no way certain, and is of even less import. What we are beginning to understand about the complex relationship between oral and written texts in rhetorical cultures, however, suggests that the oral existence of the Magdalene stories may have been in every way as essential as that of the written text.[5] This insight serves as an invitation, if not an imperative, to examine once again the relationship between the written versions of the Magdalene stories for traces of oral composition and/or circulation. If such evidence can be found, then

---

"Les femmes au tombeau," *NTS* 15 (1969) 184; Léopold Sabourin, *The Gospel according to St Matthew* (Bombay: St. Paul Press, 1982) 929; Nikolaus Walter, "Eine Vormatthäische Schilderung der Auferstehung Jesu," *NTS* 19 (1973) 416.

[3] John E. Alsup considers the fact that the gospels of Matthew and John both record an appearance of Jesus to Mary Magdalene a coincidence, since he maintains that Matthew invented the appearance narrative but John drew his account from oral tradition (*The Post-Resurrection Appearance Stories*, 113).

[4] Alsup, *The Post-Resurrection Appearance Stories*, 120; C. H. Dodd, "The Appearances of the Risen Christ," in idem, *More New Testament Studies* (Manchester: University of Manchester Press, 1968) 130; Sherman E. Johnson, *A Commentary on the Gospel According to St. Mark* (London: A & C Black, 1977) 266; and Harold Riley, *The Making of Mark* (Macon, Ga.: Mercer University Press, 1989) 200 (who also challenges the Two-Source Hypothesis and proposes that Mark was composed from Matthew and Luke).

[5] On the close relationship between oral and written text see also Mary J. Carruthers, *The Book of Memory* (Cambridge: Cambridge University Press, 1990) 10–13; A. N. Doane, "Oral Texts, Intertexts, and Intratexts," in Jay Clayton and Eric Rothstein, eds., *Influence and Intertextuality in Literary History* (Madison: University of Wisconsin Press, 1991) 80; Ruth H. Finnegan, *Oral Poetry: Its Nature, Significance, and Social Context* (Cambridge: Cambridge University Press, 1982) 161; Jack Goody, *The Interface between the Written and the Oral* (Cambridge: Cambridge University Press, 1987) 106; Eduard Nielsen, *Oral Tradition Studies in Biblical Theology* (London: S.C.M., 1954) 34–35; Bruce Rosenberg, "The Complexity of Oral Tradition," *Oral Tradition* 2 (1987) 77; Archer Taylor, "Folklore and the Student of Literature," in Alan Dundes, ed., *The Study of Folklore* (Englewood Cliffs, N.J.: Prentice-Hall, 1965) 37.

the way is clear to consider how these stories were constitutive of social life in contexts beyond those framed by the gospel narratives: in other words, to begin formulating a picture of how these stories functioned as living traditions in early Christian communities.

Method

The close relationship between writing and speech in rhetorical cultures makes it difficult to distinguish one from the other with absolute certainty. Nonetheless, students of folklore, medieval history, classics, ethnography, and biblical studies have developed various criteria that may be employed to identify traces of oral composition and performance in written texts.[6] Drawing on the experience of these studies, I propose four criteria against which to measure each of the Magdalene stories (Matt 28:9-10, John 20:1-18, and Mark 16:9-11) in order to determine whether the stories exhibit traces of oral composition and/or circulation. The criteria, presented in the form of questions, are as follows:

(1) Is there evidence that the story was copied from an earlier written text?[7] This criterion must be judged on the basis of degree. A story that has been copied will not necessarily agree with the original in every detail. Nonetheless, there is a point at which the supposed "copy" diverges so far from the proposed original that it no longer represents a "copy," but a separate version. The existence of two or more versions of the same story points persuasively toward independent circulation of the story as an oral tradition.[8]

[6] For specific studies see notes for individual criteria.

[7] Oivind Andersen, "Oral Tradition," in Henry Wansbrough, ed., *Jesus and the Oral Gospel Tradition* (Sheffield: JSOT Press, 1991) 27; Taylor, "Folklore and the Student of Literature," 48; Dan Ben-Amos, *Folklore in Context* (New Delhi: South Asian Publishers, 1982) 4; Alan Dundes, *Holy Writ as Holy Text* (New York: Rowman & Littlefield, 1999) 18–19; Dennis R. MacDonald, *The Legend and the Apostle* (Philadelphia: Westminster, 1983) 18; Francis Lee Utley, "Folk Literature: An Operational Definition," in Dundes, ed., *The Study of Folklore*, 61. However, the inadequacy of "oral transmission" for a definition of oral tradition has often been noted, since the medium of transmission does not offer a definition of the thing created (Ben-Amos, *Folklore in Context*, 9; Alan Dundes, "Text, Texture, and Context," *Southern Folklore Quarterly* 28 (1964) 251; Finnegan, *Oral Poetry*, 74).

[8] Jan H. Brunvand, *The Study of American Folklore* (New York: W. W. Norton & Co., 1986) 7.

(2) Does the story exhibit a clear beginning, middle, and end describing a single story line?[9] These are the basic elements necessary to designate a text as "story." If it can be shown that the Magdalene texts exhibit the basic elements of "story," then the possibility exists that they circulated independently of the longer written texts in which they are presently embedded.

(3) Does the story exhibit characteristics that are associated with oral text?[10] These characteristics include conventionality in form,[11] the use of only two characters in a scene,[12] the presence of memory devices such as repetition, patterns, and verbal echoing,[13] the use of interpretive comments, illustrations, or asides,[14] unanticipated shifts in the narrative resulting in illogical structure,[15] and tolerance of inconsistencies.[16] While some of these characteristics are shared by written texts, their

[9] Bultmann, *History of the Synoptic Tradition*, 32; Doane, "Oral Texts, Intertexts, and Intratexts," 78; Walter J. Ong, *Orality and Literacy* (London: Methuen, 1982) 141, 144; Robert H. Stein, "What is Redaktionsgeschichte?" *JBL* 88 (1969) 56; Taylor, "Folklore and the Student of Literature," 38; Gerd Theissen, *The Miracle Stories of the Early Christian Tradition* (Philadelphia: Fortress, 1983) 192.

[10] Walter J. Ong, "Text as Interpretation: Mark and After," *Semeia* 39 (1987) 14.

[11] Ernest L. Abel, "The Psychology of Memory and Rumor Transmission and their Bearing on Theories of Oral Transmission in Early Christianity," *JR* 51 (1971) 276; Anderson, "Oral Tradition," 31; Brunvand, *The Study of American Folklore,* 7; Doane, "Oral Texts, Intertexts, and Intratexts," 78; Burke O. Long, "Recent Field Studies in Oral Literature and the Question of Sitz im Leben," *Semeia* 5 (1976) 193; Taylor, "Folklore and the Student of Literature," 38; Vincent Taylor, *The Formation of the Gospel Tradition* (New York: St. Martin's, 1964) 208.

[12] Bultmann, *History of the Synoptic Tradition,* 32; Axel Olrik, "The Epic Laws of Folk Narrative," in Dundes, ed., *The Study of Folklore,* 135. A "character" may be either an individual or a group that functions as a single party in an interchange of dialogue or action.

[13] Joanna Dewey, "Oral Methods of Structuring Narrative in Mark," *Int* 43 (1989) 35; Ian H. Henderson, "Didache and Orality in Synoptic Comparison," *JBL* 111 (1992) 294; Charles H. Lohr, "Oral Techniques in the Gospel of Matthew," *CBQ* 23 (1961) 407, 409; Olrik, "The Epic Laws of Folk Narrative," 132–33; Ong, *Orality and Literacy,* 48; Theissen, *The Miracle Stories of the Early Christian Tradition,* 191.

[14] Dewey, "Oral Methods of Structuring Narrative in Mark," 35; Henderson, "Didache and Orality in Synoptic Comparison," 294; Theissen, *The Miracle Stories of the Early Christian Tradition,* 191.

[15] Dewey, "Oral Methods of Structuring Narrative in Mark," 35; Theissen, *The Miracle Stories of the Early Christian Tradition,* 193.

[16] Henderson, "Didache and Orality in Synoptic Comparison," 294; MacDonald, *The Legend and the Apostle,* 32; Theissen, *The Miracle Stories of the Early Christian Tradition,* 192.

presence must also be viewed as possible evidence of circulation as an oral composition.

(4) Does the story diverge from the literary tendencies of the author?[17] All narrators, whether speaking or writing, leave their imprint on the text by employing favored words and other characteristic elements of style. The presence of words, expressions, or ideas that differ significantly from those of the author may indicate that the text owes its origin to an independent source. This source may be written, but where no written source can be found the evidence points toward oral tradition as the source of the story.

No single criterion, on its own, is adequate to demonstrate composition or circulation as oral tradition. However, if any one of the stories can be shown to satisfy all four criteria—i.e., it does not show evidence of being copied from an earlier written text, it can stand on its own as "story," it exhibits stylistic characteristics of oral text, and it diverges from the literary tendencies of the evangelist—then a persuasive case can be made that the Magdalene story circulated as oral tradition.

I begin by examining the most recent text first: Mark 16:9-11. This text is generally dated to the early part of the second century.[18] I will then move backward chronologically, examining John 20:1-18 next, and concluding with Matt 28:9-10.[19] I move in this direction because the more recent texts are thought to have been constructed from the earlier text(s).

Analysis of Mark 16:9-11

The post-resurrection appearance to Mary Magdalene recorded in Mark 16:9-11 belongs to the Longer Ending of Mark (16:9-20). Most scholars concur that the Longer Ending was not authored by the

[17] Barry W. Henaut, *Oral Tradition and the Gospels: The Problem of Mark 4* (Sheffield: JSOT Press, 1993) 119.

[18] Hugh Anderson, *The Gospel of Mark* (Grand Rapids: Eerdmans, 1981) 358; James A. Kelhoffer, *Miracle and Mission: The Authentication of Missionaries and their Message in the Longer Ending of Mark* (Tübingen: J.C.B. Mohr [Paul Siebeck], 2000) 175; Charles S. C. Williams, *Alterations to the Text of the Synoptic Gospels and Acts* (Oxford: Blackwell, 1951) 42.

[19] The Gospel of Matthew is thought to have been written about 85–90 C.E. and the Gospel of John about 90 C.E. (Dennis Duling and Norman Perrin, *The New Testament* [New York: Harcourt Brace, 1994] 333, 409).

evangelist.[20] The evidence pointing to this conclusion may be summarized as follows: (1) The Longer Ending differs significantly in style, vocabulary, and content from the rest of Mark's gospel. (2) The addition of vv. 9-11 creates an illogical storyline. Mary Magdalene is described in v. 9 as if she is being introduced for the first time, when she has been mentioned previously in 15:40, 47 and 16:1. The women who accompanied her in 16:1 have suddenly disappeared. The reader has been led to expect an appearance to the disciples in Galilee and is taken entirely unawares when Jesus appears "first" to Mary. (3) The Longer Ending is absent from the important Greek manuscripts Sinaiticus and Vaticanus.[21] What I will seek to determine is whether the Longer Ending has been created by copying from the written texts of Mark, Matthew, Luke, and John or show signs of originating as an oral composition.

Is there evidence that the story was copied from an earlier written text?

The Magdalene story in the Longer Ending shares a number of words with the Magdalene stories in Matthew, Luke, and John: πρωϊ ("early": John 20:1; see also Mark 16:2), σάββατον ("Sabbath": Mark

[20] Anderson, *The Gospel of Mark,* 358; C.E.B. Cranfield, *The Gospel According to St. Mark.* Cambridge Greek Testament Commentary (Cambridge: Cambridge University Press, 1977) 472; James R. Edwards, *The Gospel According to Mark* (Grand Rapids: Eerdmans, 2002) 497–99; Joseph Hug, *La Finale de L'Évangile de Marc: Mc 16,9-20* (Paris: Gabalda, 1978) 25–32; Sherman E. Johnson, *A Commentary on the Gospel According to St Mark,* 266; Kelhoffer, *Miracle and Mission,* 121; Rudolf Pesch, *Das Markusevangelium* (Freiberg: Herder, 1977) 2:544; Vincent Taylor, *The Gospel According to St. Mark,* 610; contra William R. Farmer, *The Last Twelve Verses of Mark* (Cambridge: Cambridge University Press, 1974). Although the majority of Greek manuscripts include these verses, they are omitted by א, B, it^{k}, syr^{s}, and by some Armenian, Ethiopic, and Georgian manuscripts. Eusebius and Jerome also considered these verses inauthentic because of their absence from the Greek manuscripts known to them (Cranfield, *The Gospel According to St Mark,* 471).

[21] By the latter part of the second century C.E. Irenaeus refers to Mark 16:19 as if it were the end of Mark, indicating that by this time vv. 9-20 had been incorporated into at least some manuscripts of the gospel (Irenaeus, *Adv. Haer.* 3.10.6). Neither Clement of Alexandria nor Origen knew of the Longer Ending (John R. Donahue and Daniel J. Harrington, *The Gospel of Mark.* SP 2 [Collegeville: The Liturgical Press, 2002] 462).

16:2; Luke 24:1; Matt 28:1; 20:1), ἑπτὰ δαιμόνια ("seven demons": Luke 8:2), ἀνίστημι ("rise": Luke 24:7; John 20:9), ἐκείνη ("she": John 20:15, 16), πορεύομαι ("go": Matt 28:7; John 20:17), and ἀπαγγέλλω ("announce": Matt 28:10; Luke 24:9; John 20:18), ζάω ("live": Luke 24:5, 23), and ἀπιστεύω ("disbelieve": Luke 24:11). While this at first seems to suggest a clear dependence on the gospel narratives, it is important to consider how the author of the Longer Ending employs each word as well as how the author strings them together to construct the Magdalene narrative. I will begin by examining how the author employs the words.

The Longer Ending describes Mary coming to the tomb πρωῒ πρώτῃ σαββάτου ("early on the first of the week"). Although John also describes the hour as πρωῒ, the closer parallel is Mark 16:2: λίαν πρωῒ τῇ μιᾷ τῶν σαββάτων ("very early on the first of the week"). The parallel is not exact. The Longer Ending omits "very" (λίαν), expresses "first" with πρώτῃ rather than τῇ μιᾷ, and employs the genitive singular rather than the genitive plural for "Sabbath."[22] Thus, while the Longer Ending picks up a phrase closely associated with the women coming to the tomb, it renders it in a very different way. It could be argued that this phrase represents a stable point in oral tradition and is included by the author of the Longer Ending for this reason.

With the Gospel of Luke, the Longer Ending shares the reference to Mary Magdalene as the one from whom Jesus cast out seven demons. The phrases are very close. However, the Longer Ending employs the passive of ἐκβάλλω rather than ἐξέρχομαι for "had gone out" and renders the phrase "from whom" with the preposition παρά rather than ἀπό. Although ἐκβάλλω is used consistently in reference to casting out demons, ἐκβάλλω with παρά occurs nowhere else in the Second Testament.[23] In addition, Luke, at this point in the text, refers to Mary as "the one called Magdalene" (Μαρία ἡ καλουμένη Μαγδαληνή), whereas the Longer Ending uses the familiar "Mary Magdalene." Since the phrase occurs in the Longer Ending as an "aside," a technique employed in

[22] Only here and in 1 Cor 16:2 and Luke 18:12 is the singular σαββάτου employed instead of the plural σαββάτων (Hug, *La Finale de L'Évangile de Marc,* 45; Pesch, *Das Markusevangelium,* 550; Riley, *The Making of Mark,* 201; Henry B. Swete, *The Gospel According to St. Mark* [New York: MacMillan, 1898] 376). The phrase πρώτῃ σαββάτου ("Sabbath") occurs nowhere else in the Second Testament (Swete, *The Gospel According to St. Mark,* 376).

[23] Pesch, *Markusevangelium,* 550; Taylor, *The Gospel According to St. Mark,* 611.

oral texts, the similarities between the two texts in content do not point conclusively toward dependence on the written text of Luke.

"Rise" (ἀνίστημι) is used frequently by both first- and second-century writers in reference to the resurrection.[24] Although this verb is employed in Luke and John as well as the Longer Ending, this can hardly be taken as evidence of literary dependence. It is more likely a case of common usage. Consistent with second-century texts, the Longer Ending employs the participial form, which is never used in other Second Testament texts in reference to the resurrection.[25]

'Εκείνη ("she") represents a case of the demonstrative pronoun "that" used as an absolute. While this usage is not common, it is not unknown in the Second Testament. It is found most often in John, but occurs in Matthew (13:11; 20:4). What makes this seem at first glance to be a striking connection with the text of John is the use of the feminine form, which is rare.[26] It is rare, however, only because female subjects are rare. The author of the Longer Ending uses the masculine demonstrative pronoun as an absolute also in vv. 11, 13, and 20. This suggests that the author of the Longer Ending favors this usage. Dependence on John at this point is far from certain.

Two words, πορεύομαι ("go"), and ἀπαγγέλλω ("announce"), occur in both the Johannine (20:17, 18) and Matthean (28:7, 10) Magdalene stories as well as the Longer Ending.[27] One, ἀπαγγέλλω, is found also in Luke 24:9. In John, Luke, and the Longer Ending the verb ἀπαγγέλλω is used to describe the women "announcing" what has happened to Jesus' followers.[28] Both Luke and the Longer Ending employ the aorist indicative. In each case what Mary (or, in Luke, the women) announce is different, the ones to whom they make the announcement are described differently, and in Luke the one from whom the message is received is an angel rather than Jesus. However, the action is the same in all three narratives. A similar correspondence is found in the use of

[24] Hug, *La Finale de L'Évangile de Marc*, 40–45; Kelhoffer, *Miracle and Mission*, 54. Hug detects an increase in the use of ἀνίστημι during the second century (*La Finale de L'Évangile de Marc*, 44).

[25] See especially Justin Martyr, *Apol.* I.50.12; I.63.16; *Dial.* 63.1; Kelhoffer, *Miracle and Mission*, 54; Pesch, *Markusevangelium*, 550.

[26] Kelhoffer, *Miracle and Mission*, 74.

[27] In John the cognate form ἀγγέλλω is used.

[28] In Matthew, Jesus commands the women to "announce" to the disciples that they will see him in Galilee. The women are never actually described "announcing" this message to the disciples.

the verb πορεύομαι. In John, Jesus commands Mary in 20:17 to "go" (πορεύου) to his brothers, while both Matthew and the Longer Ending employ the participle to describe the action of Mary (or the women) "going" to the disciples. Since both verbs occur frequently in the gospel narratives, their appearance in the Longer Ending may suggest no more than that the author is employing common words.

The remaining two words, ζάω ("live") and ἀπιστεύω ("disbelieve"), both occur in Luke's account of the women coming to the tomb (Luke 24:5,11, 23). This is notable since Mark 16:11, where these two words occur, closely resembles the episode recorded in Luke 24:1-12, 23 in which the women report that the angel has said Jesus lives and the disciples disbelieve them.[29] Yet the account in the Longer Ending is no more than the briefest summary of the events described in Luke, so much so that it is impossible to say with confidence that the episode in Luke is presumed by the author of the Longer Ending. A glance at the differences between the Longer Ending and the account in Luke makes this clear: In the Longer Ending the appearance is by Jesus rather than an angel; the appearance is to Mary Magdalene alone rather than to a group of women; the Longer Ending makes no mention of "disciples" but rather of "those who had been with him"; the latter are described as "mourning and weeping," a description never applied to the followers of Jesus elsewhere in the Second Testament.[30]

This analysis of vocabulary suggests several potential points of contact with the gospels. With Mark the Longer Ending shares a variant form of the phrase "early in the morning," and with Luke the words "seven demons," the reference to the risen Jesus as one who "lives," and the "disbelief" of the disciples. Four words, ἀνίστημι, ἐκείνη, πορεύομαι, and ἀπαγγέλλω, although shared with the Longer Ending, are so common that it is difficult to claim any kind of contact.

[29] Although the disbelief of the disciples in reference to the report of the women is mentioned only in Luke, the doubt and disbelief are associated with the disciples in Matthew (28:17), Luke (24:25, 41), and John (20:24-29), as well as in second-century texts (Hug, *La Finale de L'Évangile de Marc,* 71–72).

[30] This expression occurs elsewhere in the Second Testament (Luke 6:25; Jas 4:9; Rev 18:11, 15, 19), but not in reference to the followers of Jesus (Riley, *The Making of Mark,* 201). However, the disciples are described as mourning and weeping in the *Gospel of Peter* 2:7, 15:59 and the *Apocryphon of James* 10:6 (Pesch, *Markusevangelium,* 551; see also Hug, *La Finale de L'Évangile de Marc,* 68–69). In the *Gospel of Mary* (PBerol. 9.5-20) Mary Magdalene comforts the disciples, telling them not to weep and be sorrowful.

The points of contact begin to lose their force, however, when we consider how the author of the Longer Ending strings them together to construct the Magdalene narrative. Following the sequence suggested by common vocabulary, the Longer Ending picks up a phrase from Mark ("early in the morning"), draws on John for the appearance to Mary Magdalene alone, borrows from Luke the description of Mary Magdalene as the one from whom Jesus cast out seven demons, returns to Matthew for the participle "go," but to John or Luke for "announce," then turns again to Luke for the word "lives" to describe Jesus and the "disbelief" of "those who had been with him." While this pattern of "cutting and pasting" does not eliminate perforce the possibility that the author is copying from the written texts of the canonical gospels, it highlights at the very least that the author is using whatever sources have been employed in a remarkably free way.

This becomes even more apparent when we consider ways in which the Longer Ending differs from the canonical texts. Although the Longer Ending shares with Luke the aside that Jesus cast out seven demons from Mary, in Luke this occurs in a pre-resurrection setting. Similarly, while the Longer Ending also shares with Luke the report that the disciples did not believe the news that Jesus lives, in Luke it is three women who bring the news, and they have seen an angel, not the risen Jesus. The appearance to Mary Magdalene alone is consistent with John, but Mary does not respond to Jesus' sudden appearance, and Jesus speaks no words of comfort, nor does he give a command. Only following the appearance does Mary respond by going to the disciples on her own initiative. To these elements the author of the Longer Ending adds one not found anywhere else in the Second Testament: the claim that Jesus appeared to Mary Magdalene first.[31]

In conclusion, mention should be made of vocabulary employed by the author of the Longer Ending that is utterly inconsistent with usage in the Second Testament. In v. 9 the author uses ἐφάνη to express "Jesus

[31] Although this claim is implied in the Gospels of Matthew and John, it is never made explicit. Neither is it stated in 1 Cor 15:5 that Peter was the first to see the risen Jesus, but the structure of the text leaves no doubt that this is the case. (See Martin Hengel, "Maria Magdalena und die Frauen als Zeugen," in Otto Betz, Martin Hengel, and Peter Schmidt, eds., *Abraham unser Vater: Juden und Christen im Gespräch über die Bibel* [Leiden: Brill, 1963] 248–50; Jane Schaberg, *The Resurrection of Mary Magdalene* [New York: Continuum, 2002] 201). Hug views πρῶτον as a marker, indicating a succession in the structure of the text (*La Finale de L'Évangile de Marc*, 51).

appeared," while the writers of the Second Testament consistently use ὤφθη.[32] In v. 10 the disciples are referred to as τοῖς μετ᾽ αὐτοῦ γενομένοις ("those who were with him"), a phrase that occurs nowhere in the Second Testament.[33] "Weeping and mourning" (v. 10) is not otherwise used of the disciples.[34] In v. 11 the verb θεάομαι is used to report that Mary "has seen" Jesus, yet this verb is never employed for this purpose in the appearance stories.[35] Finally, although κακεῖνοι occurs in all four gospels, it is never used in reference to the disciples nor does it occur in the appearance stories.[36]

Was the author of the Longer Ending dependent on the written texts of the canonical gospels for the account of the post-resurrection appearance to Mary Magdalene? While some of the evidence may point in that direction, it is far from conclusive. The "cut and paste" manner in which words, phrases, and episodes have been borrowed from the canonical gospels, the variations in vocabulary and verb forms, and the introduction of elements found nowhere in the Second Testament suggest strongly that the Longer Ending was constructed from oral traditions.[37]

[32] Luke 24:34; 1 Cor 15:5, 6, 7, 8. Φαίνω (the root of ἐφάνη) is never used in reference to the resurrection and occurs rarely in the Second Testament. It is employed in connection with theophanies and appearances by other divine beings, both in the New Testament and LXX (Josef Ernst, *Das Evangelium nach Markus* [Regensburg: Pustet, 1981] 493; Hug, *La Finale de L'Évangile de Marc,* 53–54, 58–59; Johnson, *The Gospel According to St. Mark,* 266; Riley, *The Making of Mark,* 201; Swete, *The Gospel According to St. Mark,* 376).

[33] Hug finds similar, if not identical, phrases in the gospels: e.g., Mark 1:36 and Luke 22:59 (*La Finale de L'Évangile de Marc,* 67–68); Kelhoffer sees an imitation of Marcan style, citing ὦσιν μετ᾽ αὐτοῦ in 3:14 (*Miracle and Mission,* 73). Harold Riley (*The Making of Mark,* 201) believes this expression is a modification of οἱ μετ᾽ αὐτοῦ in Mark 1:36 (cf. also 5:40).

[34] See n. 30 above.

[35] Cf. Matt 28:7, 10, 17; Mark 8:7; Luke 24:39; John 20:18, 25, 29.

[36] Taylor, *The Gospel According to St. Mark,* 611.

[37] Anderson, *The Gospel of Mark,* 358; Raymond E. Brown, *The Gospel According to John,* AB 29, 29A. 2 vols. (Garden City, N.Y.: Doubleday, 1966–1970) 1003; Ernst, *Das Evangelium nach Markus,* 492; Reginald Fuller, *The Formation of the Resurrection Narratives* (New York: MacMillan, 1971) 157; Pesch, *Markusevangelium,* 549; Taylor, *The Gospel According to St. Mark,* 610. Williams (*Alterations to the Text of the Synoptic Gospels and Acts,* 41) thinks Mark 15:9-11 was composed on the basis of Luke, Matthew, and oral tradition.

Does the story exhibit a clear beginning, middle, and end describing a single story line?

As the text presently stands vv. 9-11 have been integrated into the narrative scheme of vv. 9-20. This is achieved in several ways: The first two pericopes (vv. 9-11 and 12-13) share a parallel construction (Jesus appears; the appearance is reported; the report is disbelieved). Temporal references in vv. 12 ("after these things,"μετὰ δὲ ταῦτα), 14 ("later," ὕστερον), and 19 ("after speaking to them," μετὰ τὸ λαλῆσαι αὐτοῖς), link each episode with the one that preceded.[38] Each episode contains a reference to the resurrection being announced (ἀπαγέλλω; vv. 10, 13a) or proclaimed (κηρύσσω; v. 20a) to others.[39] The first two episodes, with their reports of disbelief on the part of the disciples, anticipate the third (vv. 14-20) where Jesus upbraids the disciples for their unbelief.[40] It is evident, therefore, that vv. 9-20 are intended to form a literary unit.[41]

However, while the verses that follow (vv. 12-20) are linked through temporal referents to what precedes, vv. 9-11 are able to stand on their own, apart from vv. 12-20.[42] Nothing in these verses suggests that additional narrative is anticipated. They represent a complete narrative with a beginning (Jesus appears to Mary Magdalene), middle (she goes to the disciples), and end (the disciples, having heard her report, do not believe her) that follows a single story line (the appearance of Jesus to Mary Magdalene). Further, within the unit each verse is dependent on the one that precedes: v. 10 is dependent on v. 9 for the antecedent of ἐκείνη ("that one/she"); v. 11 is linked temporally to v. 10 ("when they had heard"; κἀκεῖνοι ἀκούσαντες). Thus vv. 9-11 represent a discrete episode that could have circulated independently.

[38] Paul A. Mirecki, "Mark 16:9-10: Composition, Tradition and Redaction," (Th.D. diss., Harvard University, 1986) 26; Pesch, *Markusevangelium,* 549.

[39] Mirecki, "Mark 16:9-10: Composition, Tradition and Redaction," 29.

[40] I concur with Kelhoffer (*Miracle and Mission,* 164–69) and Mirecki ("Mark 16:9-10: Composition, Tradition and Redaction," 26–30) that the Longer Ending is divided into three sections by temporal references, but differ slightly from both in my divisions: 9-11, 12-13, 14-20.

[41] On the literary unity of Mark 16:9-20 see Hug (*La finale de l'évangile de Marc,* 174–75), Kelhoffer (*Miracle and Mission,* 164–69), Mirecki, "Mark 16:9-10: Composition, Tradition and Redaction," 28–32.

[42] The Longer Ending consists of three episodes strung together (vv. 9-11, 12-13, 14-20). While the author of the Longer Ending has woven the three into a unit, the removal of the temporal referents allows each episode to stand on its own.

Does the story exhibit characteristics associated with oral text?

Two characteristics associated with oral text are present in Mark 16:9-11. First, there are never more than two characters in the scene at any one time: Jesus appears with Mary, Mary appears with the disciples. The two do not overlap. Second, the narrator interjects an aside in which Mary Magdalene is identified as the one from whom Jesus cast out seven demons. This is typical of oral performance, where characters are identified by an attribute or association. These dynamics suggest that vv. 9-11 may have originated in oral performance.

Does the story diverge from the literary tendencies of the author?

Since we possess only a fragment of text produced by the author of the Longer Ending it is difficult to identify with any certainty the literary tendencies of that author. Nonetheless, a few observations can be made. For example, the author uses the aorist tense almost exclusively for indicative verbs, and the present and aorist tenses for participles.[43] The author frequently begins clauses with a participial phrase (vv. 9a, 10a, 11a, 12a, 13a, 14a, 15b, 16a, 17a, 20a). Certain vocabulary is favored, such as "go" (πορεύομαι, vv. 10, 12, 15), "announce" (ἀπαγγέλλω, vv. 10, 13), "that one/these" (ἐκείνος; κἀκεῖνοι, vv. 10, 11, 13, 20), "see" (θεάομαι, vv. 11, 14), "believe" (πιστεύω, vv. 13, 14, 16, 17), "cast out" in reference to demons (ἐκβάλλω, vv. 9, 17), "appear" (φανερόω, vv. 12, 14), and "speak" (λαλέω, vv. 17, 19). The author tends toward absolute uses of ἐκεῖνος and κἀκεῖνος.[44] These examples are sufficient to suggest that it is possible to speak of "literary tendencies" with respect to the author of the Longer Ending.

This makes one difference in vocabulary between vv. 9-11 and vv. 12-20 worthy of mention. In v. 9 the phrase "he appeared" is rendered by the aorist passive of φαίνω. In vv. 12 and 14 the same phrase is rendered by the aorist passive of φανερόω. What makes the use of different verbs for "appear" in v. 9 and vv. 12 and 14 more striking is the number of

[43] Exceptions for the indicative include v. 9, "had cast out" (perfect tense), v. 11, "he lives" (present tense), and vv. 16, 17, and 18, where the future is employed in reference to future events. For participles, exceptions include v. 14, where a perfect participle occurs, "had been raised" (ἐγηγερμένον).

[44] Mark 16:10a, 11a, 13, 20a (Kelhoffer, *Miracle and Mission,* 72).

words that occur in both vv. 9-11 and 12-20 (πορεύομαι, ἀπαγγέλλω, ἐκείνος, κἀκεῖνοι, θεάομαι, ἐκβάλλω), revealing the hand of the author shaping these verses. This raises the question of whether φαίνω belongs to a source or to the author of the Longer Ending.

A second, less clear-cut example is found in the way the author expresses the act of "disbelief." In v. 11 the author uses the verb ἀπιστεύω ("disbelieve"), while in vv. 13 and 14, we find the phrase οὐ πιστεύω ("not believe"). In each instance the "disbelief" is attributed to Jesus' followers who fail to believe in the proclamation of his resurrection. Verse 11 stands apart from vv. 13 and 14 by the use of the negative verb, ἀπιστεύω. Although this verb also occurs in v. 16, this occurrence is set apart from that in v. 11 by its form (participle) and context. When the participle is employed in v. 16 it refers to those who do not believe the proclamation of the eleven disciples. In v. 11 the indicative refers to "those who were with him [Jesus]." Complicating matters, however, is the use of the noun ἀπιστία in v. 14. In this instance the noun does refer to the disbelief of Jesus' followers, offering a close parallel to v. 11. Yet since the noun occurs in the gospels, while the verb does not, it may be that a distinction should be drawn between the use of the verb and the use of the noun. Thus the use of the indicative of ἀπιστεύω in v. 11 may indicate a second example of a divergence in the literary style of the author of the Longer Ending.

Summary

Despite similarities between the Longer Ending and the Magdalene stories in the canonical gospels, it is difficult to make a strong case for literary dependence.[45] None of the shared vocabulary points necessarily toward the author of the Longer Ending copying from the written text of the gospels. Too many of the words may be explained away as words in "common usage" or stable points in oral tradition. The inclusion of the "aside" in v. 9 also points toward origin in oral tradition,

[45] Anderson, *The Gospel of Mark,* 358; Brown, *The Gospel According to John,* 1003; Ernst, *Das Evangelium nach Markus,* 492; Fuller, *The Formation of the Resurrection Narratives,* 157; Hug, *La Finale de L'Évangile de Marc,* 164–65; Pesh, *Markusevangelium,* 549; Vincent Taylor, *The Gospel According to St. Mark,* 610. Contra Kelhoffer, *Miracle and Mission,*150, and Williams, *Alterations to the Text of the Synoptic Gospels and Acts,* 41.

and the striking use of φαίνω suggests a source other than the gospels. In addition, the presence of two elements not found in the canonical gospels—the explicit reference to Mary as the first to see Jesus and the description of the disciples as mourning and weeping—offers clear evidence that the author of the Longer Ending is drawing on sources other than the canonical gospels. This evidence, in combination with the way in which the points of contact with the canonical stories have been reshaped into a story that resembles none of gospel texts, suggests that the story of the post-resurrection appearance to Mary Magdalene recorded in Mark 16:9-11 originated in oral tradition. Since this new story has the capacity to stand on its own, apart from the Longer Ending, it may have been among the several versions of the Magdalene story circulating in early Christian communities.

Analysis of John 20:1-18

The twists and turns in John 20:1-18 indicate that the story, as it presently stands, has been constructed from two or more separate sources. Raymond E. Brown, among others, argues that vv. 3-10 represent a separate tradition that has been woven into the Magdalene story.[46] He notes, for example, that Mary Magdalene disappears after v. 2 and suddenly returns in v. 11, as if the events of vv. 3-10 had never happened. She looks into the tomb, but where the disciples have seen linen wrappings, Mary sees angels. These incongruities suggest that two independent

[46] Brown, *The Gospel According to John*, 988; Rudolf Bultmann, *The Gospel of John*, trans. G. R. Beasley-Murray (Philadelphia: Westminster, 1971) 681; Albert Descamps, "La structure des récits évangéliques de la résurrection," *Bibl* 40 (1959) 732; Fuller, *The Formation of the Resurrection Narratives*, 134; Percival Gardner-Smith, *Saint John and the Synoptic Gospels* (Cambridge: Cambridge University Press, 1938) 77; Ernst Haenchen, *John*. Hermeneia (Philadelphia: Fortress, 1984) 2:208; Susanne Heine, "Eine Person von Rang und Namen: Historische Konturen der Magdalenerin," in Dietrich-Alex Koch, Gerhard Sellin, and Andreas Lindemann, eds., *Jesu Rede von Gott und ihre Nachgeschichte im frühen Christentum* (Gütersloh: Gerd Mohn, 1989) 186; Barnabas Lindars, *The Gospel of John*. New Century Bible (London: Oliphants, 1972) 603; Gerd Lüdemann, *The Resurrection of Jesus* (Minneapolis: Fortress, 1994) 156; Willi Marxsen, *The Resurrection of Jesus of Nazareth* (Philadelphia: Fortress, 1970) 57; Pheme Perkins, *Resurrection* (Garden City, N.Y.: Doubleday, 1984) 173. Rudolf Schnackenburg, *The Gospel According to St. John* (New York: Crossroad, 1982) 3:301 groups vv. 1-10 together, and Hans Grass (*Ostergeschehen und Osterberichte*, 54) groups vv. 2-10 together.

stories have been combined.[47] Further, vv. 3-10 shape their own discrete storyline with a clear beginning (the two disciples go to the tomb), middle (they see the linen wrappings), and end (because they do not understand the scriptures they return home). For these reasons I will not consider these verses in the discussion of the post-resurrection story.

The omission of vv. 3-10 raises the question of the relationship between vv. 1, 2 and 11-18. Verse 2, in particular, poses a problem because of the incongruous "we." Although Mary comes to the tomb alone, she reports to the disciples that "we do not know where they have laid him." There have been various attempts to explain this "we," none of them satisfactory.[48] A similar story recorded in Luke 24:1-12, in which Peter runs to the empty tomb not having believed the report of the women, suggests the possibility that John 20:2 belongs with vv. 3-10.[49]

[47] Frans Neirynck maintains that Luke 24:12 cannot be separated from the empty tomb narrative; therefore he concludes that John 20:1-10 must be viewed as a unit with the Mary Magdalene episode that follows ("Tradition and Redaction in John XX.1-18," in Elizabeth A. Livingstone, ed., *Papers Presented to the fifth International Congress on Biblical Studies held at Oxford, 1973.* Studia Evangelica 7 [Berlin: Akademie Verlag, 1982] 362).

[48] Several scholars have proposed that the "we" reflects a manner of speech and should not be read as a genuine plural (Bode, *The First Easter Morning,* 74; Bultmann, *The Gospel of John,* 684, n. 1; 134, n. 3; Grass, *Ostergeschehen und Osterberichte,* 54; Haenchen, *John,* 2:208). In the examples cited, however, the individual who is speaking represents an identifiable group with which he or she is associated, such as the Jews or the Samaritans (see John 3:2, 11; 4:22; 9:31; 14:5). Yet nowhere in John's text is Mary Magdalene associated in the same way with an identifiable group. Although Mary Magdalene is listed with the mother of Jesus and Mary, the wife of Clopas, in 19:25, this can hardly be considered a group in the same way as those represented by the authors cited above. Thus the "we" in 20:2 is difficult to explain as a manner of speech. Gerd Lüdemann maintains that the "we" does not necessarily mean that several women went to the tomb (*Resurrection of Jesus,* 152). Paul S. Minear proposes that John uses "we" for the Christian community ("'We Don't Know Where. . . .' John 20:2," *Int* 30 [1976] 126).

[49] The relationship of John to the synoptic gospels is a subject of much debate. To engage this question fully is beyond the scope of this study. However, a few remarks are in order. Raymond E. Brown observes that, while John tends to agree with Mark and Luke more often than with Matthew, over a series of scenes he does not agree consistently with any one gospel; therefore in order to propose literary dependence one would have to conclude that John knew all three gospels and chose eclectically among them (*The Gospel According to John,* xiv). These observations are confirmed by my own analysis of the narrative of the post-resurrection appearance to Mary Magdalene. While John does share some sayings and stories with the synoptics (primarily with Mark), outside of the Passion narrative this contact is

The incongruous "we" could then be explained as a carryover from a source in which several women went to the tomb.[50] If v. 2 is removed, the narrative moves with relative ease from v. 1 to v. 11.[51] This seems to me the most persuasive scenario since, in John, the appearance to Mary is clearly linked to the tomb.[52] For the purposes of this discussion I will treat vv. 1, 11-18 as a single story.[53]

---

relatively small (D. Moody Smith, "John and the Synoptics: Some Dimensions of the Problem," *NTS* 26 [1980] 428–29). Then the question must be raised whether it is possible to determine what came undisputedly from the hand of the author of Mark and what came from tradition (ibid. 437). In addition, there is the question of why, if John knew the synoptics, he did not make greater use of them (ibid. 427). Finally it comes down to this: "Is it easier to explain the similarities on the basis that John did not know the synoptics than to explain the differences assuming John did?" (ibid. 443). I believe it is easier to explain the similarities on the assumption that John did not know the synoptics.

[50] C. K. Barrett, *The Gospel According to St. John* (Philadelphia: Westminster, 1978) 563; Brown, *The Gospel According to John,* 1000; Mary Catherine Carson, "They Said Nothing to Anyone: A Redaction-Critical Study of the Role and Status of Women in the Crucifixion, Burial and Resurrection Stories of the Canonical and Apocryphal Gospels" (Ph.D. diss., University of Newcastle upon Tyne, 1990) 262. John E. Alsup proposes that v. 2 is a redactional element, introduced by the author of John in an attempt to link vv. 3-10 with vv. 1 and 11-18 (*The Post-Resurrection Appearance Stories,* 100).

[51] Grass, *Ostergeschehen und Osterberichte,* 54; Fuller, *The Formation of the Resurrection Narratives,* 134. Lindars links vv. 1-2 with vv. 11-18 (*The Gospel of John,* 595).

[52] Raymond E. Brown (*The Gospel According to John,* 1000) and Pheme Perkins (*Resurrection,* 172) view vv. 1-2 as an independent, if abbreviated, episode.

[53] Yet another proposal for how these verses may be reconstructed is that of Gert Hartmann, who links v. 11a with vv. 1-10 and 14b-18. His proposal is based on the assumption that the race to the tomb, as recorded in the tradition, was between Peter and Mary Magdalene ("Die Vorlage der Osterberichte in Joh 20," *ZNW* 55 [1964] 198, 200). He notes that v. 8 (which states that the Beloved Disciple "believed") stands in tension with v. 9 (which implies that neither disciple understood the significance of the empty tomb because they did not yet know the Scripture saying that it was necessary for Jesus to be raised), and he suggests that v. 8 was inserted into the tradition by John. If v. 8 is removed, then this tension is resolved. Further, if the race to the tomb originally took place between Peter and Mary Magdalene, then the tension between vv. 10 and 11 is resolved: Verse 10 would speak of Peter returning to his home, while in v. 11a Mary would remain at the tomb (ibid. 201, 204–205). Hartmann goes on to suggest that the tradition picks up again at v. 14b, runs through v. 16, part of v. 17, and concludes with v. 18a (ibid. 206–209). He views the appearance of the angel as a late interpolation by the redactor (ibid. 205). According to this scheme the "race to the tomb" tradition would conclude with the appearance of Jesus to Mary Magdalene. In addition, it reflects the competition that

Is there evidence that the story was copied from an earlier written text?

Was John 20:1, 11-18 constructed from Matt 28:1-10?[54] The two texts share a number of elements in common. In both, the appearance of Jesus is linked to the narrative of the empty tomb and is preceded by the appearance of angels. Both texts emphasize Mary Magdalene: Matthew by naming her first among the women, and John by singling her out to come to the empty tomb. Both texts involve the element of "touch," and in both Jesus commands the women to go to "my brothers."[55]

More notable, however, are the many differences between them. In Matthew the appearance is to two women, while in John it is to Mary Magdalene alone;[56] further, the Gospel of John gives no evidence of knowing the other Mary named in Matthew. The appearance is only tangentially linked to the empty tomb story in the Gospel of Matthew, taking place as the women depart, while in John it is thoroughly integrated into the scene at the tomb. In Matthew there is one angel who rolls away the stone and then sits on it outside the tomb. In John there are two angels who sit inside the tomb and are wholly unconnected with the removal of the stone. The angel in Matthew gives the women a message to carry to the disciples, while in John the two angels ask why Mary is weeping. In Matthew the women recognize Jesus immediately. In John, Mary does not recognize Jesus, mistaking him for the gardener. In Matthew the women do not speak, while in John, Mary does speak. Jesus welcomes the women's touch in Matthew, but in John, Jesus tells Mary "do not touch" him.[57] The message the women are

---

is set up between Mary Magdalene and Peter in the Gospel of Mary and the Gospel of Thomas. It also lends support to the theory that the disciple Jesus loved is Mary Magdalene. However, there is no way of establishing Hartmann's thesis.

[54] Since John 20:1-11 includes an appearance by angels it is necessary to consider whether John is drawing not only on the appearance by Jesus, but also the appearance by the angels in Matthew.

[55] Frans Neirynck also thinks that the χαίρετε in Matthew's text represents a recognition motif. He goes on to suggest that since χαίρετε is usually followed by a proper name, the Μαριάμ in John 20:16 may reflect this greeting in Matt 28:9 ("John and the Synoptics: the Empty Tomb Stories," *NTS* 30 [1984] 168).

[56] As Neirynck observes, John does have a tendency to individuate characters, so this difference, at least, could be attributed to Johannine style ("John and the Synoptics," 167).

[57] There is some debate as to whether or not Mary Magdalene actually touches Jesus in John's narrative. For a current discussion of the issues see Harold W. Attridge, "'Don't Be Touching Me': Recent Feminist Scholarship on Mary Magda-

to carry to the disciples in each gospel is completely different.[58] These many differences point to two independent versions of a common story rather than literary dependence.

An examination of vocabulary bears out this conclusion. Most of the words shared by the two texts, such as "Sabbath" (σαββάτων), "come" (ἔρχομαι), "stone" (λίθος), and "angel" (ἄγγελος), are too common to provide credible evidence of literary dependence. At only two points is the similarity so striking that it is worthy of mention: both texts use Μαριάμ for Mary, and in both Jesus sends Mary to ἀδελφοί μοῦ ("my brothers"). Yet these points of contact are more easily explained as stable elements in oral tradition than evidence that the author of John has copied from Matthew's text. By analogy, one might argue that the use of "Goldilocks" and the phrase "someone's been sitting in my chair" indicates that the writer has clearly copied from a written text of "Goldilocks and the Three Bears." Yet anyone who has been called upon to recite this story knows that, no matter how else you might alter it, these elements must find their way into the tale. Neirynck suggests one additional point of contact. He notes that ἅπτομαι ("touch," John 20:17) can be interchanged with κρατέω ("take hold of," Matt 28:9) (e.g., Matt 8:15//Mark 1:31).[59] Yet in the one verse where John employs κρατέω (20:23) it takes on the sense of δέω ("bind") rather than ἅπτομαι. Some of these differences can be attributed to variations in literary style, while others may be the result of John's adapting the story to fit the narrative scheme of the gospel. Yet the sheer number of differences between the texts militates against the literary dependence of Gospel of John on the Gospel of Matthew for this story.

Does the story exhibit a clear beginning, middle, and end describing a single story line?

A single storyline can be traced through vv. 1, 11-18, exhibiting a clear beginning (Mary standing outside the tomb), expanded middle

lene," in Amy-Jill Levine, ed., *A Feminist Companion to John* (London: Sheffield Academic Press, 2003) 143, n. 6. The phrase is probably best left ambiguous.

[58] Frans Neirynck, arguing in favor of John's dependence on Matthew, comments that Matthew merely adapts the message of Mark's angel, and that John has no place for Galilee in his gospel ("John and the Synoptics," 169–70).

[59] Neirynck, "John and the Synoptics," 168; "Les femmes au tombeau," 187. See also Brown, *The Gospel According to John,* 992.

(dialogue with the angels, followed by dialogue with Jesus), and end (Mary departing to the disciples).[60] A twist in the story line exists where Mary speaks to the angels, then turns around and begins the conversation all over again with Jesus. However, it does not derail the flow of the story. Verses 1, 11-18 could have circulated as a story independent of John's text.

Does the story exhibit characteristics associated with oral text?

Numerous characteristics associated with oral text are found in John 20:1, 11-18. The story exhibits conventionality in form, as identified by John E. Alsup and others: (1) an appearance (vv. 14-15); (2) a verbal or nonverbal response to the appearance (vv. 16-17a); (3) words of comfort or a command spoken by the one appearing (v. 17).[61] In this version the form is expanded, with the addition of extended dialogue and a nonrecognition motif.

No more than two characters appear at one time. Mary comes to the tomb, where she encounters two angels. The latter inexplicably melt from the scene when Jesus appears. This strict adherence to the "law of two characters" leads to abrupt shifts in the storyline over which the reader stumbles in the written text, but which would easily be passed over by a hearer who is more interested in what comes next than in how one event leads smoothly to another.

Inconsistencies and illogical twists are found in nearly every verse. Mary is called Μαρία in vv. 1 and 11, but Μαριάμ in vv. 16 and 18.[62] The angels suddenly disappear, yet no explanation is given for their disappearance nor is it treated as surprising or in any other way unusual. When Jesus asks Mary the same question asked by the angels she offers a different response, but she does not question or show surprise at being asked a second time why she is weeping. In v. 17 Jesus tells Mary

[60] Fuller, *The Formation of the Resurrection Narratives,* 134; Grass, *Ostergeschehen und Osterberichte,* 54; Lindars, *The Gospel of John,* 595; Lüdemann, *The Resurrection of Jesus,* 156; contra Schnackenburg, *The Gospel According to St. John,* 306.

[61] John E. Alsup, *The Post-Resurrection Appearance Stories of the Gospel Tradition* (Stuttgart: Calwer, 1975) 211; James A. Bailey and Lyle D. Vander Broek, *Literary Forms in the New Testament* (Louisville: Westminster John Knox, 1992) 144, 154; Dodd, "The Appearances of the Risen Christ," 104; Joachim Gnilka, *Das Matthäusevangelium* (Freiburg: Herder, 1986) 1:491.

[62] See also Μαρία in 19:25 and 20:1.

to "stop holding me," yet no mention has been made of Mary taking hold of him. Finally, in v. 18 the text shifts abruptly from direct discourse to indirect discourse: "Mary Magdalene went and announced to the disciples, 'I have seen the Lord'; *and she told them that he had said these things to her.*" These inconsistencies and unexpected turns are difficult to explain if the story originated as a written composition. To the contrary, they point persuasively toward oral composition.[63]

Does the story diverge from the literary tendencies of the author?

The story of the post-resurrection appearance to Mary Magdalene is characteristic of John in nearly every way.[64] This makes the few words that do not seem to belong to John's literary tendencies all the more notable. These include: ἄγγελλοι ("angels"), ῥαββουνί ("teacher"), ἅπτομαι ("touch"), and ἀδελφοί ("brothers").[65]

[63] The numerous repetitions that occur in these verses may also indicate oral composition, but they are more difficult to assess. The author regularly uses patterns of repetition to develop themes throughout the gospel. Because of this practice it is not possible to discern which repetitions belong to the author and which might be evidence of oral composition. The same may be said of asides, such as that in v. 15 ("supposing him to be the gardener"), since these occur throughout the gospel (e.g., 1:15; 2:9; 4:2; 7:2, 39; 8:20; 11:5-7, 51; 18:14; 19:31). One might venture that the author of the Gospel of John has a very oral aural style, despite the emphasis on the gospel having been written (John 20:30; 21:25). On this subject see Joanna Dewey, "The Gospel of John in Its Oral-Written Media World," in Robert T. Fortna and Tom Thatcher, eds., *Jesus in Johannine Tradition* (Louisville: Westminster John Knox, 2001) 236–52.

[64] Alsup, *The Post-Resurrection Appearance Stories,* 209; Pierre Benoit, "Marie-Madeleine et les disciples au tombeau selon Jean 20, 1-18," in Walther Eltester, ed., *Judentum, Urchristentum, Kirche. Festschrift für Joachim Jeremias* (Berlin: A. Töpelmann, 1960) 146; Barnabas Lindars, "The Composition of John XX," *NTS* 7 (1960–1962) 145. See, for example: v. 14: οἶδα (Matthew = 25x; Mark = 23x; Luke-Acts = 44x; John = 83x); v. 15: γύναι ("women") (the vocative is employed by John 4x [2:4; 4:21; 19:26]; 1x only in Matthew [15:28] and Luke [13:12]); vv. 11, 13, 15: κλαίω ("weep") (not employed often, but significantly at the death of Lazarus [11:31, 33] and in 16:20 ["you will weep" when I/Jesus am gone]); v. 15: ζητέω ("seek") (a Johannine theme: 1:38; 6:26; 7:18, 34, 36; 8:21; 13:33; 16:19; 18:4, 7, 8); v. 16: Ἑβραιστι ("Hebrews") (appears only in John [5:2; 19:13, 17, 20; 20:16] and Revelation); v. 17: ἀναβαίνω ("go up": 3:13; 6:62. However, the theme of ascending is found also in 7:33, 13:1, 3; 14:4, 28; 16:5, 17, 28; 17:13 [C. K. Barrett, *The Gospel According to John,* 565]); v. 18: μαθητής ("disciple") (used consistently by John for the followers of Jesus).

[65] Rudolf Schnackenburg believes κῆπος ("gardener") originated with John's source material (*The Gospel According to St. John,* 317). Because of the strong garden

Although ἄγγελλοι ("angels") is a common word, it stands out here because of the lack of references to angels in John's gospel. While the synoptic gospels have numerous references to angels and appearances by angels, the Gospel of John contains only two references and one appearance.[66] In John 1:51 Jesus tells Nathanael that he "will see heaven opened and the angels of God ascending and descending upon the Son of man," and in 12:29 the crowds mistake the voice of God for the voice of an angel.[67] Therefore the sudden, unanticipated appearance by the angels in ch. 20 combined with their ambiguous role in the story suggests that they derive from a source other than the author.

Although Jesus is addressed as ῥαββί eight times in John, only in John 20:16 is he called ῥαββουνί.[68] This raises the question of whether ῥαββουνί is a variant introduced by the author or derives from a source employed by the author.[69] It is noteworthy that both terms are translated for the reader: ῥαββί ("teacher") the first time it appears in 1:38 and ῥαββουνί (also translated "teacher") in 20:16. It is possible that the author recognizes ῥαββουνί as a new title, sufficiently different from ῥαββί to require translation.[70] This may point to its origin in source material.

῞Απτομαι ("touch") appears only this one time in the Gospel of John, although people are described touching other persons elsewhere in the gospel. In 9:15, 16 Jesus anoints (ἐπιτίθημι) the eyes of the blind man with clay. In 20:25, 27 Thomas touches the wound in Jesus' side (βάλλω, φέρω). Two additional verbs are employed to describe taking hold of

---

imagery in the gospel (the tomb is said to be located in a garden [κῆπος {19:41}]; further, in the Gospel of John, Jesus is arrested in a garden [18:1, 26], in contrast to the synoptics where Jesus is arrested on the Mount of Olives [Mark 14:32//Matt 26:30//Luke 22:39]) I am less confident, although it is striking that the word occurs only this one time in the Second Testament.

[66] Matthew has 20 references to ἄγγελλοι; Mark has 6; Luke has 26.

[67] There also is a text variant in ch. 5 that adds a fourth verse to the chapter describing an angel coming down to stir the waters of the pool at the Sheep Gate, but the manuscript evidence in support of the variant is weak (e.g., A K L Δ f^{13}).

[68] ῾Ραββούνι appears elsewhere in the NT only in Mark 10:51.

[69] Robert G. Maccini thinks it originated with the author and was intended to signify a close personal bond between Mary Magdalene and Jesus (*Her Testimony is True: Women as Witnesses According to John* [Sheffield: Sheffield Academic Press, 1996] 213).

[70] Forms of ῥαββουνί are known from the Targums, including the fragment from the Cairo Geniza and the Targum of Onkelos (Barrett, *The Gospel According to St. John,* 565; Brown, *The Gospel According to John,* 991).

Jesus with the intent to arrest him: πιάζω and συλλαμβάνω.[71] It could be argued that the author employs distinct vocabulary in order to distinguish between the kinds of "touch" involved. Yet since the "touch" by Mary Magdalene is unanticipated and creates an illogical structure in the story, origin in source material seems more probable.[72]

Ἀδελφοί ("brothers"), as a reference to Jesus' disciples, also appears only this one time in the Gospel of John.[73] This is not the first time a unique expression has been used in relation to the disciples. In 15:15 Jesus tells the disciples: "No longer do I call you servants . . . but I have called you friends, for all that I have heard from my Father I have made known to you" (see also 13:16; 15:20). Some scholars have suggested that "brothers" signifies the fulfillment of Jesus' mission to enable all who believe in him to become children of God (1:12; see also 11:52) so that Jesus may truly speak of ascending to "my father and your father" (20:18), but the fit is not perfect.[74] In 15:15, when Jesus calls the disciples his φίλοι ("friends"), a climactic shift is effected in the status of the disciples' relationship to Jesus. It is not evident from the text that a further shift in this relationship is to be expected. The shift to "brothers" in 20:17 comes as a surprise. Only in the words that follow ("my father and your father") is the awkwardness smoothed over.[75]

Summary

This examination of the post-resurrection appearance to Mary Magdalene in John 20:1, 11-18 reveals that John is a skilled storyteller, able to clothe the story in language and images that resonate with the rest of

[71] Πιάζω 7:30, 32, 44; 8:20; 10:39; 11:57. In 21:3, 10 it is used in reference to catching fish. Συλλαμβάνω is in 18:12.

[72] Hartmann, "Die Vorlage der Osterberichte in John 20," 207; Rudolf Schnackenburg, *The Gospel According to St. John*, 318.

[73] Elsewhere it refers to Jesus' blood relations, who function as a distinct group within the gospel.

[74] Bultmann, *The Gospel of John*, 688; Sandra M. Schneiders, "Women in the Fourth Gospel and the Role of Women in the Contemporary Church," in Mark W. G. Stibbe, ed., *The Gospel of John as Literature: An Anthology of Twentieth-Century Perspectives* (Leiden: Brill, 1993) 140; Robert H. Smith, *Easter Gospels: The Resurrection of Jesus According to the Four Evangelists* (Minneapolis: Augsburg, 1983) 165.

[75] Dodd ("The Appearances of the Risen Christ," 147), Hartmann ("Die Vorlage der Osterberichte in Joh 20," 207) and Schnackenburg (*The Gospel According to St. John*, 320) think that ἀδελφοί reflects John's source.

the gospel narrative. At the same time, the story exhibits twists and turns that make it evident the author has cobbled it together from a variety of sources. The probability of the written text of Matthew's gospel being one of those sources is slight. The lack of verbal similarities and the number of differences in story line, content, and characterization argue strongly against literary dependence. Rather, the quantity of oral characteristics exhibited in the text points to dependence on oral tradition.[76]

Analysis of Matthew 28:9-10

The post-resurrection appearance to the women in Matt 28:9-10 is the earliest extant version of this story in writing. The absence of an earlier written text makes it impossible to examine the appearance story in relation to the first criterion. It does not, however, eliminate the possibility that the story was copied from a written source. I will address this possibility in the summary, after first examining Matt 28:9-10 in

[76] Benoit, "Marie-Madeleine et les disciples au tombeau selon Jean 20, 1-18," 145, 151; François Bovon, "Le privilège pascal de Marie-Madeleine," *NTS* 30 (1984) 50; Brown, *The Gospel According to John,* 1003; Nils A. Dahl, "The Passion Narrative in Matthew," in Graham Stanton, ed., *The Interpretation of Matthew* (Philadelphia: Fortress, 1995) 46; Fuller, *The Formation of the Resurrection Narratives,* 137; Gnilka, *Das Matthäusevangelium,* 492; Hengel, "Maria Magdalena und die Frauen als Zeugen," 255; Charles Masson, "Le tombeau vide: essai sur la formation d'une tradition," *RTP* 32 (1944) 167; Perkins, *Resurrection,* 130; Schnackenburg, *The Gospel According to St. John* 3:308; Mary R. Thompson, *Mary of Magdala: Apostle and Leader* (Mahwah, N.J.: Paulist, 1995) 69; David Wenham, "The Resurrection in Matthew's Gospel," *TynBul* 24 (1972) 35. A question can be raised whether the narrative in John is dependent on Matthew indirectly, through the re-oralization of Matthew's text. If this is the case, then the re-oralized version must have gone through several transformations before circulating to the author of John. Another approach would be to argue that John invented the narrative of the post-resurrection appearance to Mary Magdalene. However, in addition to the points discussed in the main text, two observations militate against such a theory: (1) Outside of the empty tomb and appearance narratives Mary Magdalene plays a minor role in John's gospel. Whereas she is listed first among women who witness the crucifixion in Mark and Matthew, in John she is listed third. In addition, she does not witness where Jesus is buried. (2) John is determined that the disciple whom Jesus loved will be the first to "believe." The awkward way in which John brings this about suggests that the tradition of a post-resurrection appearance to Mary Magdalene must have been dominant enough that John could not supplant it.

relation to the other three criteria. The text of Matthew invites an additional question, not asked of the other two texts: Did the author of the Gospel of Matthew invent the story of the appearance to the women?

Does the story exhibit a clear beginning, middle, and end describing a single story line?

Despite its brevity, the appearance story in Matt 28:9-10 exhibits a distinct beginning (Jesus appears), middle (the women respond), and end (Jesus commissions the women to go to the disciples) that follows a single storyline. Similarly brief appearance stories can be found in Greco-Roman literature and inscriptions (see Appendix E) as well as in the Babylonian Talmud (see Appendix F). It is not uncommon in these stories for references to the temporal and spatial setting to be omitted, as in Matt 28:9-10, nor is it uncommon for the stories to conclude with the words of the one appearing (see especially the examples from the Second Testament in Appendix G). Hence the post-resurrection appearance to the women in Matt 28:9-10 is not unusual, but conforms to an established pattern.[77]

In addition, it is notable how little the story has been woven into the surrounding text. Verse 1 introduces the women and provides the temporal and spatial setting for vv. 9-10. The reference to the women's departure in v. 11 similarly creates a transition from the appearance story to the events that follow. However, neither v. 1 nor v. 11 is necessary to satisfy the structure of the story. Both may be explained as an effort by the author to link the post-resurrection appearance with the surrounding text. The success of this endeavor has been called into question. Alexander Sand observes that if vv. 9-10 are removed from the text, the narrative reads as smoothly as if they had never been there at all.[78] Matthew 28:9-10, therefore, does represent a discrete episode that could have circulated independently of Matthew's gospel.[79]

[77] Gnilka, *Das Matthäusevangelium*, 491. See also Alsup, *The Post-Resurrection Appearance Stories in the Gospel Tradition*, 211; Bailey and Vander Broek, *Literary Forms in the New Testament*, 144, 154; Dodd, "The Appearances of the Risen Christ," 104.

[78] Alexander Sand, *Das Evangelium nach Matthäus* (Regensburg: Pustet, 1986) 591.

[79] Brun, *Die Auferstehung Christi in der urchristlichen Überlieferung*, 86; Descamps, "La structure des récits évangéliques de la résurrection," 730; Gnilka, *Das Matthäusevangelium*, 490, 491; Heine, "Eine Person von Rang und Namen," 186; Lüdemann,

Does the story exhibit characteristics associated with oral text?

Although the story exhibits conventionality in form and only two characters appear in the scene, neither of these observations carries much weight. The brevity of the scene hardly allows for more than two characters, and the form may be modeled on the earlier appearance by the angel.[80] More notable is the illogical structure that results from the appearance story following on the story of the empty tomb. The angel tells the women to tell the disciples that "you will see" (ὄψεσθε) Jesus in Galilee. The disciples do see Jesus in Galilee, but only after the women have seen Jesus first, somewhere in the vicinity of Jerusalem. Nothing has prepared the reader for the appearance of Jesus to the women.[81] Even if the reader concludes that the women are among the disciples, the confusion persists because the appearance does not take place in Galilee as the angel said it would. This awkwardness suggests that Matthew has joined two traditions together.[82]

An inconsistency also exists within the story. When Jesus first appears to the women, he greets them (v. 9a). They respond by approaching him, taking hold of his feet, and worshiping him (v. 9b). Jesus then says to them, "do not fear" (v. 10). Although this is a traditional formula in appearance stories, in the context of vv. 9-10 it is nonsensical.[83]

Resurrection of Jesus, 131; Masson, "Le tombeau vide," 167; Wilhelm Michaelis, *Die Erscheinungen des Auferstandenen* (Basel: Heinrich Majer, 1944) 16; Sand, *Das Evangelium nach Matthäus*, 585.

[80] This is the view held by Alsup, *The Post-Resurrection Appearance Stories in the Gospel Tradition*, 110; Bode, *The First Easter Morning*, 56; Brun, *Die Auferstehung Christi*, 54; Bultmann, *History of the Synoptic Tradition*, 288; Hill, *The Gospel of Matthew*, 359; Neirynck, "Les femmes au tombeau," 184; Sabourin, *The Gospel According to St. Matthew*, 929. Reginald Fuller thinks that the Christophany probably arose from the angelophany at an earlier date (*The Formation of the Resurrection Narratives*, 78 (so also Brun, *Die Auferstehung Christi*, 54).

[81] Descamps, "La structure des récits évangéliques de la résurrection," 730; Fuller, *The Formation of the Resurrection Narratives*, 78.

[82] Descamps, "La structure des récits évangéliques de la résurrection," 731; Fuller, *The Formation of the Resurrection Narratives*, 78; John T. Larson, "The Application of Redaction Criticism to the Resurrection Accounts of the Synoptic Gospels" (M.A. thesis, Graduate Theological Union, 1971) 31; Michaelis, *Die Erscheinungen*, 16; Sand, *Das Evangelium nach Matthäus*, 591.

[83] Perkins, *Resurrection*, 130. See also Gen 15:1; 22:17; Luke 1:13, 30; 2:10. Robert Gundry (*Matthew* [Grand Rapids: Eerdmans, 1982, 591) and George Dunbar Kilpatrick (*The Origins of the Gospel According to St. Matthew* [Oxford: Clarendon Press, 1946] 48) view φοβέομαι as Matthean. In two instances Matthew introduces

There is nothing in the behavior of the women to suggest that they are afraid.[84] Jesus' initial greeting elicits not fear, but piety. Thus the response "do not fear" may be a carryover from source material, which the author of Matthew has altered so that the response by the women conforms to a literary theme developed in the gospel.[85]

Does the narrative diverge from the literary tendencies of the author?

These two short verses contain a number of words that are distinctly Matthean. At least two are almost certainly from the hand of the author: προσέρχομαι ("go") and προσκυνέω ("worship"). In addition, there are words and phrases the author has likely borrowed from the appearance of the angel to the women in Mark 16:1-8: ὑπάγω ("go"), εἰς τὴν Γαλιλαίαν ("to Galilee"), and ὁράω ("see").

Nonetheless, three words diverge from Matthew's literary tendencies. The first is ὑπαντάω ("meet"). This verb occurs twice in Matthew (8:28 and 28:9). The first occurrence is taken over from Matthew's source, Mark 5:2. The second belongs either to the hand of Matthew or to another source. Matthew also employs the noun cognates ὑπάντησις ("meeting") (8:34; 25:1) and ἀπάντησις ("meeting") (25:6).[86] An examination of the three occurrences of the nouns, along with the use of the verb in 8:28, suggests a pattern. Both 8:28 and 8:34 belong to the same pericope. In 8:28 two demoniacs meet (ὑπήντησαν) Jesus; in 8:34, the whole city comes out to meet (ὑπάντησιν) Jesus and beg him to leave their neighborhood. The verb and the noun, therefore, are used in a parallel construction. The same phenomenon occurs in 25:1 and 25:6. In 25:1 ten virgins take lamps and go to meet (ὑπάντησιν) the bridegroom. In 25:6 a cry goes out, "Behold, the bridegroom! Come out to

---

the expression μή φοβεῖσθε into the text (10:26; 17:7) and in a third (28:5) modifies his source (Mark 16:6) by changing the words of the angel from μὴ ἐκθαμβεῖσθε to μὴ φοβεῖσθε. Yet because it is a common expression it may as easily reflect a source in 28:10 as the hand of Matthew.

[84] Frans Neirynck ("Les femmes au tombeau," 182) argues that the women's fear in v. 8 must be overcome. But since the women are already on their way to tell the disciples what the angel has said when they encounter Jesus, whatever the nature of their fear, it was no obstacle in need of being overcome.

[85] See the discussion in ch. 5 on προσκυνέω.

[86] The cognate ἀπαντάω does not occur in Matthew. Robert Gundry, noting that the cognate ὑπάντησις occurs only three times in the NT, but twice in Matthew, includes this in his list of Matthean vocabulary (*Matthew*, 591).

meet (ἀπάντησιν) him!" Again a parallel construction is employed. The only other occurrence of some form of the word is in 28:9. But here there is no parallel construction. Further, in the four instances where the verb or a cognate form is employed prior to 28:9 it is a person or group who meets Jesus/the bridegroom. Only in 28:9 is this pattern reversed. This makes the use of the verb in 28:9 an anomaly.[87]

The second word is κρατέω ("take hold of"). This word occurs twelve times in Matthew.[88] Of these occurrences seven are taken over from Mark, one is found in "Q" (22:6), two are additions to the text by Matthew (12:11; 26:57), and two are either Matthean additions or come from another source, such as "M" (18:28; 28:9). In nine of the twelve verses κρατέω is used in reference to seizing someone with the intent to do them harm or to arrest them.[89] In one case (9:25, *par.* Mark 5:41) Jesus takes a girl by the hand, healing her. In another (12:11) he speaks of grabbing a sheep out of a pit. Only in 28:9 is the word used in reference to taking hold of Jesus' feet. Elsewhere this is an expression Matthew avoids.[90] In two instances Matthew substitutes προσκυνέω ("worship") for Mark's description of someone "falling (πίπτω) at Jesus' feet" (Mark 5:22; 7:25).[91] Hence the use of κρατέω in 28:9 is an anomaly in Matthew.[92] A closer look at the verse supports this thesis. Κρατέω is sandwiched between two words favored by Matthew, προσέρχομαι and προσκυνέω.[93] It may be that Matthew employs these two words in order to smooth over an expression normally avoided, ἐκράτησαν αὐτοῦ τοὺς πόδας

[87] Gundry includes ὑπαντάω and ὑπάντησις in his list of Matthean words, but not ἀπάντησις (*Matthew*, 681, 674).

[88] Matt 9:25 (//Mark 5:41); 12:11; 14:3 (//Mark 6:17); 18:28; 21:46 (//Mark 12:12); 22:6; 26:4, 48, 50, 55 (//Mark 14:1, 44, 46, 49); 26:57; 28:9.

[89] Matt 14:3; 18:28; 21:46; 22:6; 26:4, 48, 50, 55, 57.

[90] Gnilka, *Das Matthäusevangelium*, 493, n. 12. This conclusion is upheld when one examines Matthew's use of πούς: 4:6 (//Luke 4:11); 5:35; 7:6; 10:14 (//Mark 6:11); 15:30; 18:8 (//Mark 9:45); 22:13; 22:44 (// Mark 12:36); 28:9.

[91] Προσκυνέω may imply prostration; however, the emphasis seems to be on the worship of a superior, such as a god or king (Henry George Liddell and Robert Scott, *A Greek-English Lexicon* [Oxford: Clarendon Press, 1940] 1918). On three occasions Matthew combines πίπτω with προσκυνέω (2:11; 4:9; 18:26 ["M"]) to render, "fall and reverence."

[92] It is unlikely that Matthew includes this detail in order to emphasize that the risen Jesus is a body and not a phantom, since Matthew shows no interest in this issue in 28:16-20 (Neirynck, "Les femmes au tombeau," 178; contra Gnilka, *Matthäusevangelium*, 195; John P. Meier, *Matthew* [Wilmington: Michael Glazier, 1980] 364).

[93] Gundry (*Matthew*, 591); Kilpatrick, *The Origins of the Gospel*, 48.

("they took hold of his feet").[94] This suggests that Matthew may be drawing on source material at this point.

The third word is ἀδελφοί ("brothers"). There is little doubt that "brothers" is a word favored by Matthew.[95] However, since it is a word that was used extensively by Paul when addressing fellow Christians it was presumably a common expression within early Christian communities.[96] This raises a question of whether the reference to "brothers" in 28:10 belongs to a source employed by Matthew or is the work of Matthew's hand.[97]

A review of how Matthew employs the expression "brothers" lends support to the possibility that Matthew is drawing on a source in 28:10.[98] The most extensive use of "brothers" occurs in the Sermon on the Mount.[99] These teachings are addressed to both the disciples and the crowds (5:1, but also 7:28-29). The references to the behavior of "brothers," therefore, seem to be intended for all believers.[100] The same may be said of the teachings in 18:15, 21, 35. Here the teachings are addressed specifically to the disciples. However, those that involve the behavior of "brothers" are set in the context of the whole body of believers (18:17; see also 19:29; 23:8; 25:40).[101] The one exception to this pattern is 12:49, where it is stated that Jesus, "stretching out his hand toward his disciples," said, "Here are my mother and my brothers." This seems to intimate that it is the disciples specifically who are the "brothers." However, v. 50 redirects the expression to the whole body of believers, stating that "whoever does the will of my Father in heaven is my brother, and sister, and mother." When the reader arrives at 28:10,

[94] Neirynck thinks ἐκράτησαν αὐτοῦ τοὺς πόδας is probably nothing more than a formula building on the act of worship ("Les femmes au tombeau," 179). However, this does not explain why Matthew avoids this expression elsewhere.

[95] Gundry, *Matthew,* 591.

[96] E.g., Rom 1:13; 8:12; 15:30; 1 Cor 1:10; 6:5-6; 15:1; Gal 1:11; 4:12; 5:13; Phil 1:12; 3:1; 4:21; 1 Thess 1:4; 4:13; 5:25.

[97] Gundry thinks ἀδελφοί is Matthean (*Matthew,* 591), as does Neirynck, "Les femmes au tombeau," 183.

[98] Matt 5:22, 23, 24, 47; 7:3, 4, 5; 12:46, 47, 48, 49, 50; 18:15, 21, 35; 19:29; 23:8; 25:40; 28:10. As a reference to blood relatives see 4:18, 21; 10:2; 10:21; 13:55; 14:3; 17:1; 20:24; 22:24, 25.

[99] Matt 5:22, 23, 24, 47; 7:3, 4, 5.

[100] The question whether "disciples" should be understood as a reference to the whole community of believers is taken up in Chapter Five. I conclude that it should not.

[101] Note that 23:8 also is addressed to both the crowds and the disciples.

then, and sees the word "brothers," does she hear this as a reference to the community of believers, or to the disciples? The situation is clarified by the time she arrives at v. 16, when the eleven are specified, but is this what the reader would have expected based on earlier uses of the word "brothers"?[102] Since in only one verse is it implied that "brothers" should be heard as "disciples" (12:49) it seems more likely that the reader will hear "community of believers." Thus even though "brothers" fits well within the realm of Matthew's vocabulary, its use in 28:10 is less obviously Matthean.[103] The possibility exists, therefore, that "brothers" could have as its source oral tradition rather than the hand of Matthew.

It is worth noting that the "non-Matthean" interpolations both describe action. Taken together, the following sequence is revealed: "he met . . . they took hold of his feet. . . ." It may be possible to add to this sequence: "do not fear . . . brothers. . . ." These bits and pieces come close to suggesting the outline of a narrative.[104] Studies of oral text reveal that it is just such a core structure that tends to remain stable in transmission, while details and dialogue may shift at the discretion of the narrator and the demands of the audience.[105] Thus the places in the text where the story diverges from Matthew's literary tendencies may also indicate a source for the narrative other than the author.

Summary

This examination of Matt 28:9-10 has sought to clarify whether these verses were invented by the author or have their origin in source material. The presence of Matthean vocabulary, along with efforts by the author to weave the verses into the stories that precede and follow, show

[102] Neirynck thinks it is ("Les femmes au tombeau," 182). Michaelis is less certain (*Die Erscheinungen des Auferstandenen,* 18).

[103] Michaelis does not think that ἀδελφοί in 28:10 is consistent with Matthean usage (*Die Erscheinungen des Auferstandenen,* 18). See also Wenham, "The Resurrection in Matthew's Gospel," 34.

[104] Wenham sees this pattern as evidence of a tradition inherited by Matthew ("The Resurrection in Matthew's Gospel," 35).

[105] Kenneth E. Bailey, "Informal Controlled Oral Tradition and the Synoptic Gospels," *Asia Journal of Theology* 5 (1991) 42; Ben-Amos, *Folklore in Context,* 25–26; Finnegan, *Oral Poetry,* 52–72; Long, "Recent Field Studies in Oral Literature," 37; Albert Bates Lord, *The Singer of Tales* (Cambridge, Mass.: Harvard University Press, 1964) 43.

that the author has shaped the appearance story to fit the narrative scheme of the gospel. That the author invented the story is less certain. As the preceding analysis reveals, the verses can stand as an independent episode, exhibit characteristics of oral text, and diverge at three points from Matthew's literary tendencies. Further, the non-Matthean words point to an underlying narrative structure. Therefore there is good reason to doubt that vv. 9-10 were invented by the author.

If they were not invented by the author, did the author draw on an oral or written source? Since neither is accessible to us, we can only speak in terms of probability. There are four reasons why I believe an oral source is more probable:

(1) Each gospel contains stories not found in the other gospels. This indicates that there was a large pool of stories circulating, from which individual authors selected the stories best suited to the needs of their narrative.

(2) Within the gospels we have examples of the free circulation of stories. Two striking examples are the woman caught in adultery and the "miraculous catch of fish." The woman caught in adultery is printed in most Bibles as John 7:53–8:11. However, in the manuscripts it proves to be a "floating" story looking for a home. Some manuscripts place it after Luke 21:28, others after Luke 24:53, still others following John 7:36, while numerous manuscripts omit it altogether. The manuscript evidence suggests that the story was circulating freely and that, over time, it was integrated into two written texts, at different points in each text. The "miraculous catch of fish" presents a similar example. This story is recorded in John 21:4-8 as a post-resurrection appearance by Jesus to Peter and other disciples. In Luke 5:1-11 it is recorded as the call of Simon [Peter]. The similarities between the stories suggest a common source, but their different locations in the two gospels indicate that they did not belong to a fixed narrative setting. Both examples point to the ongoing circulation of stories and their performance in different narrative contexts.

(3) Verses 9-10 exhibit characteristics of oral as well as written text, pointing to circulation as oral tradition.

(4) In the predominantly oral aural environment of the first century C.E., described in Chapters One and Two, the vast majority of people had limited recourse to written texts and relied almost exclusively on memory and the spoken word. While a written text of the Magdalene story *may* have existed, an oral version almost certainly did. In the end there is no final answer to the question, yet in view of the evidence it

seems more probable that the author has adapted an oral tradition to the text.[106]

Conclusion

We have inherited three separate versions of a post-resurrection appearance to Mary Magdalene. Despite shared story lines and, in some instances, shared vocabulary, there is insufficient evidence to posit conclusively that these three versions, recorded in Matthew, John, and the Longer Ending of Mark, were copied from earlier written texts. The variables between them, in combination with their common elements, suggest that the more plausible explanation is access to versions of the Magdalene story circulating as oral tradition among early Christian communities.[107] This circulation did not stop when the story was written down.[108] In a time and place when so few could read or write, it strains credibility to believe that written texts brought an end to storytelling, particularly when these written texts had not yet formed any authority of their own.[109] Further, since these written texts would, by

[106] A number of scholars think the post-resurrection narrative in Matthew is drawn from oral tradition: Benoit, "Marie-Madeleine et les disciples au tombeau selon Jean 20, 1-18," 145, 151; Peder Borgen, "John and the Synoptics in the Passion Narrative," *NTS* 5 (1958–59) 247; Bovon, "Le privilège pascal de Marie-Madeleine," 51; Brown, *The Gospel According to John,* 1002; Dahl, "The Passion Narrative in Matthew," 46; Descamps, "La structure des récits évangéliques de la résurrection," 731; Gardner-Smith, *St. John and the Synoptic Gospels,* viii; Gnilka, *Das Matthäusevangelium,* 490; Heine, "Eine Person von Rang und Namen," 186; Hengel, "Maria Magdalena und die Frauen als Zeugen," 255; Kilpatrick, *The Origins of the Gospel,* 49; Lüdemann, *The Resurrection of Jesus,* 131; Masson, "Le tombeau vide: essai sur la formation d'une tradition," 167; Michaelis, *Die Erscheinungen des Auferstandenen,* 16; Sand, *Das Evangelium nach Matthäus,* 585; Wenham, "The Resurrection in Matthew's Gospel," 33. n. 40. Roman Kuhschelm thinks the angelophany and Christophany may represent two versions of the same experience ("Angelophanie-Christophanie in den synoptischen Grabesgeschichten," in Camille Focant, ed., *The Synoptic Gospels: Source Criticism and the New Literary Criticism* [Leuven: Leuven University Press, 1993] 563).

[107] Pheme Perkins thinks that the number of differences between the narratives indicates there was no unified tradition regarding the appearance to Mary Magdalene (*Resurrection,* 91).

[108] See remarks on Chapter Three in Chapter One, "Introduction."

[109] C. H. Dodd, "Thirty Years of New Testament Study," *Religion in Life* 47 (1978) 324–25; John Miles Foley, *Traditional Oral Epic* (Berkeley: University of California Press, 1990) 5; Robin Lane Fox, "Literacy and Power in Early Christianity," in Alan

necessity, be read aloud, the stories were not confined to the written page but reentered the free-flowing world of oral exchange as they joined the repertoire of first one storyteller and then another.[110]

The realization that the Magdalene stories circulated orally has several implications for our understanding of the tradition. It indicates that the Magdalene story was valued and kept alive through repeated performance in early Christian communities. It confirms that we are not looking at a fixed text, but a text that has the capacity to be recreated again and again. This is evident from the written versions that have come down to us. No single text, then, represents the Magdalene tradition. Finally, it reminds us that the Magdalene tradition was formed and transformed by its performance context. No single meaning can be assigned to the text, and careful attention must be given to the context in which it is told, the interests it serves, and the interests it argues against. In the next chapter I will consider the tradition as performance in an oral, storytelling environment—apart from the restraints of a written gospel narrative—and how it functioned to shape social life in early Christian communities.[111]

K. Bowman and Greg Woolf, eds., *Literacy and Power in the Ancient World* (Cambridge: Cambridge University Press, 1994) 127; Eduard Nielsen, *Oral Tradition: A Modern Problem in the Old Testament Introduction.* Studies in Biblical Theology 11 (London: S.C.M., 1954) 34–35; Helmut Koester, "Written Gospels or Oral Traditions?" *JBL* 113 (1994) 29.

[110] Gilbert L. Bartholomew, "Feed My Lambs: John 21:15-19 as Oral Gospel," *Semeia* 39 (1987) 74; Thomas E. Boomershine, "Peter's Denial as Polemic of Confession: The Implications of Media Criticism for Biblical Hermeneutics," *Semeia* 39 (1987) 74; Jack Goody, *The Interface between the Written and the Oral* (New York: Cambridge University Press, 1987) 106; Nielsen, *Oral Tradition,* 34–35; Rosenberg, "The Complexity of Oral Tradition," 73–90.

[111] One would like to be able to speculate on the date of the tradition, but any suggestion would be exactly that—speculation. The evidence of this chapter indicates that it predates the gospels. Those who favor an early date cite in support the tenacity of the Magdalene tradition and the improbability of fabricating an appearance to a woman (Bovon, "Le privilège pascal de Marie-Madeleine," 51; Brown, *The Gospel According to John,* 692, n. 12; Heine, "Eine Person von Rang und Namen," 185; Schneiders, "Women in the Fourth Gospel and the Role of Women in the Contemporary Church," 140). Some speculate that narrative traditions may bear an earlier date than summary lists of witnesses (Peter Carnley, *The Structure of Resurrection Belief* [Oxford: Clarendon Press, 1987] 206; Ahn Byung-Mu, "The Transmitters of the Jesus-Event," *CTC Bulletin* [Dec 1984–April 1985] 27). If this was the case, then the post-resurrection appearance to Mary Magdalene might predate the lists recorded in 1 Cor 15:5-8.

Chapter Four

Functions of the Mary Magdalene Tradition in Storytelling Circles

Oral narratives, by definition, exist only in performance, when a storyteller and an audience come together in the same location.[1] In a strict sense these narratives are lost to us. While we have the stories, we neither hear the rhythmic voice of the storyteller nor sit elbow-to-elbow with a first-century audience. We have limited access to the common desires, experiences, and relationships that would have drawn them together and, more importantly, we have no way to capture the moment in which these four—storyteller, story, audience, and context—came alive in performance. In view of these limitations, this chapter undertakes a self-consciously heuristic task: to "re-oralize" the Magdalene story in a first-century context.

To re-oralize a written text requires the identification of four elements: the storyteller, the story, the audience, and the context, recognizing that each of these elements is not "fixed" but ever shifting, and that together they constitute an almost infinite number of possibilities. Furthermore, it is not enough to simply identify these elements. It is necessary to describe how they interact to create the moment called "performance," a moment that has no existence beyond itself. It is also

[1] Richard Bauman, *Verbal Art as Performance* (Rowley, Mass.: Newbury House, 1977) 42; Dan Ben-Amos, *Folklore in Context* (New Delhi: South Asian Publishers, 1982) 13; Beverly Long, "Recent Field Studies in Oral Literature and Their Bearing on Old Testament Criticism," *VT* 26 (1976) 189.

necessary to recognize that what is described is not itself a performance, but only points to the possibility of performance. Inadequate as this may be, it has the potential to offer us a glimpse of ways in which the Magdalene stories functioned as a living tradition in early Christian communities.[2]

I will begin with a brief description of potential storytellers, audiences, and performance contexts, drawing on the reconstruction of storytelling in Chapter Two. This will be followed by a lengthier analysis of the Magdalene stories in relation to the genre, legend. In this analysis particular emphasis will be placed on the stories as texts that are not fixed, but both stable and variable. The variable elements reveal where a storyteller was most able to shape the story; the stable elements reveal where the story became fixed through repeated performance. This analysis will provide the basis for the concluding discussion, in which I propose ways these four elements—storyteller, story, audience, and context—came together in performance.

Storytellers and Audiences in Context

The story of the post-resurrection appearance to Mary Magdalene was told and retold in early Christian communities. Each telling of the story would have been different, shaped by the particular configuration of storyteller and audience, the setting in which the story was told, and the occasion that was the cause of their gathering together.[3] We can catch glimpses of these multiple storytelling contexts by drawing on the earlier reconstruction of storytelling in the world of antiquity in Chapter Two.

[2] Two recent studies that also focus on the oral nature of written texts are Antoinette Clark Wire, *Holy Lives, Holy Deaths: A Close Hearing of Early Jewish Storytellers* (Atlanta: Society of Biblical Literature, 2002) and Richard A. Horsley with Jonathan A. Draper, *Whoever Hears You Hears Me: Prophets, Performance and Tradition in Q* (Harrisburg: Trinity Press International, 1999). Wire undertakes a close "hearing" of the text in order to identify performance cues. Horsley and Draper focus on Q as oral communication.

[3] Robert A. Georges, "Toward an Understanding of Storytelling Events," *JAF* 82 (1969) 324; Ilhan Basgöz, "The Tale Singer and His Audience," in Dan Ben-Amos and Kenneth S. Goldstein, eds., *Folklore: Performance and Communication* (The Hague: Mouton, 1975) 159; Dell H. Hymes, *"In Vain I tried to tell you": Essays in Native American Ethnopoetics* (Philadelphia: University of Pennsylvania Press, 1981) 86.

The Magdalene story gives every indication of being an "in-house" story, told within communities of believers rather than to persons outside those communities. There is no attempt to explain or justify the sudden appearance of Jesus. In each extant version of the story Mary goes to fellow believers with the news that Jesus is risen. The intimate exchange between Mary and Jesus in John's version and the women's worshipful response to Jesus in Matthew's version describe behavior of persons who are already followers of Jesus and for whom the resurrection of Jesus is a vindication of their faith. This is a story that belongs to the community and helps the community to identify itself in the midst of the dominant culture.[4]

The settings in which the Magdalene story may have been told are aligned with the activity of daily life: in the home, over meals, at work. Two of the contexts, the "home" and "meals," may signal gatherings of the community for worship and the sharing of the Lord's Supper. Since the Magdalene story itself evokes the presence of the risen Jesus it is possible that the story was told whenever the community gathered to recall the resurrection. The response by the women in Matthew's version suggests the telling of this story in the context of worship. Yet there is no reason to assume that the story was restricted to this context. With the possible exception of the recitation of Jesus' words at the Lord's Supper, nothing in our evidence points to restrictions or regulations that governed telling the stories of Jesus.

Other possible settings are suggested by the contexts of "home, meals, work." The Magdalene story may have been told among or within families in the evening after a meal, particularly in communities that lifted up Mary Magdalene among the leaders of the early church. It may have been told by women as they worked side by side at common tasks such as spinning or weaving, or when they gathered to prepare a body for burial. It may have been told by men who contemplated the promise of resurrection even as they watched one another being worked to death, hauling out their wares in the marketplace or traveling to the next village, where they heard that laborers were needed. Perhaps it was told by a mother or father to children as they rested after tending the family's plot of vegetables, to remind them that there was a savior other than Caesar who promised them life. Ultimately the storyteller

[4] William H. Jansen, "The Esoteric-Exoteric Factor in Folklore," in Alan Dundes, ed., *The Study of Folklore* (Englewood Cliffs, N.J.: Prentice-Hall, 1965) 46–49.

and audience would determine whether a context was appropriate for the telling of any one particular story.

In gatherings of the community the audience would have consisted of women, men, and children of varying ages and status within the community. In these larger gatherings it is likely that status within the community determined who assumed the role of storyteller. The writings of the Second Testament suggest that status was defined in different ways by different communities. In the text of John the "disciple whom Jesus loved" is given privilege of place; in Corinth it is those who demonstrate spiritual gifts; in Acts it is the apostles in Jerusalem, but individual stories suggest that among the widows Dorcas was particularly respected, and Priscilla, a coworker of Paul's, was recognized as a teacher. There are, in addition, the women who are said to have provided financial support for the mission of the early church, such as Mary Magdalene, Joanna, and Phoebe. They, too, may have been among the first chosen to address the community. Within large gatherings of the community storytelling could be used to entertain, to teach, to exhort, to encourage, to persuade, and to settle disputes. In the case of the latter, the storyteller was in a position of particular influence but could find that the next storyteller might propose a different course of action by the story she chose to tell.

Smaller gatherings of families, or "fictive kin" would have formed a similar mixed audience, but the dynamics would have differed somewhat from those of larger gatherings. In these smaller gatherings status may still have determined who spoke first, but status was more likely determined by gender or age, or perhaps by who was recognized as the most gifted storyteller. While the role of storyteller in larger gatherings was probably restricted to a few, the evidence from Chapter Two suggests that in smaller gatherings it might be passed from person to person. This is likely to have been the case in work settings, where storytelling was used to pass the time.

Since women are central figures in the Magdalene story it is probable that the story was favored by women. The evidence from Chapter Two suggests that in gatherings of women it may have been told to support the experience of other women or to show one another what was possible, although in larger gatherings of women it may have been told to promote status by association. This agonistic use of the story is more likely to have occurred in gatherings of men, where one and then another might tell a story of an appearance by Jesus that established the precedence of his community or patron.

In each gathering the Magdalene story would have taken on a different shape, molded by the intersection of storyteller, audience, and setting. This review of storytellers and audiences in context underlines the degree to which stories about Jesus belonged to the community rather than to individuals or leaders within the community. It also underlines the capacity of the stories to be adapted to a variety of contexts, which, in turn, would shape how the stories were told. As the shape of the story shifted, so too would its function in the life of the community. I turn next to the Magdalene tradition, to consider in what ways the tradition could be shaped to address the life of the community.

The Magdalene Tradition as Story

The stories of the post-resurrection appearance to Mary Magdalene belong to the broad genre of legend.[5] The identification of the stories' genre is important for two reasons. First, genre produces a "horizon of expectation" in both storyteller and audience: that is, a set of shared assumptions about how a story will unfold and how it should be received.[6] Identifying the genre of the Magdalene stories will enable us to align our own expectations more nearly with those of a first-century audience. Second, the identification of the stories' genre allows us to compare the Magdalene stories with other, similar legends. This comparative analysis will assist in uncovering how the Magdalene stories conform to and diverge from other appearance stories in the world of

[5] D. Felton, *Haunted Greece and Rome* (Austin: University of Texas Press, 1999) 2. The identification of genre is open to some debate, both because there is a lack of agreement with respect to definition and because narratives often may belong to more than one genre. Although I have elected to identify the post-resurrection narratives as "legends," it also is possible to speak of them as commissioning narratives or epiphanies. I have avoided "epiphany" because it assumes the appearance of a divine being. Although Jesus has been raised from the dead, not all the post-resurrection narratives ascribe to Jesus an exalted status as a divine being (M. Eugene Boring, *Sayings of the Risen Jesus: Christian Prophecy in the Synoptic Tradition* [Cambridge: Cambridge University Press, 1982] 47). Similarly, I have avoided "commissioning narrative" because not all the post-resurrection narratives involve a commissioning.

[6] Elizabeth Tonkin, *Narrating Our Pasts: The Social Construction of Oral History* (Cambridge and New York: Cambridge University Press, 1992) 2.

antiquity and suggest ways they may have functioned in early Christian communities. The primary collection of stories for comparison will be the post-resurrection stories recorded in the Second Testament.[7] In addition, I will consider the stories of a post-death appearance by Romulus recorded in Greco-Roman literature, and stories of post-ascent appearances by Elijah recounted in the Talmud.[8] To assist in this process I have created tables that compare the stories with respect to the following: temporal setting, spatial setting, persons in the story, reaction to the appearance, words spoken within the story, and expansion of the basic structure (see Appendices E, F, and G).[9]

Dan Ben-Amos defines legends as narratives that are about the human world, associated with local or real personalities, and believed to be historically reliable by the communities that perpetuate them.[10] Although their primary setting is the human world they may involve interaction with the divine world. The purpose of this interaction, according to Ben-Amos, is to abrogate the boundary between the human and divine worlds by the intrusion of the one into the other.[11] The form of the legend is relatively flexible. While the central thread tends to remain stable, details may change from version to version.[12] In this way the storyteller is able to weave the legend into the life of the community through the use of local referents.[13]

[7] I do not include in this list the stories of the appearances by Jesus to Paul in Acts because in these stories Jesus never actually appears (Acts 9:1-9; 22:6-11; 26:12-18). Paul sees a blinding light. However, the voice he hears is the voice of Jesus.

[8] The stories of Romulus and Elijah provide close parallels to the appearance stories in the Second Testament because all three provide multiple versions of stories involving appearances by the same person.

[9] These categories correspond, roughly, to the elements of narrative identified by Theon (*Progymnasmata* V.4-11): (1) the character (which may be one or many); (2) the act done by the character; (3) the place where the activity is done; (4) the time during which the activity is done; (5) the manner of the activity; (6) the reason for the activity.

[10] Dan Ben-Amos, "Narrative Forms in the Haggadah" (Ph.D. diss., Indiana University, 1967) 76. See also William R. Bascom, "The Forms of Folklore: Prose Narratives," *JAF* 79 (1965) 5.

[11] Ben-Amos, "Narrative Forms in the Haggadah," 87.

[12] Kenneth Bailey, "Informal Controlled Oral Tradition and the Synoptic Gospels," *Asia Journal of Theology* 5 (1991) 42; Heda Jason, "Concerning the 'Historical' and the 'Local' Legends and Their Relatives," in Américo Paredes and Richard Bauman, eds., *Toward New Perspectives in Folklore* (Austin: University of Texas Press, 1972) 143.

[13] Frederic C. Bartlett, "Some Experiments on the Reproduction of Folklore," in Dundes, ed., *The Study of Folklore*, 251.

What "horizon of expectation" does the genre "legend" produce? First, both storyteller and audience will expect the story to be about a person who is recognized by the audience and who may be significant for the life and history of their community. Second, they will expect the story to be located in this world but anticipate the possibility of an intrusion into this world by the divine world. Third, the audience will expect to be able to recognize the central thread of the story, while the storyteller will expect to be able to embellish this central thread in order to shape the story to her audience, the needs suggested by the context, and, of course, her own interests.[14] The ensuing discussion of the Magdalene stories will be organized around this "horizon."

Persons Recognized by the Community

The storyteller begins, "Now Mary Magdalene. . . ." The numerous references to Mary Magdalene in the gospels suggest that she was among persons who would be recognized by early Christian communities and with whom they might associate a part of their history and identity. As the story unfolds they would recall other stories they had heard about her: the one in which she was exorcised of seven demons by Jesus (Luke 8:1-3; Mark 16:9), for example, or her journey from Galilee to Jerusalem where she witnessed the crucifixion (Mark 15:40-41 // Matt 27:55-56), and the story of her going to the tomb (Mark 16:1-8 // Matt 28:1-8 // Luke 24:1-10).[15] Whenever she is mentioned in conjunction with other women, the audience would expect her name to be mentioned first—and it *is* always mentioned first, since she holds a place of honor among the women (Mark 15:40, 47; 16:1; Matt 27:56, 61; 28:1; Luke 8:2; 24:10). When we examine the literary remains left to us we observe that while a number of persons among the followers of Jesus have individual stories associated with their names, Mary Magdalene is among the few who are both associated with more than one story and about whom different stories are told in different gospels.[16]

[14] Linda Dégh, *Narratives in Society: A Performer-Centered Study of Narration* (Helsinki: Suomalainen Tiedeakatemia, 1995) 132.

[15] She is also mentioned as present at the burial of Jesus. However, the central figure in the story of the burial is Joseph of Arimathea (Mark 15:42-47 // Matt 27:57-61).

[16] Peter (e.g., Mark 8:27-30 // Matt 16:13-20 // Luke 9:18-21; Mark 9:2-10 // Matt 17:1-9 // Luke 9:28-36; Mark 14:66-72 // Matt 26:69-75 // Luke 22:56-62 // John 18:25-27; Matt 17:24-27; Luke 5:1-11; John 21:7-14); Judas (Mark 14:10-11 // Matt

Among those to whom Jesus is said to appear, Peter is the only other who can claim this honor.[17] Yet she stands apart even from those to whom Jesus appears because, along with the "other Mary" in Matthew, she is the only named person to whom Jesus appears in the canonical Gospels outside of the Twelve (see Appendix G). When the audience hears the name of Mary Magdalene, she will be recognized.

Intrusions Into This World by the Divine World .

"Mary turned and said to him, 'Teacher!' . . ." The appearance to Mary Magdalene takes place in this world, near a tomb set in a garden or on a road leading back to Jerusalem. The storyteller can describe the spatial setting in a variety of ways. It is not fixed. The other post-resurrection stories bear this out. In two the appearances are described taking place on the road while the persons involved travel from one destination to another (Matt 28:9-10; Luke 24:1-32). One story is set along a lakeshore (John 21:1-8). Two more take place inside a house (John 20:19-23, 26-29) while yet another occurs on a mountain in Galilee (Matt 28:16-20). The extent of variation is notable since spatial setting is one of the relatively stable elements in the Romulus stories (see Appendix E). With the post-resurrection stories the storyteller has more latitude. In some of the stories there seems to be an interest in linking the appearance with a specific geographic location: i.e., Galilee (Matt 28:16-20; John 21:1-14), Emmaus (Luke 24:1-32), and possibly Jerusalem (Luke 24:33-53). In the other stories the interest seems to be

26:14-16 // Luke 22:3-6; Mark 14:17-21 // Matt 26:20-25 // John 13:21-30; Mark 14:43-52 // Matt 26:47-56 // Luke 22:47-53 // John 18:2-12; Matt 27:3-10; John 12:1-8; 13:2); Matthew (Matt 9:9-13) or Levi (Mark 2:13-17 // Luke 5:27-32); Thomas (John 11:7-16; 14:1-7; 20:24-29; 21:1-14); Nathanael (John 1:43-51); Andrew (Mark 1:16-20 // Matt 4:18-22; John 1:35-42; 6:1-14; 12:20-26); Philip (John 1:43-51; 6:1-14; 12:20-26; 14:8-14); the sons of Zebedee (Mark 1:16-20 // Matt 4:18-22 // Luke 5:1-11; Mark 9:2-10 // Matt 17:1-9 // Luke 9:28-36; Mark 10:35-45 // Matt 20:20-28; John 21:1-8); the mother of the sons of Zebedee (Matt 20:20-28; 27:56); Mary and Martha (Luke 10:38-42; John 11:1-44; 12:1-8); Nicodemus (John 3:1-21; 19:38-42); Joseph of Arimathea (Mark 15:42-47 // Matt 27:57-61 // Luke 23:50-56 // John 19:38-42); and the Beloved Disciple (John 13:21-30; 19:26-27; 20:1-10; 21:1-24).

[17] The sons of Zebedee are mentioned in John 21 as among those to whom Jesus appears. However, in the appearance story itself only Peter and the Beloved Disciple are named. For this reason I do not count them in the same category as Peter and Mary Magdalene.

in the kind of space in which the appearance takes place. This is the case in the extant Magdalene stories: one version links the appearance to the tomb (John 20:1-18) while the other locates the appearance on a road as the women depart from the tomb (Matt 28:9-10). In each story the space is defined by the trappings of our earthly existence.

In this world Jesus draws near (Luke 24:15), stands (Luke 24:36), enters (John 20:19), is seen (Matt 28:17), approaches (Matt 28:18), or meets (Matt 28:9). The storyteller never says that he "appears" (ὤφθη).[18] The post-resurrection stories closely resemble the Elijah stories at this point. Elijah enters the scene as casually as if he had walked through the door.[19] By introducing Jesus into the scene in this same casual manner the storyteller shifts focus away from Jesus' sudden intrusion into this world to the words spoken by Jesus.[20] The divine world

[18] Hans Grass, *Ostergeschehen und Osterberichte* (Göttingen: Vandenhoeck & Ruprecht, 1962) 134–38.

[19] The New Testament also records an appearance narrative involving Elijah as well as Moses (Matt 17:1-9 // Mark 9:2-10 // Luke 9:28-36). Although the narrative states that Elijah and Moses speak with Jesus, the conversation is not recorded. Rather, the narrative has been constructed in such a way as to shift attention away from the interaction between Elijah, Moses, and Jesus to focus entirely on the transfiguration of Jesus. The effect more nearly resembles the Greco-Roman narratives, which emphasize the divine nature of the one who appears. However, in this case the ones who appear serve merely to corroborate the divine nature of Jesus. Thus, instead of Elijah entering into the human realm, Jesus enters into the divine realm. While this marks a significant shift from the narratives recorded in the Talmud, it should be noted that even in the Talmudic narratives Elijah always appears to a rabbi: someone of elevated status within the community. The transfiguration of Jesus also stands apart from the other appearance stories recorded in the Second Testament because it includes a detailed description of his appearance. This emphasis is, for the most part, absent from the post-resurrection narratives.

An appearance story recorded in Acts 9:10-16 more nearly resembles the Elijah narratives. This appearance story is different from the others included in this study in that it states that Jesus appears in a vision. As in the Elijah narratives, the structure consists of an appearance and an expanded dialogue. No setting is given, and the dialogue simply comes to an end (although it is followed immediately by a related scene). The emphasis of the narrative is entirely on the spoken word. Further, Ananias exhibits no reaction to the appearance. It is presented as neither unexpected nor out of the ordinary. And, as in the Elijah narratives, the focus is on the interaction of the divine with the human realm. Indeed, one could say that Jesus has been substituted for Elijah within the narrative pattern. This points to the close structural relationship between these appearance narratives.

[20] The two exceptions are, of course, Luke 24:13-32, where the appearance to the disciples on the road to Emmaus is subordinated to the appearance to Peter, and

intrudes into our world because it has something to say.[21] Yet this is no disembodied voice.[22] Jesus is present in body as well as spirit.

Stable and Variable

"Jesus said to her, 'Do not hold on to me. . . .'" "They took hold of his feet and worshiped him." The Magdalene stories are striking not only for their similarities but also for their differences. They vary from each other almost as much as they vary from the other post-resurrection stories. What describes the core thread the storyteller was compelled to follow? At what points did the storyteller have latitude to let her own voice speak through the voice of the story?

The post-resurrection appearance stories recorded in the Second Testament exhibit the following core elements:[23] (1) a setting is established;

Mark 16:9-11, where the lack of dialogue similarly places emphasis on the appearance of Jesus rather than the interaction between Jesus and Mary Magdalene. In this passage also the narrator is careful to note that Mary Magdalene is the first person to whom Jesus appears, indicating that some authority or status is to be attributed to her on the basis of this appearance. I also recognize that the idea of "seeing" Jesus is not completely absent from some of the other post-resurrection narratives: see especially John 20:26-29. In stark contrast to the post-resurrection stories are the summary lists of witnesses to the risen Jesus in 1 Cor 15:3-5 and Luke 24:34, where emphasis is similarly placed on those to whom Jesus appears. However, there is a subtle, yet notable difference between them. In the appearance "lists" the focus is on Jesus' appearing (ὤφθη). In terms of those to whom Jesus appears, it is *seeing* Jesus that is important and it is from this *seeing* that the individual to whom Jesus appears derives authority (Gerald O'Collins, "Peter as Easter Witness," *HeyJ* 22 [1981] 1, 17; Hans von Campenhausen, *Der Ablauf der Osterereignisse und das leere Grab* [Heidelberg: Universitätsverlag C. Winter, 1966] 15). This suggests that the appearance stories serve purposes different from those of the summary lists of witnesses. Ahn-Byung-mu observes that Paul focuses on the meaning of the Jesus-event while the gospel narratives not only describe the Jesus-event but witness to an existential situation ("The Transmitters of the Jesus-event," *CTC Bulletin* [Dec. 1984–April 1985] 30, 31). Mary R. Thompson observes a similar distinction but sees the function of the post-resurrection narratives as the authentication of the authority of the recipients of the appearance (*Mary of Magdala: Apostle and Leader* [Mahwah, N.J.: Paulist, 1995] 20).

[21] Sometimes the divine world intrudes because it has something to show. In some of the narratives this purpose is to demonstrate the corporeality of Jesus' risen body: Luke 24:36-43; John 20:26-29; 21:1-14.

[22] In contrast to the appearances to Paul (Acts 9:1-9; 22:6-11; 26:12-18).

[23] In oral tradition stability refers to traditional story patterns, themes, and phraseology (Werner Kelber, "Jesus and Tradition" *Semeia* 65 [1994] 148).

(2) characters are identified; (3) Jesus enters the scene; (4) there is a reaction; (5) Jesus speaks.[24] This same pattern of core elements is exhibited in the Greco-Roman appearance stories (see Appendix E), while the Elijah stories consist of only two core elements: (1) Elijah appears; (2) a dialogue ensues between Elijah and the one to whom he appears. Some of the Second Testament stories are expanded to include a dialogue between Jesus and those to whom he appears (Luke 24:13-32; John 20:11-18; John 21:4-8), resembling more nearly the Elijah stories, or to include a non-recognition/recognition motif (Luke 24:13-32; John 20:11-18; John 21:1-23), an element also found in one of the Elijah stories (*b. Sota* 49a-b). The storyteller might add a demonstration or proof of Jesus' identity or corporeality (Luke 24:36-43; John 20:26-29), or other additional scenes (Luke 24:13-32; Luke 24:33-35; John 20:2-10; John 21:15-23). The Magdalene story in John includes both a dialogue and a non-recognition motif, while the versions in Matt 28:9-10 and Mark 16:9-11 include none. The pattern of these stories, then, is very flexible. Minimally, the storyteller would be expected to identify the characters involved, describe Jesus "drawing near" and a reaction to his presence, and offer some words spoken by Jesus. Within and around this "core structure" the storyteller had latitude to weave a story very much of her own making.

[24] Similar proposals regarding the structure of the post-resurrection appearance stories have been offered by John E. Alsup and C. H. Dodd. Alsup proposes the following structure: (1) participants are in a state of crisis; (2) Jesus appears unexpectedly; (3) he is seen, but not recognized; (4) there is a verbal exchange; (5) Jesus is recognized (*The Post-Resurrection Appearance Stories of the Gospel Tradition: A History-of-Tradition Analysis; With Text-Synopsis* [Stuttgart: Calwer, 1975] 211). Dodd proposes a similar five-part structure: (1) the followers of Jesus are bereft; (2) Jesus appears; (3) there is a word of greeting; (4) the followers recognize Jesus; (5) Jesus gives a word of command to his followers ("The Appearances of the Risen Christ," in idem, *More New Testament Studies* [Manchester: University of Manchester Press, 1968] 104). Alsup and Dodd tend to mingle content with structure. Martin Albertz divides the post-resurrection appearance stories into two groups according to what he identifies as their function: (1) those that establish apostolic authority; (2) those to individuals emphasizing that Jesus lives ("Zur Formgeschichte der Auferstehungsberichte," *ZNW* 21 [1922] 259–60). Dodd ("The Appearances of the Risen Christ," 127–28) and Gerald O'Collins (*The Easter Jesus* [London: Darton, Longman and Todd, 1980] 80) make the same distinction, with some variation on the interpretation of the appearances to individuals. In contrast, Pheme Perkins (*Resurrection* [Garden City, N.Y.: Doubleday, 1984] 89) suggests that the appearance traditions may have served more generally than their use as commissionings might indicate.

One of the choices left open to the storyteller was the identity of the persons to whom Jesus appeared. In five of the stories the individuals are named: Mary Magdalene and the "other Mary" (Matt 28:9-10), Mary Magdalene alone (John 20:11-18; Mark 16:9-11), Thomas (John 20:26-29), and Peter, Thomas, Nathanael, the sons of Zebedee, and the Beloved Disciple, plus two unnamed disciples (John 21). Although there is no story recording the appearance, Peter also is named in Luke 24:34 as having seen the risen Jesus. In four other stories Jesus appears to some combination of unnamed disciples (see Appendix G).[25]

In every case those to whom Jesus appears are identified as followers of Jesus. There are no "outsiders" involved. This "in-group" or esoteric quality of the stories is further indicated by the absence of any descriptive statements about those to whom Jesus appears. The storyteller makes no mention of their occupation, social standing, or origin, short of the designation "disciple." The one exception is Mark 16:9-11, where Mary is identified as the one from whom Jesus had cast out seven demons. However, this would not identify Mary to outsiders; rather, it distinguishes this Mary from other Marys known to the community (Mary being a popular name). This pattern stands in contrast to two of the Romulus stories, where Julius Proculus is introduced in a way that assumes he is not known to the audience (see Appendix E). In these examples the descriptions of Julius vary significantly, indicating that the stories are addressed to two quite different audiences.[26] The post-resurrection stories more nearly resemble, in this respect, the Elijah stories in which Elijah appears to a number of different religious leaders. In these stories, too, the storyteller offers no description of the one to whom he appears. It is assumed the audience will recognize the persons by name alone. It seems the storyteller may choose, within limits, the one to whom Jesus appears. The literary remains indicate that, to be named, the person must be among those who were closest to Jesus while he was on earth.

[25] These unnamed disciples may have included women as well as men since, in Greek, the masculine plural is employed to denote a group composed of both genders (Herbert W. Smyth, *Greek Grammar* [Cambridge: Harvard University Press, 1984] 244).

[26] In Plutarch's *Romulus* (XXVIII.1-3) he is described as a patrician of noble birth who is a colonist of Alba, while in Dionysius' *Roman Antiquities* (II.63.3) he is described as a husbandman, descended from Ascanius. These two descriptions clearly reflect the voice of the storyteller, who is attempting to describe Julius in a way that will promote a particular reaction from the audience.

In describing the reaction to the appearance by Jesus, the storyteller had considerable room for expression. These reactions range from fear to doubt to rejoicing, with no two stories reporting the same reaction. In three of the stories the "reaction" is replaced by a non-recognition/recognition motif (Luke 24:13-32; John 20:11-18; John 21:4-8), while in Mark 16:9-11 the reaction is described by Mary's going to the disciples to report what she has seen.[27] A similar pattern is found in the reaction by Julius to the appearance of Romulus in the Greco-Roman stories. In terms of storytelling strategy the "reaction" plays a significant role because it invites the audience to participate in the story, either by identifying with the reaction expressed or rejecting it. It is of particular interest that the three versions of the Magdalene tradition vary to such a degree at this point. While the two Marys recognize Jesus immediately in Matthew 28 and respond in worship, the Mary Magdalene of John 20 does not immediately recognize Jesus, while the Mary of Mark 16 responds simply by reporting what she has seen to the disciples. We should envision a different audience for each story.

Finally, the words spoken by Jesus differ from story to story. For example, in Matthew 28 the disciples are instructed to baptize the nations and to teach all that Jesus has commanded them, in Luke 24:13-32 Jesus presents the events surrounding his death in the context of the Scriptures, while in John 20:26-29 Jesus praises those who have "not seen, yet believe." A similar pattern of variance is found in both the Romulus and Elijah stories.[28] Of all the places in the story where the storyteller has a free hand this is, perhaps, the most important. Here the storyteller is able not only to shape the story but to add power and authority to her words by addressing the audience through the voice of Jesus (see Appendix G). In the Magdalene stories the storyteller may be somewhat more constrained. The versions in Matthew and John both report that Jesus commands the women to "go, tell my ἀδελφοί" (brothers and sisters) and to repeat the words Jesus has spoken to them.[29] It is possible

[27] The recognition/non-recognition motif is distinguished from proofs of Jesus' identity or corporeality.

[28] In the Elijah stories the emphasis is entirely on the spoken word. The wide range of topics covered in the conversations between prophet and sage reveals that these appearance narratives provide a flexible medium through which the storyteller is able to address the community directly.

[29] Jesus' command to "go tell my . . ." can be read as instruction to go to a group of male disciples or to a group of both male and female disciples (see n. 25 above). Only context will determine which the correct reading should be. In a storytelling

that this phraseology has become fixed through repeated performance or that it is in some way viewed as part of the "core" of the Magdalene stories.[30]

Summary

As the storyteller begins, the audience is all expectation. Who will this story be about? Will it be about someone known by us or only known to us? At what point will Jesus appear? Where will this encounter take place? How will those present react? Will they recognize him? Will Jesus have to demonstrate that it is truly he, or that he is, indeed, present in body as well as spirit? Do we approve of their reaction? Would we react differently? What will Jesus say? Above all, what will Jesus say? How the storyteller and audience choose to answer these questions will give shape to the stable core that they both know by heart. It is precisely this "shape" which will make this version of the story different from all the others—which will make it come alive in performance.

The Intersection of Storyteller, Story, Audience, and Context in Performance

For a story to be effective, the sympathy of the audience must be engaged,[31] and for that purpose a sense of identity between a real situation and its artificial embodiment as story has to be established.[32] We may assume, therefore, that the stories of the post-resurrection appearance to the women reflected in some way the experience of early Chris-

---

environment this context may shift from performance to performance, depending on the purpose for which the story is being employed.

[30] Dell Hymes observes that performance is a "mode of existence and realization that is partly *constitutive* of what the tradition is" (*"In vain I tried to tell you,"* 86)

[31] Roger D. Abrahams, "Introductory Remarks to a Rhetorical Theory of Folklore," *JAF* 81 (1968) 147; idem, "Personal Power and Social Restraint in the Definition of Folklore," in Paredes and Bauman, eds., *Toward New Perspectives in Folklore,* 19; John Blacking, "The Concept of Identity and Folk Concepts of Self: A Venda Case Study," in Anita Jacobson-Widding, ed., *Identity: Personal and Socio-Cultural* (Uppsala: Academiae Upsaliensis, 1983) 48.

[32] Abrahams, "Introductory Remarks to a Rhetorical Theory of Folklore," 148.

tian communities. Exactly how is more difficult to pinpoint. That is a part of what I want to explore in this section.

To assist our imaginations in bringing together storyteller, story, audience, and context, I propose a storytelling event:

> They have gathered in the courtyard, because the evening is warm. With both mother and child safely delivered the women can rest now. One of them comments, "It's a pity. I will miss hearing Hannah's voice in worship, but with three children she will have other things to occupy her mind." The women murmur in agreement. It is difficult to juggle the tasks of household and children and community. "There are some of the men," says another, "who wouldn't mind seeing a few more women less able to raise their voices." "I don't suppose that would include your husband?" asks Joanna. The silence that follows answers "yes." They all know that Lydia's husband is not alone in his views, and he has some powerful supporters. Finally Esther, a widow who rarely speaks and, consequently, is all the more respected, says, "I will remind them. I will remind them of how, on the first day of the week, it was Mary Magdalene. . . ."

Roger Abrahams describes the social function of traditional narrative as an attempt to address recurring social problems that threaten the existence of the community.[33] What problems might a storyteller address through a performance of the Magdalene post-resurrection stories? An obvious one would be the question presented by the empty tomb, but this is a question addressed by all of the post-resurrection stories. One will do just as well as another. However, features peculiar to the three extant versions of the Magdalene stories suggest two problems that could be addressed through a performance of these particular stories.

The three extant Magdalene stories, despite differences between them, are consistent with respect to two things: those who see the risen Jesus are all women, one of whom is Mary Magdalene, and in each story the women go to the disciples to report what they have seen and heard. Two of the versions share a third element: the initial words spoken by Jesus to "go, tell my ἀδελφοί" (brothers and sisters).[34] This

[33] Ibid. 146. See also William R. Bascom, "Four Functions of Folklore," in Dundes, ed., *The Study of Folklore,* 290; Eric A. Havelock, *Preface to Plato* (Cambridge: Harvard University Press, 1963) 100; Jan Vansina, *Oral Tradition: A Study in Historical Methodology* (London: Routledge, 1965) 78.

[34] See n. 29 above.

suggests that these features may have been points of stability within the Magdalene tradition. Using these features as guideposts, I propose that the Magdalene stories were performed to resolve tensions around the relationship of women to the now risen Jesus, and to demonstrate one way in which the risen Jesus was to be reintegrated into the social life of the community.

It is not difficult to imagine that the death of Jesus precipitated a crisis within communities of his followers. While the resurrection of Jesus ameliorated this crisis to a degree by replacing the earthly Jesus with the risen Jesus, it was not a completely satisfactory solution. Although Jesus was "present," he was not present in the same way. This, perforce, called for both a reordering of the social structure of the communities in their various locations throughout Galilee and in and around Jerusalem, and a reintegration of Jesus into the life of these communities.

The active role of women in early Christian communities is not disputed.[35] This is evidenced in the Magdalene stories themselves. Nothing in the way the stories are preserved suggests that it was considered fantastical for the women to have seen the risen Jesus, nor is any objection recorded against their addressing the community of believers. However, other texts such as 1 Cor 14:33-36 and 1 Tim 2:11-15 point to rising tensions within some communities around the role of women. In order to counteract this marginalization of women, a storyteller might perform one of the Magdalene stories in an attempt either to maintain an existing social order (for example, where women assumed active roles in the community) or to impose an alternative reality on an existing situation (where the roles of women were being restricted).[36] Using the story to demonstrate that women had been called not only by the earthly Jesus but also by the risen Jesus to speak words of encouragement to the community, the storyteller could endeavor to actively persuade the community to effect a continuity between past and present

[35] Ute E. Eisen, *Women Officeholders in Early Christianity: Epigraphical and Literary Studies.* Translated by Linda M. Maloney (Collegeville: The Liturgical Press, 2000); Ross S. Kraemer, *Her Share of the Blessings* (Oxford: Oxford University Press, 1992) 174–90; Elisabeth Schüssler Fiorenza, *In Memory of Her: A Feminist Theological Reconstruction of Christian Origins* (New York: Crossroad, 1984) 160–204.

[36] Richard Bauman, "Differential Identity and the Social Base of Folklore," in Paredes and Bauman, eds., *Toward New Perspectives in Folklore,* 38; idem, *Story, Performance, and Event* (Cambridge: Cambridge University Press, 1986) 4–5; Ben-Amos, *Folklore in Context,* 29.

through imitation.[37] She could also hope to influence the future by establishing the story as part of the community's memory.[38]

The Magdalene story may also have been performed to address the question of how the post-resurrection Jesus was to be reintegrated into the life of early Christian communities. This is a concern addressed by several of the post-resurrection stories.[39] For example, in Matt 28:16-20 the risen Jesus charges the eleven to teach disciples to observe all that he has commanded them; thus one of the ways Jesus continues to be present within the community is through the observance of Jesus' instruction. In Luke 24:28-32 Jesus' presence is made known in the breaking of bread, and in Luke 24:44-49 Jesus' presence is to be continued through the witness of the disciples in the proclamation of the message of Scripture. In the Mary Magdalene stories recorded in Matthew and John, Jesus' presence is continued in a way that is distinct from those described in the other post-resurrection stories. In the Magdalene stories Jesus instructs the women to "go and tell my brothers and sisters"—that is, the women are instructed to speak the words of the risen Jesus to the community of gathered disciples. This is unique among the post-resurrection stories. In contrast, the eleven in Matt 28:16-20 are instructed to teach the words of the earthly Jesus. Only the women are told to speak the words of the risen Jesus.[40] This strongly suggests that the Magdalene stories may have been told to legitimate the prophetic activity of women (and perhaps men) who claimed that their speech was authorized by the risen Jesus.[41] Support for this suggestion is

[37] Jerzy J. Smolicz and Robert Crotty, "The Role of Tradition in the Study of Religion," *Religious Traditions* 3/2 (1980) 87.

[38] Tonkin, *Narrating Our Pasts,* 12.

[39] Matt 28:9-10, 16-20; Luke 24:13-35, 44-53; John 20:11-18, 19-23. I came to this insight through an article on the animation of corpses at old-time wakes in Ireland (Ilana Harlow, "Creating Situations: Practical Jokes and the Revival of the Dead in Irish Traditions," *JAF* 110 [1997] 152). Marianne Sawicki makes a similar observation in *Seeing the Lord* (Minneapolis: Fortress, 1994) 78. Elisabeth Schüssler Fiorenza, in contrasting 1 Corinthians 15 with the empty tomb narratives, observes that the former emphasizes the absence of Jesus while the latter emphasizes his presence (*Jesus: Miriam's Child, Sophia's Prophet* [New York: Continuum, 1995] 126).

[40] I do not mean to suggest what form these prophetic words may have taken, only that they are thought in some way to derive from the risen Jesus.

[41] There is a similarity here with the situation referred to by Tertullian (*On Baptism,* 1.17) in which women are reported to be employing the story of Paul and Thecla to legitimate women baptizing. Susanne Heine ("Eine Person von Rang und Namen: Historische Konturen der Magdalenerin," in Dietrich-Alex Koch, Gerhard Sellin,

found in the references to women prophets in the Second Testament as well as in the letters of Paul where he claims to speak a "word of the Lord."[42]

When Esther, in the scenario that opened this section, tells the story of Mary Magdalene, these are the issues she has in mind. Speaking to a group of women, all of whom are known to each other as neighbors, relations, and members of the same Christian community, she tells the story in an effort to reinforce the present reality in which women serve as prophetic leaders in the community, and to offer support to the women who feel this leadership role is being threatened. It is evident that the Magdalene story is already known to those present and that Mary Magdalene is a person of status within the life and memory of the community. It is likely that Mary serves as a model for these women, demonstrating that they, too, are called by the risen Jesus and commissioned to speak to the community in the name and power of

---

and Andreas Lindemann, eds., *Jesu Rede von Gott und ihre Nachgeschichte im frühen Christentum* [Gütersloh: Gerd Mohn, 1989] 187–88) emphasizes the close connection between Christophanies and leadership function, noting that the appearances serve the purpose of legitimation, although not only this purpose.

[42] References to women prophets are found in Acts 21:10, 1 Corinthians 11, and Rev 2:20. References to a "word of the Lord" in Paul are found in 1 Cor 7:10, 12, 25; 11:23; 14:27, and 1 Thess 4:15-17. Which of these represents a prophetic word and which represents a saying of the historical Jesus is contested. However, David Aune, whose study of prophetic sayings is the most comprehensive to date, believes that 1 Thess 4:15-17 belongs to prophecy (David Aune, *Prophecy in Early Christianity and the Ancient Mediterranean World* [Grand Rapids: Eerdmans, 1983] 253–56). The subject of early Christian prophecy is one on which there is divided opinion as well as a need for more study. Nonetheless, there is no question that women prophets were active in the early church. See, for example, Mary Rose D'Angelo, "Re-membering Jesus: Women, Prophecy, and Resistance in the Memory of the Early Churches," *Horizons* 19/2 (1992) 199–218; Eisen, "Prophets," in *Women Officeholders in Early Christianity*, 63–87; Karen L. King, "Early Christian Women as Prophetic Leaders," *Harvard Divinity Review* 24/3 (1995) 7; Mary Rose D'Angelo, "(Re)Presentations of Women in the Gospels: John and Mark," in eadem and Ross S. Kraemer, eds., *Women & Christian Origins* (Oxford: Oxford University Press, 1999) 132; Karen Jo Torjesen, *When Women were Priests* (San Francisco: HarperSan Francisco, 1993) 23–30; Antoinette C. Wire, *The Corinthian Women Prophets* (Minneapolis: Fortress, 1990). On the phenomenon of prophecy in the early church see the work by Aune mentioned above; Boring, *Sayings of the Risen Jesus* (see n. 5 above); Gerald F. Hawthorne, "The Role of Christian Prophets in the Gospel Tradition," in idem, with Otto Betz, eds., *Tradition and Interpretation in the New Testament: Essays in Honor of E. Earle Ellis for his Sixtieth Birthday* (Grand Rapids: Eerdmans, 1987); David Hill, *New Testament Prophecy* (Atlanta: John Knox, 1979).

Jesus. In addition, there is an expectation that her story can function as a paradigm for the life of the community.[43] The interaction of the risen Jesus with Mary demonstrates to the community that it ought to recognize and approve the voices of the women. Jesus' words and actions serve as guides for the life of the community together. While young women may serve as leaders in the community, it is Esther, an older widow, who tells the story. Age, status, and experience lend her an authority the other women do not yet enjoy. There also is an expectation that if she tells the Magdalene story to the larger community she will be listened to in a way that the younger women will not. Because she is a widow there is no man who can claim authority over Esther, and her age and wisdom demand respect. Yet this is only one scenario. There are others to consider.

In performance, the construction of the story is in the hands of the storyteller.[44] How the storyteller chooses to fill in those elements that are flexible can utterly alter the shape of the story. Imagine, for example, another scenario. Esther's community has gathered for worship. Men and women, with their children, are packed together in the home of one of their members—a merchant who, because he has a storage room in the back, can fit more people into the larger front room. Because it is the first day of the week, stories of appearances by the risen Jesus are told. The community is well aware of the tension that has been brewing for some months, and knows each storyteller will carefully shape her story to speak to this tension in some way. Because the merchant has a guest with him, a member of another Christian community, the guest is invited to tell the first story. The story is this:

> The day of crucifixion begins our resurrection story. Although many had fled, the women remained by the cross all that day, and watched to see where the body was buried. Then, early on the first day of the week, Mary Magdalene went to the tomb. The stone had been rolled away and, looking inside, she saw that the tomb was empty. In bewilderment and grief Mary sat outside the tomb weeping, not knowing what to do. A voice behind her caused her to

[43] Kenneth Bailey, "Informal Controlled Oral Tradition," *Asia Journal of Theology* 5 (1991) 42; Vincent Taylor, *The Formation of the Gospel Tradition* (New York: St. Martin's, 1964) 59–60; Thomas Luckmann, "Remarks on Personal Identity: Inner, Social and Historical Time," in Jacobson-Widding, ed., *Identity: Personal and Socio-Cultural* (see n. 31 above) 85.

[44] Werner Kelber, *The Oral and the Written Gospel* (Philadelphia: Fortress, 1983) 93.

> turn. "Mary," said Jesus. Mary in the joy of recognition reached out to touch him, but Jesus said, "Do not touch me, for I have not yet ascended to my Father." Then Jesus said to her, "Go, and tell my brothers and sisters that I have been raised from the dead and that I will be with them." Mary departed from the tomb, full of fear and confusion. When she reported what she had seen and heard, the disciples were baffled by her words and did not know what to make of them. One of them said, "Let us wait and see what happens."

Perhaps the storyteller is cautioning the women in the community to be patient, to "wait and see what happens." Or perhaps the storyteller is suggesting that the testimony of women (or prophets) should be subject to scrutiny before it is accepted. The meaning, not entirely clear to us, may not be clear to the audience either. Some may hear it one way and some another.[45]

This ambiguity may be deliberate on the part of the storyteller. According to James Scott, "Oral traditions, due simply to their means of transmission, offer a kind of seclusion, control and even anonymity that make them ideal vehicles for cultural resistance."[46] One way in which oral traditions can be employed as a mode of resistance is through encoding.[47] Encoding occurs when there is a situation of dominance, oppression, or risk for a particular group and opposition to this situation cannot be made explicit.[48] A code may be complicit (the receiver does not realize a code is being employed) or explicit (the receiver knows there is a code regardless of whether he or she can understand it or not).[49] It may also be implicit: that is, the encoding may not be deliberate on the part of the storyteller, but nonetheless is perceived by members of the audience.[50] In the story above, for example, the oblique reference to those who had fled (i.e., the disciples) could be heard by some members of the audience as irony: those who fled are also the ones who question Mary's experience, yet it is to Mary that Jesus ap-

[45] Joan Newlon Radner, "Preface," in eadem, ed., *Feminist Messages: Coding in Women's Folk Culture* (Chicago: University of Illinois Press, 1993) vii.

[46] James C. Scott, *Domination and the Arts of Resistance* (New Haven: Yale University Press, 1990) 160.

[47] Ibid. 18-19, 121.

[48] Ibid. 158; Joan Newlon Radner and Susan Sniader Lanser, "Strategies of Coding in Women's Culture," in *Feminist Messages*, 9.

[49] Ibid. 6.

[50] Ibid.

pears.[51] While members of the audience who belonged to the dominant group would hear the story as a reinforcement of their perspective, those who recognized that a code was being employed would hear in the story an affirmation of their experience rather than a negation or diminishing of it.[52] Each performance of the story, therefore, raises questions concerning what the storyteller seeks to gain by employing this particular story in this particular setting and in this particular way.[53]

The role of the storyteller is not without limits. Not all stories and storytellers were held in equal regard.[54] A concern raised by Greco-Roman, Jewish, and Christian texts alike is credibility. Since the story is passed on in public, the audience, through its approval or censure, participates in the determination of what is considered a faithful rendering of the story.[55] Stories that were considered fabulous were dismissed as "old wives' tales," a phrase found everywhere in Greco-Roman literature.[56] This expression is employed also by the author of 1 Timothy in 4:7 and is implied in 5:13 of the stories told by widows as they go from house to house. Those who listened to these stories were put down as rude and uneducated, having no more sense than children.[57] Yet on occasion even "literate" individuals might find themselves persuaded, if not by the tale, then by the credibility of the one who told it.[58] A common defense in the face of a doubting audience was the claim to have witnessed or experienced the events oneself, in the hope that

[51] Ibid. 19.

[52] Scott, *Domination and the Arts of Resistance,* 93. Radner and Lanser note that coding always risks reinforcing the ideology it is designed to critique; hence "coding must always signify a freedom that is incomplete" ("Strategies of Coding in Women's Culture," 23).

[53] Abrahams, "Personal Power and Social Restraint," 28.

[54] Georges, "Toward an Understanding of Storytelling Events," 324. See also Josephus, *Antiquities* 1.22; *Against Apion* 1.304; 3.420; Plato, *Republic* III.397E, 198E; Philostratus, *Life of Apollonius* 5.14; Plutarch, *Theseus* 28.1.

[55] Bailey, "Informal Controlled Oral Tradition," 42; Long, "Recent Field Studies in Oral Literature and their bearing on Old Testament Literature," 191.

[56] Cicero, *Nature of Gods* 3.5; Horace, *Satires* 2.6.77; Lucian, *Lover of Lies* 9; Plato, *Gorgias* 527A; Quintilian, *Institutes* 1.8.19; Strabo, *Geography* 1.2.3.C16. See also 1 Tim 4:7.

[57] Ovid, *Metamorphoses* VIII.611; Quintilian, *Institutes* 5.11.19; Strabo, *Geography* 1.2.8.

[58] Ovid, *Metamorphoses* XII.532; Plutarch, *Solon* 3.2.1.

one's own credibility would win credibility for the story.[59] Without the assent of the audience, however, the credibility of both story and storyteller would be lost.[60] Although the Magdalene stories could be made to serve quite different rhetorical purposes, it is possible that some versions of the story were granted greater credibility than others. Whether a particular version was accepted might also be related to the credibility of the storyteller in relation to the audience.

Credibility may have been an issue not only within communities but also between communities. An indication that this might be the case is found in one of the relatively stable elements in the post-resurrection stories: the temporal setting.[61] In all but two of the post-resurrection stories the appearance by Jesus is described as taking place on the first day of the week.[62] This is fairly remarkable, especially when one considers that each of these appearances is to a different group of persons and occurs in a different location.[63] It is possible that these stories represent attempts by various communities to claim a post-resurrection appearance "on the first day of the week" for someone closely associated with their community.[64] Such a possibility is suggested by Luke 24:13-35, where the story makes it clear that Jesus appeared to Peter before appearing to the disciples traveling to Emmaus, and Mark 16:9-11, where it is stated that Jesus appeared first to Mary Magdalene. If this is the case, then one community's claim that their local hero was present on the first day of the week may not be recognized by another commu-

[59] Apuleius, *Metamorphosis* II.20; Ovid, *Metamorphoses* VIII.615-17.

[60] This is true even in the case of encoded texts. James C. Scott observes that such texts require a public: practices and discourses of resistance cannot exist "without tacit or acknowledged coordination and communication within the subordinate group" (*Domination and the Arts of Resistance,* 118).

[61] In contrast, two entirely different temporal settings are employed in the Romulus stories.

[62] This time referent stands in contrast to 1 Cor 15:4, where it is stated that Jesus was raised "on the third day." The appearance to Thomas (John 20:26-29) is said to take place eight days after the appearance on the first day of the week. This places it on the first day of the following week.

[63] The two exceptions (Matt 28:16-20 and John 21:1-14) occur at some time other than the first day of the week, although the exact time is not specified, and both take place in Galilee.

[64] Taylor, *The Formation of the Gospel Tradition,* 59–60. However, this does not seem to be the case with the appearances that occur in Galilee. Here the geographic location is made explicit, suggesting that the narrator wants to connect the appearance with that region.

nity making a similar claim.[65] Richard Bauman notes that oral narrative may be employed by kinship groups that are competing for status.[66] Viewing early Christian communities as fictive-kinship groups, we may consider it possible that the post-resurrection stories were employed agonistically by the communities in an attempt to gain status over one another.[67] The prominence of Mary Magdalene's name in these and other stories and their preservation in written documents signals her importance within at least some communities.

Conclusion

While we cannot recapture the Magdalene stories as they existed in performance, we can try to appreciate the dynamics that would bring the stories to life in performance. As we do so it is essential to recognize that there was no single setting in which the stories were told, no fixed text, no one purpose for which they were employed, and no certain response to them on the part of the audience. The text was in the control of the storyteller, who could freely build on the core structure of the story, limited only by her need to win the assent of her audience. Her purpose might be encouragement or sheer entertainment, but it might also be an attempt to persuade her audience to a particular point of view or course of action. The audience, for their part, might find in the story a source of common identity—one that, perhaps, set their community apart from other communities—or they might hear implicit support for a dominant group within their community or resistance on the part of those in the community who feared being marginalized. This capacity of the Magdalene stories to be shaped and reshaped draws attention to their function as a living tradition in early Christian communities. It also calls our attention to storytelling as a field of engagement where storyteller and audience meet in order to resolve

[65] According to Kenneth Bailey, stories about important individuals in the history of a community can only be told within communities that consider these stories important for their identity ("Informal Controlled Oral Tradition," 42).

[66] Bauman, "Differential Identity and the Social Base of Folklore," 38.

[67] Albertz, "Zur Formgeschichte der Auferstehungsberichte," 260; François Bovon, "Le privilège pascal de Marie-Madeleine," *NTS* 30 (1984) 50; Heine, "Eine Person von Rang und Namen," 189; William O. Walker, "Postcrucifixion Appearances and Christian Origins," *JBL* 88 (1969) 163.

tensions in the life of the community and establish the parameters of their life together.

The persistence of the Magdalene stories in written documents argues strongly for the credibility and importance attributed to them by early Christian communities. It also raises a question: Why were these particular versions of the story preserved while others were not? The answer may lie in the points of stability shared by these three versions. The prominent role of the women and their commission to be the voice of the risen Jesus suggests that these particular versions were central to a larger conversation concerning the role of women as leaders within early Christian communities and, more specifically, their role as bearers of the words of the risen Jesus to communities of the risen Jesus. The written record of the Magdalene stories in Matthew 28, John 20, and the Longer Ending of Mark indicates that some storytellers and/or audiences may have expected, or perhaps even demanded, the inclusion of these stories in any narrative of the life of Jesus that was directed toward the ongoing life of the Jesus communities. It remains to be explored how the storytellers behind the Gospel of Matthew and the Gospel of John tell the Magdalene story and, more importantly, to what end.[68]

[68] Although I have included Mark 16:9-11 in my inquiry up to this point, I do not go on to examine the Longer Ending as part of the rhetorical argument of the Gospel of Mark for two reasons: First, the Longer Ending does not appear to have become associated with the Gospel of Mark until the second century. Therefore it is further removed from the interests and conflicts of the pre-gospel period, which is the primary interest of this study. Second, the second-century date of these verses and the elements they share in common with Gnostic texts require that they be examined in relation to the Gnostic movement. Such an undertaking is beyond the scope of the present study.

Chapter Five

Storytelling Strategies in Matthew: The Function of the Mary Magdalene Tradition in Its Literary Context

Behind every story is a storyteller. This is no less true of a written document than of an oral tradition. When a story is performed orally the storyteller is present for all to see. When it is written, that individual is hidden and is discernible to the audience only through inferences in the text. In the case of the Gospel of Matthew, the teller of the story is an enigma.[1] Although tradition identifies the storyteller as the apostle Matthew (9:9; 10:3), there are numerous reasons to question this ascription.[2] In the end the identity of the storyteller remains a mystery. What

[1] I use the term "storyteller" for what, in literary theory, would be called the "implied author." According to Seymour Chatman the implied author is the one who shapes the story in a particular way (*Story and Discourse: Narrative Structure in Fiction and Film* [Ithaca: Cornell University Press, 1978] 148). I have elected to use the term storyteller in order to maintain continuity with earlier discussions of oral text and because I believe that the term "storyteller" more nearly suggests the active role of the "implied author."

[2] The earliest connections between the apostle Matthew and the gospel ascribed to him date to the second century, several decades after the gospel first appeared. Most scholars believe the gospel to have been written between 80 and 90 C.E. It is unlikely that a follower of Jesus, even if a young man or woman at that time, would still be alive during the last decades of the century. Further, the author never identifies himself as an eyewitness of the events that are reported. Finally, the literary skill of the author seems inconsistent with what one would expect of a Galilean tax collector whose first language would have been Aramaic.

we do know is that the storyteller made a self-conscious decision to include the post-resurrection appearance to Mary Magdalene tradition in the gospel narrative.[3] It falls to the audience to discern why.

What would be particularly helpful to know is the relationship between the storyteller and the audience. Is the storyteller a person of status within the community? Has someone within the community commissioned this individual to tell a particular version of the Jesus story? Would this version of the story have been acclaimed by the community, or contested? Although we cannot know the answers to these questions, they remind us that the story contained in the Gospel of Matthew is a particular story, told by a particular individual. Moreover, the storyteller is not neutral, but has chosen this story as a vehicle for promoting specific values and interests, at least some of which are shared by those to whom it is addressed.[4] It is only by a careful reading of the story that we can determine what those values and interests are.

In this chapter I will explore how the storyteller narrates the tradition of the post-resurrection appearance to Mary Magdalene in the context of the story that is the Gospel of Matthew. By weaving the tradition into the larger context of the Gospel narrative the storyteller has shaped and framed the tradition so that it no longer stands on its own, but interacts with and is interpreted by the story that surrounds it. I will show how the women provide continuity to the events of the crucifixion, burial, and resurrection, filling a void created by the departure of the disciples from the narrative, and serve as a foil to the disciples' "little faith." Through this close study of how "Matthew" weaves the tradition into the larger narrative I will reveal that a strategy is at work, both in the telling and in the hearing.[5]

[3] Assuming the four-source hypothesis, Matthew's primary sources, the Gospel of Mark and "Q," contain no resurrection appearances. Whether Matthew inherited the Mary Magdalene tradition from "M" or another source is not known.

[4] This is not universally true of all tellers of stories. Depending on the context, one might tell a story that blatantly contradicts the values one holds. However, since the gospels are an attempt to persuade people to accept a particular understanding of Jesus and also to promote specific kinds of behavior within the community, it may be assumed that the values and commitments promoted in the narrative are shared by the historical author of the narrative (Mark Alan Powell, *What is Narrative Criticism?* [Minneapolis: Fortress, 1990] 26).

[5] Hereafter I will refer to the storyteller as "Matthew" or "the evangelist." I remain open to the possibility that "Matthew" is a woman, recognizing that attempts to determine gender on the basis of content or subject matter are highly problematic.

Weaving the Tradition into the Gospel Narrative

In ch. 28 the storyteller combines the tradition of the post-resurrection appearance to Mary Magdalene and the other Mary (28:9-10) with the tradition of the women's visit to the empty tomb (28:1-8) to create a single narrative. This is indicated in three ways. First, the women are identified by name only in 28:1. The audience understands that the women to whom Jesus appears in v. 9 are the same women who come to the tomb in v. 1. Second, the women are shown departing from the tomb in v. 8. This movement brings to conclusion the scene at the tomb and at the same time becomes the setting for the appearance of Jesus in vv. 9 and 10. Finally, the scene at the tomb anticipates the appearance of Jesus to the women: The angel informs the women that Jesus has been raised from the dead and they will see him; in the next scene this prediction is fulfilled when the women see Jesus for themselves.[6] Parallel structures further help to shape the two traditions into a single narrative unit. In both there is an appearance by a being who represents the divine realm, the appearance is punctuated by the expression "behold" (vv. 2, 9), a command ("do not fear") is spoken by the one who appears (vv. 5, 10), and a charge is given to go to the disciples with the news that they will see Jesus in Galilee (vv. 7, 10).[7] In these ways the two traditions are woven together as one.

Yet the narrative of the women finds its beginning before ch. 28. The women are first named in 27:55-56 and again in 27:61. Table 1 (below) reveals that these verses are linked not only through repeated references to the women but also through repetition of vocabulary and grammatical forms. Both 27:55 and 27:61 begin with the same phrase, "and there were" (ἦσαν δε ἐκεῖ), while the verse in between (27:56) employs the collective form of the verb "to be," ἦν.[8] This repetition of the verb "to be" (27:55, 56, 61) underlines the presence of the women three

[6] Janice Capel Anderson, *Matthew's Narrative Web: Over, and Over, and Over Again* (Sheffield: JSOT Press, 1994) 68. Anderson (p. 170) also observes that the words of the angel are retrospective as well as prospective (cf. 16.21; 17:9b, 23; 20:19; 26:32). See also David R. Bauer, *The Structure of Matthew's Gospel* (Sheffield: Almond Press, 1988) 103.

[7] John E. Alsup, *The Post-Resurrection Appearance Stories in the Gospel Tradition: A History-of-Tradition Analysis; with Text-Synopsis* (Stuttgart: Calwer, 1975) 109; David Hill, *The Gospel of Matthew* (Grand Rapids: Eerdmans, 1972) 359.

[8] Robert H. Gundry, *Matthew: A Commentary on His Handbook for a Mixed Church Under Persecution* (Grand Rapids: Eerdmans, 1982) 582; Keith Howard Reeves, *The Resurrection Narrative in Matthew: A Literary-Critical Examination* (Lewiston, N.Y.:

times in three short verses. The verses are also linked through the repetition of the preposition "from" (ἀπό) as well as the use of participles to describe the activity of the women: "watching," "serving," "sitting" (θεωροῦσαι, διακονοῦσαι, καθήμεναι). These patterns of repetition indicate that vv. 55-56 and v. 61 should be read together as a unit rather than as two independent scenes.

Repetition also links 27:55-56 and 27:61 with the scene that begins in 28:1, revealing them to be of a piece. In both 27:55 and 28:1 the women "see" the tomb (θεωρέω, the only two times this verb occurs in the Gospel of Matthew).[9] The tomb is the object of focus in both 27:61 and 28:1 and in both verses the identical phrase, "Mary Magdalene and the other Mary" is used to identify the women.[10] In this way the scenes involving the women are carefully woven together as one.

The final reference to Mary Magdalene and the other Mary is found in 28:11. The reference is oblique ("as they were going," πορευομένων δὲ αὐτῶν), therefore easy for the reader to overlook. However, that is not the intention of the storyteller. The use of the genitive absolute makes the women's departure to the disciples the introduction to the final episode in the narrative of the guards. Although the women are not heard from again, this construction indicates that their action continues to shape the narrative: the chief priests are instructing the guards to say that the disciples stole the body at the same time that the audience knows the women are going to the disciples to say that Jesus has been raised.[11]

Mellen Biblical Press, 1993) 12; Elaine M. Wainwright, *Towards a Feminist Critical Reading of the Gospel according to Matthew* (Berlin: Walter de Gruyter, 1991) 140.

[9] Reeves, *Resurrection Narrative*, 55. The first occurrence is taken over from Mark, who employs the word seven times. The second is a Matthean addition. Elaine Wainwright proposes that since θεωρέω appears only in 27:61 and 28:1 it may be that it is employed to highlight the two central proclamations of the early church: that Jesus was crucified and that he was raised (*Towards a Feminist Critical Reading*, 295). She suggests that the role of women as witnesses to these central proclamations may have created tensions within Matthew's community. In order to call attention to the women's witness, Matthew employs unique terminology while at the same time avoiding terms such as μαρτευρέω that might cause offense by suggesting some sort of official testimony (ibid. 140–41, 296). She also acknowledges that θεωρέω may simply serve to bridge these two verses together (ibid. 300).

[10] Reeves, *Resurrection Narrative*, 20; Wainwright, *Towards a Feminist Critical Reading*, 302.

[11] So also John Paul Heil, *The Death and Resurrection of Jesus: A Narrative-Critical Reading of Matthew 26–28* (Minneapolis: Fortress, 1991) 100; Daniel Patte, *The Gospel According to Matthew* (Philadelphia: Fortress, 1987) 395–96.

Table 1

27:55 and there were ἦσαν δε ἐκει	many women γυναῖκες πολλαὶ		from afar ἀπὸ μακρόθεν	watching θεωροῦσαι	
	who αἵτινες	had followed ἠκολούθησαν			Jesus τῷ Ἰησοῦς
			from Galilee ἀπὸ Γαλ.	serving διακονοῦσα	him αὐτῷ
27:56	among whom ἐν αἷς				
were ἦν					
	Mary Magdalene Μαρία ἡ Μαγδ. Mary the mother of James and Joseph Μαρία ἡ τοῦ . . .				
27:61 and there were ἦσαν δε ἐκει	Mary Magdalene Μαρία ἡ Μαγδαληνη the other Mary ἡ ἄλλη Μαρία			sitting καθήμεναι	
			across from ἀπέναντι		the tomb τοῦ τάφου

While the guards and the chief priests conspire to perpetuate a lie, the women faithfully deliver a true word, as evidenced by the gathering of the disciples in Galilee.[12]

Relative to the whole of the gospel these references to the women in chs. 27 and 28 are brief. Nonetheless, they are important because they link the events of the crucifixion and burial with those of the resurrection through the continuity of the women.[13] The role of the women in the narrative, therefore, is strategic, guiding the audience from cross to tomb to risen Jesus. By appearing in four scenes the women also play a larger role in Matthew's gospel than do other minor characters who appear in one scene and are not heard from again. This suggests that, like other characters who enjoy a sustained presence in the gospel narrative, the women are integral to the movement of the plot.

Storytelling Strategies: The Characterization of the Women

The main characters in this narrative unit are women. An examination of patterns of repetition and progression reveals how the women are moved from the periphery to the center of action to the periphery again. In 27:55 a group of "many women" is described watching from afar (Table 1). The relative pronoun "who" specifies that the entire group of women is to be numbered among those who have followed and served Jesus. "Following" and "serving" are the primary attributes of these women.[14] In 27:56 individual women within this larger group

[12] A comparison is drawn also between the soldiers and the disciples through the repetition of the verb "teach" (διδάσκω: 28:15, 20): as the soldiers teach as they are taught, so the disciples will teach as they are taught (John P. Meier, *The Vision of Matthew: Christ, Church, and Morality in the First Gospel* [Wilmington: Michael Glazier, 1980] 210).

[13] Charles Homer Giblin, "Structural and Thematic Correlations in the Matthean Burial-Resurrection Narrative (Matt. xxvii.57–xviii.20)," *NTS* 21 (1975) 407; Heil, *Death and Resurrection,* 94; Hill, *Gospel of Matthew,* 356; Meier, *Vision of Matthew,* 206; Reeves, *Resurrection Narrative,* 14; Donald Senior, *Matthew* (Nashville: Abingdon, 1998) 338. Claudia Setzer ("Excellent Women: Female Witnesses to the Resurrection," *JBL* 116 [1997] 261) views this continuity as an apologetic since some doubted the empty tomb as an effective proof of the resurrection.

[14] The repetition of the phrase ἦσαν δε ἐκει suggests that vv. 55a and 61 serve as brackets for the material in between, forming an aba' pattern. In "a" of this pattern it is stated that many women watched from afar, while in "a'" it is said that Mary

are singled out for mention: Mary Magdalene, Mary the mother of James and Joseph, and the mother of the sons of Zebedee.[15] The mother of the sons of Zebedee is the only one of the women to appear earlier in the gospel (20:20-21). Her presence among the women has the effect of lending credibility to the claim that the women have followed Jesus from Galilee.[16]

In 27:61 this group is further delimited to Mary Magdalene and "the other Mary" (who is, presumably, the aforementioned mother of James and Joseph). The repetition of these two women's names in 28:1 (// 27:61) emphasizes their role within the resurrection narrative as a whole. It is noteworthy that Mary, called the mother of James and Joseph in 27:56, is identified only as "the other Mary" in 27:61 and 28:1. As a result the two Marys who approach the tomb are identified by relationship neither to sons nor to husbands. Their behavior, then, gains honor or shame only for themselves. Thus while all the women who follow from Galilee serve Jesus, only Mary Magdalene and the other Mary are set apart for an encounter with the risen Jesus. This movement from the greater to the lesser focuses attention on these two women.

An examination of references to the various characters named in 28:1-10 shows how the scene shifts from the women, first to Jesus and then to the disciples (see Table 2). The women are named only once, in 28:1. In 28:5 they are called "the women." From then on, references take the form of second person singular commands ("you") or third-person pronouns ("they" or "them"). In contrast, the disciples are named each time they are mentioned, the third occasion employing the language of

---

Magdalene and the other Mary sat across from the tomb. In both "a" and "a'" the women are situated at a distance from the main action in the narrative which, in each instance, is related to the death of Jesus. Further, in both "a" and "a'" the activity of the women, which is described by a finite verb plus a participle, occurs in the present: that is, it occurs simultaneously with the main action in the narrative. In "b" of this pattern the activity of the women is neither spatially nor temporally related to the main action of the narrative. Rather, the activity of the women is identified as characteristic of their behavior since they first began following Jesus in Galilee. The aba' pattern formed by vv. 55, 56, and 61 indicates that "following" and "serving," as characteristic behavior, also describe the nature of the women's "watching" from afar and "sitting" across from the tomb.

[15] This movement is marked by a repetition of sounds that would capture attention in an oral performance of the text: αἵτινες and ἐν αἷς.

[16] Patte, *Gospel according to Matthew*, 391.

kinship, "brothers" (28:7, 8, 10).[17] The women depart from the narrative in 28:11, while the disciples take center stage at the conclusion of the gospel.[18] Although the women bear eyewitness testimony to the disciples that Jesus has been raised, they are silent messengers. They are never allowed to give voice to their testimony.

Despite the limitations imposed on the role of the women, the storyteller describes them as models of faithfulness and obedience. This characterization of the women is revealed through their actions, their encounters with divine beings, and their relationship to spatial settings. Each of these will be examined in turn.

Table 2

28:1	Two Marys				
28:2		angel			
28:3		angel			
28:4			guards		
28:5	women	angel		Jesus	
28:6	[you]	angel		Jesus	
28:7	[you]	angel		Jesus	disciples
28:8	they				disciples
28:9	them			Jesus	
28:10	them			Jesus	disciples/brothers
28:11	they		guards		
28:16					disciples

[17] Although elsewhere in Matthew's gospel the expression seems to include more than the eleven (see the discussion in Chapter Two), here it becomes more narrowly defined by what follows: i.e., the "brothers" turn out to be the Eleven.

[18] Mary Catherine Carson suggests that Matthew, being dissatisfied with the ending of Mark's gospel, intended to redact the disciples back into the tradition ("And They Said Nothing to Anyone: A Redaction-Critical Study of the Role and Status of Women in the Crucifixion, Burial and Resurrection Stories of the Canonical and Apocryphal Gospels" [Ph.D. diss., University of Newcastle upon Tyne, 1990] 182).

Actions

According to the storyteller, the women follow Jesus and minister to him (27:55); they stand at a distance during the crucifixion (27:55); they sit across from the tomb and watch the burial (27:61); they go to see the tomb on the first day of the week (28:1); they depart from the tomb in fear and joy to tell the disciples, as they have been instructed to do by the angel, that Jesus has been raised and will meet them in Galilee (28:8, 11); finally, they take hold of Jesus' feet and worship him before continuing on their journey to the disciples as they have been instructed, now by the risen Jesus (28:9). The reader knows that the women have fulfilled their charge when the disciples gather in Galilee (28:16). These actions portray the women as constant and obedient. They also show the women to be exemplary: They are present when the disciples are absent;[19] they heed the word of divine messengers; they worship the risen Jesus. Thus the women are significant characters to the degree that they demonstrate behavior against which other characters can be judged.[20] This comparative aspect of the narrative will be taken up below.

Encounters With Divine Beings

This positive characterization of the women is also suggested by their encounters with divine beings. The women inhabit space occupied, respectively, by crowds (27:55), a devoted follower of Jesus (27:57), and guards belonging to the chief priests and Pharisees (28:4). Yet the only characters with whom the women interact are an angel (28:2-7) and the risen Jesus (28:9-10).[21] Thus while the women dwell in the human realm and are observers of human activity, they engage with and act according to the instructions of the divine realm. This reveals to the reader that two levels of activity are taking place within the narrative: that associated with human intentions and that associated

[19] Some scholars suggest that the women stand in for the disciples at this point in the narrative (Anderson, *Matthew's Narrative Web,* 170; Richard A. Edwards, "Reading Matthew: the Gospel as Narrative," *Listening* 24 [1989] 92; Heil, *Death and Resurrection,* 91).

[20] According to Aristotle (*Poetics* 6.19-24, 1450b) character is revealed when someone chooses or avoids a course of action in circumstances where choice is not obvious.

[21] The encounter with the disciples takes place "off stage."

with divine intentions. The activity of the women is shown to be aligned with divine intentions.[22]

The encounter of the women with the angel echoes the beginning of Matthew's gospel, where Joseph is visited by a series of angels (1:20; 2:13, 19). Both the women and Joseph, instructed by the words of the angels, become agents of God's activity, and their obedience in each case testifies to their good character. Through these characters the storyteller begins and closes the gospel with a word from a divine messenger announcing that the divine is about to break into the human realm in the person of Jesus.

The angel tells the women to announce to the disciples that "you will see" (ὄψεσθε) Jesus in Galilee (28:7). It is not evident that the women are included in the "you." The women do see Jesus, but not in Galilee. This suggests that the message the women are to deliver to the disciples is intended for the disciples only (a reading supported also by Matt 26:32 where Jesus tells the disciples that after he is raised up "I will go ahead of you to Galilee"). Hence the appearance of Jesus to the women is independent of the announcement of the appearance of Jesus to the disciples. The women see Jesus because, according to the words of the angel, they seek him (28:5). Initially they seek Jesus "who was crucified" (28:5), but through the words of the angel this expectation is changed so that, departing from the tomb, they now seek Jesus who has been raised. In 28:9-10 their expectation is fulfilled and their persistence rewarded when Jesus appears to them.

The encounter of the women with the risen Jesus prefigures that of the disciples with Jesus in Galilee. Both the structure of the text and the words of Jesus indicate that the encounter of the women with the risen Jesus is intended to point toward that of the disciples with Jesus at the end of the gospel. At the same time it is significant that the women also see Jesus. This encounter ensures that the word they bear to the disciples is not a secondhand report received from the angel, but an eyewitness testimony. The word of the women, therefore, is utterly reliable.

Spatial Setting

Although the women do not appear in the narrative until the crucifixion, they are identified as residents of Galilee who have followed

[22] It is striking, also, that the storyteller both begins and ends the gospel with women: women appear in the genealogy in ch. 1 and at the tomb in ch. 28.

Jesus to Jerusalem (27:55). In addition to informing the audience that the women are not simply bystanders who have come to see the entertainment, this reference to Galilee offers insight into the character of the women.[23] Beginning with the infancy narrative, the storyteller sets up a theme of opposition between Galilee and Jerusalem.[24] Jerusalem is the place where Jesus' enemies reside and scheme against his life.[25] Galilee is the place where Jesus calls his disciples, where he carries out his ministry, and where he can retreat when threatened.[26] On the basis of this opposition the audience recognizes references to Galilee as allusions to Jesus' ministry. By describing the women as followers of Jesus from Galilee the storyteller discloses their close association with Jesus' ministry.

Between 27:55 and 28:11 the women occupy three separate spatial settings. In the first they are located at a distance from the crucifixion. The only other occurrence of the expression "from afar" in the gospel is in 26:58, where Peter is described following "from afar" after Jesus is arrested.[27] Since Peter, once he is discovered, adamantly denies his association with Jesus at the same time that the women persistently remain until Jesus' death, the storyteller seems to be drawing a contrast between the behavior of Peter and the behavior of the women.[28] Both observe from afar. However, in Peter's case the distance calls attention to his betrayal, while in the case of the women it calls attention to their faithfulness.

The women move from the edge of the setting in 27:55, where they "watch from afar," to somewhere near the middle in 27:61, where they "sit across from the tomb." Finally, in 28:1, they enter into the center of the spatial setting as they themselves approach the tomb. The tomb is the focus of much attention from characters human and divine, representing

[23] Mark does not include the phrase "who had followed Jesus from Galilee." This suggests that Matthew wants the reader to connect the women with the spatial setting "Galilee" and its referents.

[24] Heil, *Death and Resurrection,* 12.

[25] Warren Carter, *Matthew: Storyteller, Interpreter, Evangelist* (Peabody, Mass.: Hendrickson, 1996) 183; Heil, *Death and Resurrection,* 12.

[26] Carter, *Matthew: Storyteller, Interpreter, Evangelist,* 177; Heil, *Death and Resurrection,* 13. See also Jack Dean Kingsbury, *Matthew as Story* (Philadelphia: Fortress, 1988) 29.

[27] Reeves, *Resurrection Narrative,* 12. This suggests to Reeves that its use in 27:55 is intended to distance the women from the spatial-temporal plane of the event of the crucifixion.

[28] Wainwright, *Towards a Feminist Critical Reading,* 141–42.

both friend and foe.[29] Each character alters the appearance of the tomb in some way and assigns it a different meaning.[30] Among these characters the women stand apart, for only the women come to see the tomb (28:1)[31] and it becomes for the women, through the words of the angel, a place of revelation.[32] Guards, representing the chief priests and Pharisees, are also present for this moment of revelation by the angel but, unlike the women, they do not hear what the angel has to say. They are, in fact, described as becoming "like dead men" at the very moment when the angel announces that the one who was dead is alive.[33] The tomb, then, is a kind of proving ground, where the audience is invited to choose between the living and the dead. In order to choose the living, the audience must identify with the women.

As the women approached the tomb in 28:1, they now depart from it in their final scene. It is striking that the location in which the women encounter Jesus is really no location at all, but a liminal space somewhere between the tomb and Galilee. This "nowhere" space, which has no distinguishing features of its own, is landscaped by the encounter between Jesus and the women: the women, bending low to grasp Jesus' feet, offer worship; Jesus, raised up, greets the women and sends them from this "nowhere" space to tell the disciples to meet Jesus in a specific place in Galilee. This dislocation of the women focuses attention on their action. From a positive perspective it perpetuates the characterization of the women as faithful and obedient servants. From a negative perspective it signifies spatially that the encounter of the women

[29] Specifically Joseph of Arimathea, the chief priests and scribes, the guards, and the angel, in addition to the women.

[30] For Joseph it is a place to bury Jesus and, by this act, to honor Jesus; for the chief priests and Pharisees it represents a threat; for the angel it is a means to disclose God's vindication of Jesus.

[31] Warren Carter views "seeing" in Matthew as a metaphor for knowledge (*Matthew: Storyteller, Interpreter, Evangelist,* 243). See also his article "'To see the Tomb': A Note on Matthew's Women at the Tomb (Matt 28:1)," *ExpTim* 107 (1996) 210–15.

[32] Angels are similarly employed in chs. 1 and 2 in order to explain the meaning of events and to assign tasks to others (David Hill, *Gospel of Matthew,* 359; Herman Waetjen, *The Origin and Destiny of Humankind* [Corte Madera, Calif.: Omega Books, 1976] 252).

[33] Carter, *Matthew: Storyteller, Interpreter, Evangelist,* 172; Eduard Schweizer, *The Good News according to Matthew* (Atlanta: John Knox, 1975) 523; Robert Smith, *Easter Gospels* (Minneapolis: Augsburg, 1983) 72; Wainwright, *Towards a Feminist Critical Reading,* 145.

with the risen Jesus is not of the same import as the anticipated encounter of the disciples with Jesus in Galilee.

The audience, following the movement of the women in 28:9-10, also is reunited spatially with the now-living Jesus.[34] It is interesting to note that when Jesus addresses the women in this "nowhere" space the historical present is used ("he says"; λέγει).[35] This usage is significant because it draws the audience into the temporal plane of the narrative, so that the audience is located both temporally and spatially alongside the women.[36] It is as if we are there. The words spoken by Jesus to the women, then, also address the audience. Like the women, the audience has its attention directed toward the disciples for the final encounter with Jesus. However, when Jesus addresses the disciples in 28:16-20 the past tense (aorist) is employed. The audience is not invited to hear these words in the same way that they were invited to hear the words spoken to the women. In this final scene the words spoken by Jesus are reserved for the disciples. Both the women and the audience will have to approach the disciples in order to enjoy the benefit of Jesus' words.

Storytelling Strategies: The Women and the Disciples

The characterization of the women reveals them to be significant characters against which other characters can be judged. But does the storyteller view the women as disciples? Scholars are divided on this issue. Some maintain that Matthew does.[37] Others disagree.[38] At the

[34] Anderson, *Matthew's Narrative Web,* 68; David D. Kupp, *Matthew's Emmanuel: Divine Presence and God's People in the First Gospel* (Cambridge and New York: Cambridge University Press, 1996) 101.

[35] Anderson observes that in the Gospel of Matthew the historical present is reserved for the narrator and Jesus (*Matthew's Narrative Web,* 61).

[36] H. J. Bernard Combrink, "The Structure of the Gospel of Matthew as Narrative," *TynBul* 34 (1983) 88.

[37] Warren Carter, *Matthew and the Margins* (Maryknoll, N.Y.: Orbis, 2000) 538; Kathleen Corley, *Private Women, Public Meals* (Peabody, Mass.: Hendrickson, 1993) 172; Michael Crosby, *House of Disciples: Church, Economics, and Justice in Matthew* (Maryknoll, N.Y.: Orbis, 1988) 114; Sean Freyne, *The Twelve: Disciples and Apostles* (London: Sheed and Ward, 1968) 152, 170; Gundry, *Matthew,* 59, 281, 578; Ulrich Luz, "The Disciples in the Gospel according to Matthew," in Graham Stanton, ed., *A Gospel for a New People: Studies in Matthew* (Edinburgh: T & T Clark, 1992) 109, 110; Sheila McGinn, "'Not Counting the Women . . .,' A Feminist Reading of Matthew

root of this debate is the question of whether one defines "disciples" as a character group within Matthew's narrative or as those who embody the characteristics that describe the ideal follower of Jesus.[39] In the case of the women this debate rests on the interpretation of two verbs: "serve" (διακονέω) and "follow" (ἀκολουθέω).

"Serve" (διακονέω) occurs five times in Matthew's gospel (4:11; 8:15; 20:28; 25:44; 27:55) and the noun cognate "servant" (διάκονος) three times (20:26, 22:13, 23:11). The question is whether this verb indicates menial service such as waiting table (its conventional meaning) or is a metaphor for discipleship.[40] Those who believe the latter point to 20:28: ". . . the Son of Man did not come to be served (διακονηθῆναι) but to serve (διακονῆσαι)." Here "serve" is clearly employed to characterize the ministry and mission of Jesus. Further, in 20:26 and 23:11 Jesus states that the one who would be esteemed as great within the community must become a "servant" (διάκονος). As Anderson points out, although Jesus admonishes the character group "disciples" with these words, neither the verb nor the noun is actually used to describe the "disciples."[41] One might argue that "disciples," as a character group, do perform acts of service, even if the word is not employed to describe

26–28," *Society of Biblical Literature 1995 Seminar Papers*, ed. Eugene H. Lovering, Jr. (Atlanta: Scholars, 1995) 172, 174; Schweizer, *Gospel according to Matthew*, 517–18; Patte, *The Gospel according to Matthew*, 391; Mary R. Thompson, *Mary of Magdala: Apostle and Leader* (Mahwah, N.J.: Paulist, 1995) 71–72; Wainwright, *Towards a Feminist Critical Reading*, 142, 296, 335 (cf. 146, 334).

[38] Janice Capel Anderson, "Matthew: Gender and Reading," *Semeia* 28 (1983) 19–20; Raymond E. Brown, *The Death of the Messiah* (New York: Doubleday, 1994) 1155; Jack Dean Kingsbury, "The Verb *Akolouthein* ("to follow") as an Index of Matthew's View of His Community," *JBL* 97 (1978) 61; Stuart L. Love, "The Place of Women in Public Settings in Matthew's Gospel: A Sociological Inquiry," *BTB* 24 (1994) 57; Talvikki Mattila, "Naming the Nameless: Gender and Discipleship in Matthew's Passion Narrative," in David Rhoads and Kari Syreeni, eds., *Characterization in the Gospels: Reconceiving Narrative Criticism* (Sheffield: Sheffield Academic Press, 1999) 172; Setzer, "Excellent Women," 266; Wainwright, *Towards a Feminist Critical Reading*, 334 (cf. 142, 296, 335); Antoinette C. Wire, "Gender Roles in a Scribal Community," in David Balch, ed., *Social History of the Matthean Community: Cross Disciplinary Approaches* (Minneapolis: Fortress, 1991) 103, 106.

[39] Anderson, "Matthew: Gender and Reading," 16.

[40] Gundry, for example, understands both "serve" (διακονέω) and "follow" (ἀκολουθέω) as metaphors for discipleship (*Matthew*, 578). See also Celia M. Deutsch, *Lady Wisdom, Jesus, and the Sages* (Valley Forge: Trinity Press International, 1996) 139 and Wainwright, *Towards a Feminist Critical Reading*, 85, 86.

[41] Anderson, "Matthew: Gender and Reading," 19.

their activity. However, Matthew's "disciples" are far from perfect.[42] Since Jesus admonishes the "disciples" twice that they must "serve" in order to be great (20:26, 28; 25:44) it seems more probable that the storyteller has reserved "serve" as a cautionary word directed toward the "disciples."

This is borne out when we consider those who are said to "serve": the angels (4:11), Peter's mother-in-law (8:15), and the women (27:55). In each case the characters involved serve "him" (i.e., Jesus).[43] The women may serve because it fulfills a role that is consistent with their social world.[44] The angels serve because Jesus is God's chosen. Yet when "serve" is used to describe the work both of the angels and of the women, the service of the women takes on a significance beyond that of carrying out social responsibilities; it becomes service rendered to God's chosen.[45] This reading is supported by the use of "serve" in 25:44, the parable of the sheep and the goats. When the Son of Man casts out the goats they bleat: "when did we see you hungry or thirsty or a stranger or naked or sick or in prison and not serve you?" These are, of course, the actions the sheep have performed on behalf of the Son of Man. They also describe the service rendered by the angels and the women to Jesus, as well as the kind of service the Son of Man came to render.[46] Thus the service of the women must be esteemed as exemplary.

[42] David B. Howell, *Matthew's Inclusive Story: A Study in the Narrative Rhetoric of the First Gospel* (Sheffield: JSOT Press, 1990) 235; Luz, "The Disciples in the Gospel According to Matthew," 101; Wire, "Gender Roles in a Scribal Community," 102.

[43] It is significant that Matthew alters Mark's text with respect to Peter's mother-in-law: Mark states that she served "them," meaning all those gathered (1:30). Therefore in Mark she is simply carrying out her domestic duties. By changing the text so that Peter's mother-in-law serves Jesus, Matthew adds another level of meaning to her service.

[44] Anderson, "Matthew: Gender and Reading," 19.

[45] Wainwright notes that διακονέω functions at both a literal and a symbolic level (*Towards a Feminist Critical Reading*, 56, 141). See also Deutsch, *Lady Wisdom*, 213 n. 162; Carolyn Osiek and David Balch, eds., *Families in the New Testament World* (Louisville: Westminster John Knox, 1997) 135.

[46] Lorraine Caza, "Disciple et apôtre à la manière de Marie de Magdala," in Michel Gourgues and Gilles-D. Mailhiot, eds., *L'Altérité, vivre ensemble différents: approches pluridisciplinaires: actes du Colloque pluridisciplinaire tenu à l'occasion du 75e anniversaire du Collège dominicain de philosophie et de théologie, Ottawa, 4, 5, 6 octobre 1984* (Montréal: Bellarmin; Paris: Cerf, 1986) 239. The full text of 20:27-28 reads "and whoever would be first among you must also be your slave even as the Son of Man came not to be served but to serve and to give his life as a ransom for many." The

Nonetheless, it does not necessarily mean that the storyteller understands the women to be disciples. Rather, the pattern of usage for "serve" suggests that the women's behavior serves as a model for an ideal the "disciples" are urged to strive for but have not yet attained.[47]

Although a variety of people are said to follow (ἀκολουθέω) Jesus in the course of Matthew's gospel, it is evident that not all are considered disciples by the storyteller. For example, Jesus is frequently followed by crowds, but these crowds, as a group, are never called disciples.[48] The women in 27:55 offer a more ambiguous example. Kingsbury asserts that "follow" refers to discipleship only when it involves personal commitment (i.e., Jesus calls or addresses the individual who follows) and personal sacrifice (e.g., loss of family or goods).[49] On the basis of this definition Kingsbury does not consider the women to be disciples.[50] Yet one could argue that the charge the women receive from Jesus does fulfill Kingsbury's definition of personal commitment, and the verb "serve" indicates that the women have sacrificed goods on Jesus' behalf. However, other indicators in the text support the claim that the women are not viewed as disciples by the storyteller.

In 27:62-66 the chief priests and Pharisees approach Pilate for permission to place a guard at the tomb for fear the disciples will steal the body of Jesus and report that he "was raised from the dead." This strongly suggests that, for the purposes of the storyteller, it is essential that the women *not* be disciples. This is shown to be the case. When, in the scene that follows, the angel announces to the women that Jesus "was raised from the dead" (28:7), the representatives of the character group "disciples" are nowhere to be seen, having fled from the story when Jesus was arrested (26:56).[51] In addition, the storyteller takes care that Joseph of Arimathea, who is identified as one discipled to Jesus (27:57), is fully removed from the vicinity (27:60).[52] Further, the only

---

major conjunction "and" (καί) suggests "to give his life as a ransom for many" should be read as additional to "serving," not as descriptive of the service.

[47] Anderson, "Matthew: Gender and Reading," 19; Love, "The Place of Women," 57–58, 62; Wire, "Gender Roles in a Scribal Community," 104.

[48] Michael J. Wilkins, "Named and Unnamed Disciples in Matthew: A Literary/Theological Study," in *Society of Biblical Literature 1991 Seminar Papers*, ed. Eugene H. Lovering, Jr. (Atlanta: Scholars, 1991) 422.

[49] Kingsbury, "The Verb *Akolouthein*," 58.

[50] Ibid. 61.

[51] Reeves, *Resurrection Narrative*, 15.

[52] In the case of Joseph of Arimathea the verb "to disciple" (μαθητεύειν) rather than the noun "disciple" (μαθητής) is employed. This may indicate that he also is not

one among the women who is related to the disciples, the mother of the sons of Zebedee, is also excluded at this point. Thus even this oblique reference to the disciples is omitted.[53] Finally, the charge the women receive to go to "*his* disciples" confirms that this is a group to which they do not belong. This is not to say that the women do not exhibit qualities that are characteristic of discipleship. To the contrary, at the same time that the storyteller removes all hint of the "disciples'" presence at the empty tomb the women become, through their faithful presence at the crucifixion, burial, and tomb, a physical testimony to Jesus' ministry, characterized by their following and serving.[54]

Other points of comparison are drawn between the women and the "disciples" as each group encounters the risen Jesus. The women seek Jesus and find him. The "disciples" gather in Galilee not because they, too, seek Jesus, but because they have been instructed to go to Galilee by Jesus, speaking through the women. This difference between the women and the "disciples" is accented by their respective reactions to seeing the risen Jesus: The women offer unqualified worship (προσκυνέω). The "disciples" also worship (προσκυνέω), but some doubt (διστάζω). An investigation of these two words suggests that a strategy is at work.

"Doubt" (διστάζω) is another word that appears only twice in Matthew (14:31; 28:17).[55] In both instances it describes a reaction by some of the "disciples" to an appearance of Jesus, and in both instances it is used in combination with "worship" (προσκυνέω).[56] Notably, these two texts also represent the only time "worship" is used in reference to the "disciples." Since the "disciples" are, elsewhere, described as "those of little faith" (6:30; 8:26; 14:31; 16:8; 17:20), this usage is consistent with

considered a member of the character group "disciples." Rather, Wilkins thinks the description of Joseph as "discipled" anticipates the final commissioning, where the verb is employed again to describe the mission of the disciples ("Named and Unnamed Disciples," 435).

[53] The mother of the sons of Zebedee is also the only one of the three women who is named prior to the Passion narrative (20:20-28).

[54] Wainwright notes, in particular, the presence in this group of the mother of the sons of Zebedee. According to Wainwright it is the mother rather than her sons who "drinks the cup" that Jesus drinks (Matt 20:20-28) (*Towards a Feminist Critical Reading*, 142, 253; see also McGinn, "'Not Counting the Women . . .,'" 173; Osiek and Balch, *Families in the New Testament*, 236).

[55] Kupp, *Matthew's Emmanuel*, 205.

[56] Ibid.; Wainwright, *Towards a Feminist Critical Reading*, 236. In the first text doubt is followed by worship (προσκυνέω); in the second they stand side by side.

Matthew's characterization of the "disciples."[57] But this characterization stands in sharp contrast to that of the women.

The verb προσκυνέω (variously translated as "worship," "prostrate oneself before") is employed by Matthew consistently to describe a response to the person of Jesus. William G. Thompson, following the work of Johannes Horst, observes that when the verb appears in the imperfect it indicates supplication before a person of higher rank (8:2, 9:18, 15:25, 18:26); when it is used in the aorist it indicates an attitude of worship (2:2, 11, 14:33, 28:9, 17).[58] Those who worship Jesus, then, are the magi, the "disciples," and the women from Galilee, but the "disciples" also doubt. Only the magi and the women offer unqualified worship, and both do so at critical moments in the narrative: at the birth of Jesus and at his "rebirth" or resurrection. Both, also, serve as foils to others who would worship Jesus: the magi to Herod and the women to the "disciples." This positive characterization of the women, then, becomes the backdrop against which the behavior of the "disciples" in 28:16-20 is heard. The result is that, even at the end, the "disciples" are shown to be wanting.

Conclusion

The narrative of Mary Magdalene and the other Mary spans 27:55–28:11 and continues to comment on and be commented on by the narrative through 28:20. The women provide the narrative with continuity, linking together the events of the death, burial, and resurrection of Jesus. The continuity of their presence is matched by the constancy of their character: their actions are motivated by faithful service to Jesus and they continue to seek him even after his death. Their persistence is rewarded by the revelation of Jesus' resurrection, followed by an appearance of the risen Jesus. This appearance enables the women to provide the disciples with an utterly reliable testimony, that Jesus has been

[57] Ibid. 206.

[58] William G. Thompson, *Matthew's Advice to a Divided Community* (Rome: Biblical Institute Press, 1970) 214, citing Johannes Horst, *Proskynein, zur Anbetung im Urchristentum nach ihrer religionsgeschichtlichen Eigenart* (Gütersloh: Gütersloher Verlaghaus Gerd Mohn, 1932) 217–38. The verb "worship" (προσκυνέω) is used two times, in neither the aorist nor the imperfect. In 2:8, where it is used with reference to Herod, it is in the future tense; in 20:20, where it refers to the mother of the sons of Zebedee, it appears as a present participle.

raised from the dead and is going ahead to meet the disciples in Galilee. That the disciples gather in Galilee confirms that the women have faithfully carried out their charge and that, in doing so, they have been agents of divine intentionality. The women hold the narrative together when it is most in danger of unraveling.

The continuity and constancy of the women also causes them to serve as foils for other characters in the narrative. Their constancy is a measure for the inconstancy of the disciples: the women follow while Peter and the disciples flee; they are present when the disciples are absent. They serve, while the disciples seek status. They seek Jesus and find him; the disciples meet Jesus because they are commanded to do so. The women offer Jesus worship; the disciples worship, but some continue to doubt. The women are exemplary where the disciples fall short. The women also serve as counterpoints to the guards: the guards become like dead men when the tomb is opened; the women remain alert to receive news of the living Jesus. The guards deliver a dead word, a lie; the women deliver a living and true word. The guards are agents of the religious leaders; the women are agents of God.

Yet despite the important and positive role given to the women, the narrative has been framed in such a way that the women's role also has strict limits imposed upon it. For example, the women are clearly distinguished from the disciples. They do not enter the narrative until the disciples have been absented from it and they are hastily ushered off before the disciples reenter. Even as the women move center stage for their encounter with Jesus they are gradually being displaced by the disciples: the women, who are mentioned repeatedly by name in the first part of the narrative, are reduced to pronouns, while the disciples are referred to by name and in increasingly intimate language. Although the women do see Jesus, they encounter him in a "nowhere" space. The disciples see Jesus in Galilee, on a mountain—space firmly aligned with the mission and ministry of Jesus. The women are commanded to bring a message to the disciples only, while the disciples are commanded to carry a message to the world. The distinction between the tasks of the two groups is further emphasized when the storyteller, speaking through Jesus, precludes participation by the women in the final commissioning in Galilee. Thus the role of the women, while exemplary, is shown, finally, to be subordinate to that of the disciples.

These limitations imposed by the storyteller raise additional questions about the function of this narrative. Indeed, one might ask why Matthew has bothered to add the narrative of the post-resurrection appearance to the women to the gospel at all. Since it is not found in Mark, its inclusion here is a self-conscious decision on the part of the storyteller. Yet it is not entirely necessary for the narrative to work. The women are already on their way to the disciples when Jesus appears to them. Although the appearance of Jesus increases the authority of the women's message, it also seems to create a problem for the storyteller. The women are the first to see the risen Jesus. This places them in a position of significant status. The storyteller must work to construct the text in such a way that this appearance to the women is clearly subordinate to the appearance to the disciples. The result is that, in the final redaction, not all appearances by the risen Jesus are equal. This suggests that, in addition to the storytelling strategy at work within the narrative, there may be another persuasive strategy in place, one that is directed toward Matthew's historical audience and concerns the question of who speaks for the risen Jesus. Is it those who, like the women, encounter Jesus in the liminal world of visions, or those who, like the disciples, are authorized to be bearers of the tradition? This is the question I will take up in the next chapter.

Chapter Six

The Mary Magdalene Tradition and Matthean Communities: The Function of the Tradition in Response to Historical Circumstances

Behind every story is a reason. Sometimes the reason is pure entertainment, sometimes it is moral guidance, and sometimes, when a community finds itself caught between competing perspectives, it is persuasion. The teller of the Gospel of Matthew concludes the gospel with two stories of post-resurrection appearances: one to the women and another to the eleven disciples. Within the narrative of the gospel these appearances are not equal. The appearance to the women is subordinate to the appearance to the disciples. The question I will endeavor to address in this chapter is "why"? Why has the teller of the Gospel of Matthew constructed the narrative in this way?

In the conclusion to the previous chapter I suggested that the storyteller is attempting to influence the direction of a debate within Matthean communities about who has authority to speak for the risen Jesus. What is not immediately clear is whether the storyteller is driven by concerns around gender, the mode in which the words of Jesus are passed on to the community, the status of one group over another within the community, or some combination of the above. To sort out the storyteller's interests I will undertake a two-part investigation. First I will examine how the storyteller has constructed and framed narratives in which women are primary characters in order to determine what, if any, boundaries are imposed on the roles of the women.

Second, I will examine the distribution of authority with respect to teaching and speaking the words of Jesus within the gospel. Specifically, I will seek to determine whether the storyteller describes an egalitarian community, as some have suggested, or has set apart individuals within the group to act as repositories and transmitters of the words of Jesus.

Women in the Gospel of Matthew

Women, in the Gospel of Matthew, occupy the margins of the storyteller's world. The world described by the storyteller is thoroughly male-centered (androcentric). This is demonstrated in numerous ways. For example, the gospel begins with a genealogy traced through the male line;[1] women are identified by their relationship to the patriarchal household,[2] and patriarchal marriage and inheritance practices are assumed (1:18-25; 5:31-32; 19:1-12; 21:33-42; 22:23-33).[3] In 13:55-56 Jesus' brothers are identified by name, but his sisters are not.[4] Women are described as engaged in those activities one expects in a patriarchal society: giving birth (24:19), making bread (13:33), going to weddings (25:1-13), intervening for their children (15:21-28).[5] Women address Jesus in only two narratives (15:21-28; 20:20-22), while men address Jesus frequently (e.g., 8:1-4, 5-13, 18-22; 9:18-19, 27-31; 12:38-42; 15:1-9; 19:3-9). Issues related to the lives of women are discussed by men or presented from the male perspective (1:18-21; 5:27-28; 19:3-12; 22:23-33).[6] The language in significant portions of the gospel, such as the

[1] Janice Capel Anderson, "Matthew: Gender and Reading," *Semeia* 28 (1983) 7, 10; Stuart L. Love, "The Household: A Major Social Component for Gender Analysis in the Gospel of Matthew," *BTB* 23 (1993) 24; Elaine M. Wainwright, *Towards a Feminist Critical Reading of the Gospel According to Matthew* (Berlin: Walter de Gruyter, 1991) 326.

[2] Antoinette C. Wire, "Gender Roles in a Scribal Community," in David Balch, ed., *Social History of the Matthean Community: Cross Disciplinary Approaches* (Minneapolis: Fortress, 1991) 103.

[3] Anderson, "Gender and Reading," 7; Love, "The Household," 24.

[4] Wire, "Gender Roles in a Scribal Community," 103.

[5] Celia M. Deutsch, *Lady Wisdom, Jesus and the Sages* (Valley Forge: Trinity Press International, 1996) 138.

[6] Joanna Dewey, "Women in the Synoptic Gospels: Seen but not Heard?" *BTB* 27 (1997) 57, 59; Carolyn Osiek and David Balch, *Families in the New Testament World* (Louisville: Westminster John Knox, 1997) 132.

Sermon on the Mount and the parables, references the experience of men.[7] Yet in all of this Matthew reflects the world in which the storyteller and the audience lived.[8] This merely shows that the storyteller has created a world in the text that the audience would recognize and with which they could identify.

Within the gospel the role of women is episodic.[9] With the exception of the women in the narrative units described by 1:18–2:33 and 27:55–28:10, none of the women appears in more than one scene.[10] This observation would mean more were it not true of all the synoptic gospels.[11] It is also true for most of the characters within the gospels, both male and female. Thus while the episodic nature of the narratives significantly limits the role of women within the gospel, it is difficult to know how to interpret this limitation.

In order to determine whether the storyteller behind the Gospel of Matthew "consistently restricts" the role of women I will examine two aspects of the text. I will consider the degree to which the storyteller challenges the prevailing androcentric worldview and the degree to which the storyteller reinforces it in narratives involving women, and I will examine how the women and the disciples are portrayed in relation to one another in the text. It is in these that the storyteller's rhetorical strategy will be revealed. My investigation will focus on three narratives in which women play a central role: the healing of Peter's mother-in-law, the woman with the flow of blood, and the Canaanite woman.[12] In order to assist in discerning the storyteller's strategy I have selected narratives that can be compared with the Gospel of Mark, the storyteller's primary source.

[7] Amy-Jill Levine, *The Social and Ethnic Dimensions of Matthean Salvation History* (Lewiston, N.Y.: Edwin Mellen, 1988) 88; Stuart L. Love, "The Place of Women in Public Settings in Matthew's Gospel: A Sociological Inquiry," *BTB* 24 (1994) 59–60; Elaine M. Wainwright, "The Gospel of Matthew," in Elisabeth Schüssler Fiorenza, ed., *Searching the Scriptures: A Feminist Commentary* (New York: Crossroad, 1994) 637, 645; Wire, "Gender Roles in a Scribal Community," 105.

[8] Dewey, "Women in the Synoptic Gospels," 53. Dewey also observes (p. 58) that no one gospel appears to be more androcentric than another.

[9] Anderson, "Matthew: Gender and Reading," 16.

[10] In 1:18–2:33 the mother of Jesus is named several times. However, her role is clearly secondary to that of Joseph.

[11] Although Mary has an expanded role within the birth narrative in Luke.

[12] References to women in Matthew's gospel may be divided into five categories: (1) Women as protagonists (8:14-15; 9:20-22; 14:1-12; 15:21-28; 20:20-28; 26:6-13; 26:69-71; 27:19; 27:55–28:10), (2) Women as secondary characters (1:1-17; 1:18–2:33;

The Healing of Peter's Mother-in-Law (Matt 8:14-15)

In the Gospel of Mark (1:29-31), when Jesus enters the house of Simon and Andrew with James and John he is told that Peter's mother-in-law is sick with a fever. As he takes her by the hand the fever departs, and she arises to serve *them.* In Matthew the narrative is significantly altered. Jesus enters Peter's house, but no mention is made of Peter, Andrew, James, and John being present.[13] When Jesus sees Peter's mother-in-law lying sick he touches her hand, causing the fever to depart. She then arises and serves *him.*

The effect of these changes is to elevate the role of Peter's mother-in-law within the narrative. No longer is her encounter with Jesus mediated by the disciples. Rather, the initiative for the encounter rests with Jesus and she, in turn, serves him.[14] Where Mark reintegrates the woman

---

9:18-19, 23-26), (3) Women as objects of discussion (5:27-28; 5:31-32; 19:3-9; 22:23-33; 26:6-13), (4) Women as exemplars (2:18; 10:35; 12:42; 13:33; 24:41; 25:1-13), and (5) Passing references to women (11:11; 14:21; 15:38; 19:29; 24:19). Of these the following are found in Matthew only: 1:1-17; 1:18–2:33; 2:18; 5:27-28; 14:21; 15:38; 20:20-28; 25:1-13; 27:19; [28:9-10 // John 20:1-18].

[13] The passing reference to Peter leads Francis W. Beare (*The Gospel According to Matthew* [San Francisco: Harper & Row, 1981] 210) and Elaine Wainwright (*Towards a Feminist Critical Reading,* 189) to suggest that Peter's name may be a later addition to the narrative. Wainwright posits that it may represent an attempt to bring the story within the confines of patriarchal leadership.

[14] Several scholars have observed that the narrative of Peter's mother-in-law stands apart from other miracle stories in the Gospel of Matthew because the initiative for the healing is taken by Jesus rather than the supplicant (Beare, *The Gospel According to Matthew,* 210; Robert Gundry, *Matthew* [Grand Rapids: Eerdmans, 1982] 148; John Meier, *Matthew* (Wilmington: Michael Glazier, 1980) 85; Osiek and Balch, *Families in the New Testament World,* 135; Eduard Schweizer, *The Good News According to Matthew,* translated by David E. Green [Atlanta: John Knox, 1975] 217; Wainwright, *Towards a Feminist Critical Reading,* 84; eadem, "The Gospel of Matthew," 648; Wire, "Gender Roles in a Scribal Community," 104). This, in combination with the use of the verb ὁράω and the absence of witnesses (also unusual in healing stories) causes some scholars to conclude that Matthew's narrative has, in fact, been structured as a call narrative with a healing motif (Daniel Patte, *The Gospel According to Matthew* [Philadelphia: Fortress, 1987] 116; Wainwright, *Towards a Feminist Critical Reading,* 181, 188; eadem, "The Gospel of Matthew," 674). Wainwright identifies the following elements in call narratives and notes that at least two other examples may be found in Matthew (4:21; 9:9): introduction (the caller approaches and sees the one to be called); exposition (a description of the one called); middle (the call: a word or action); and conclusion (response to the call) (*Towards a Feminist Critical Reading,* 181). Thus she concludes that Matthew is drawing on a remembered call to discipleship rather than the Gospel of Mark (ibid. 179, 181). However, the verses that

into the patriarchal household once she is healed, Matthew integrates her into the new family of those who do the will of God (12:46-59; 25:31-46). Her action also becomes an example against which the disciples will be judged.[15] Amy-Jill Levine observes irony in the fact that Peter's mother-in-law rises from her bed to serve Jesus, while Peter, when asked by Jesus to watch with him, falls asleep (26:36-46).[16] A similar irony can be observed in the stories involving the mother of the sons of Zebedee: the sons seek to sit with Jesus in his kingdom, but only the mother stands with Jesus at the cross.[17] Thus on two occasions the storyteller draws a comparison between the mothers of disciples and their sons; in each case it is the disciples who are found wanting.

In addition to making changes within the narrative of the healing of Peter's mother-in-law, Matthew also places it at a different point in the gospel. In Mark it is located between two summary passages: one recording how Jesus' fame spread everywhere as a result of casting out an unclean spirit (1:28), the other recording how many who were sick or possessed were brought to him (1:32-24). In Matthew the healing of Peter's mother-in-law is the third of three healing stories. The first involves a leper and the second the slave of a centurion. Each of the three healings involves an individual who, at some level, can be described as

---

follow (8:16-17) indicate that the storyteller understands the story as a healing narrative. In addition, it is Matthew's editorial tendency to omit persons and details (Daniel J. Harrington, *The Gospel of Matthew* (Collegeville: The Liturgical Press, 1991) 116; Heinz Joachim Held, "Matthew as Interpreter of the Miracle Stories," in Günther Bornkamm, Gerhard Barth, and Heinz Joachim Held, eds., *Tradition and Interpretation in Matthew* [Philadelphia: Westminster, 1963] 233–37). Although the omission of the disciples would not necessarily preclude leaving the initiative for the healing with the supplicant (i.e., Peter's mother-in-law), Matthew seems to employ a pattern within the narratives involving women by which the women move from silence, to speaking to themselves, to speaking directly to Jesus.

[15] See the earlier discussion of διακονέω. Elaine Wainwright (*Towards a Feminist Critical Reading,* 190) suggests that the inclusion of Peter's name in the narrative may represent an attempt to bring the story within the confines of a patriarchal relationship.

[16] Amy-Jill Levine, "Matthew," in Carol A. Newsom and Sharon H. Ringe, eds., *The Women's Bible Commentary* (Louisville: Westminster John Knox, 1998) 343.

[17] Mary Rose D'Angelo notes that there are misogynist overtones in the way mother Zebedee is depicted: she deflects attention away from the inappropriate ambitions of her sons by voicing their request as her own ("(Re)Presentations of Women in the Gospel of Matthew and Luke-Acts," in Ross S. Kraemer and Mary Rose D'Angelo, eds., *Women & Christian Origins* [Oxford: Oxford University Press, 1999] 174).

an outsider: lepers, with respect to society; Gentiles, with respect to Judaism; women, with respect to an androcentric culture. With each of these healings, boundaries are being redescribed: those that separate, respectively, clean and unclean, Jew and Gentile, male and female.

The narrative of the healing of Peter's mother-in-law is followed immediately by one in which Jesus encounters two "would-be" disciples (8:18-22).[18] The inability of these "would-be" disciples to follow Jesus stands in stark contrast to the exemplary behavior exhibited in two of the preceding healings: the centurion whose faith exceeds that found in Israel (8:10) and the woman who serves (8:15). As noted in the previous chapter, the service rendered by the woman becomes a standard against which the disciples are judged. The juxtaposition of these texts further enhances the behavior of the woman.

The Woman With the Flow of Blood (Matt 9:20-22)

The story of the woman with the flow of blood (9:20-22) also differs significantly from the version found in Mark (5:25-34). Matthew eliminates the lengthy description of the woman, the reference to her internal thoughts, the woman's direct discourse, the dialogue between Jesus and his disciples, the reference to the woman's attempt to hide, and he shortens Jesus' final words to the woman.[19] The result is that the story is reduced to a bare two verses in which the woman approaches Jesus and Jesus responds to the woman. Very little is left to capture the audience's imagination or sympathy. This suggests, initially, that Matthew has reduced the story of the woman with the flow of blood to little more than a passing reference. Yet when it is considered alongside the healing of Peter's mother-in-law, some striking similarities emerge, suggesting that Matthew's minimalist approach may be driven by a strategy.[20]

[18] Patte, *The Gospel According to Matthew,* 116.

[19] Although Matthew does not have the woman speak aloud, the words she speaks to herself offer insight into her thought world. This introduces a level of intimacy that is absent in the Marcan narrative. Robert Gundry notes that the "to herself" echoes the "to themselves" (another Matthean redaction) in Matt 9:3 (*Matthew,* 173).

[20] It is Matthew's tendency to omit persons and details (Daniel J. Harrington, *The Gospel of Matthew,* 116; Held, "Matthew as Interpreter of the Miracle Stories," 233–37).

Both the story of the healing of Peter's mother-in-law and the story of the healing of the woman with a flow of blood are related in two short verses. By eliminating all references to other characters, the storyteller focuses each narrative entirely on the encounter between Jesus and the woman. No persons mediate or intervene. The intimate connection between Jesus and each woman is further underlined in two ways. In each narrative the story pivots around the moment in which the woman is touched by (ἅπτομαι) or touches (ἅπτομαι) Jesus.[21] Through this physical contact each woman is restored to wholeness. In both stories, also, Matthew has redacted the text so that emphasis is placed on Jesus seeing (ὁράω) the woman: "When Jesus entered Peter's house, he saw his mother-in-law lying in bed with a fever" (8:14); "Jesus turned, and seeing her he said, "Take heart, daughter; your faith has made you well" (9:22).[22] This "seeing" draws the audience's eyes to the woman as well, giving her a place of prominence. Finally, the qualities exhibited by each woman, respectively service and faith, are held up to the disciples as qualities to strive for, although the disciples consistently fall short of them.[23] This convergence of similarities suggests that the storyteller may have redacted the story of the woman with the flow of blood in such a way that the audience would recall the story of Peter's mother-in-law.

In Mark the story of the woman with the flow of blood is preceded by the healing of the Gerasene demoniac and followed by Jesus' return to his own country, where he astonishes those in the synagogue with his teaching. In Matthew it is preceded by the teaching on putting new wine into new wineskins and followed by the healing of the two blind men. The story of the woman can be shown to be interwoven with both pericopes. In the story of the two blind men Jesus responds to their confident belief in his ability to heal them by saying: "According to your faith be it done to you" (9:29). In contrast, the woman, who has boldly taken the initiative for her healing by touching Jesus' garment, is told that her faith has saved her (9:22). The effect is to highlight the

[21] The ἅπτομαι in the healing of Peter's mother-in-law is a Matthean redaction. Wainwright suggests that it is a carryover from Matthew's source material and notes that it seems to appear in stories where healing and discipleship motifs are combined (9:29; 20:34; 17:7) (*Towards a Feminist Critical Reading,* 186).

[22] Jesus sees Peter's mother-in-law and heals her; he sees the woman with the flow of blood and tells her that her faith has healed her.

[23] Wainwright, *Towards a Feminist Critical Reading,* 90. The disciples are referred to at several points as ὀλιγόπιστος (6:30; 8:26; 14:31; 16:8; see also 17:20).

already demonstrated faith of the woman.[24] It is noteworthy, also, that Matthew places the story of the woman with the flow of blood immediately after the teaching on putting new wine into new wineskins. The reader is led to expect that something new is about to occur.[25] That this "something new" involves a woman suggests a positive evaluation of women's involvement in the community of the faithful.

The Canaanite Woman (Matt 15:21-28)

The story of the Canaanite woman, like the previous two stories, has been significantly altered from Mark's version. In Mark the woman is identified as a Syrophoenician (Mark 7:24-30), while in Matthew she is a Canaanite.[26] In Mark the woman approaches Jesus in a house, while in Matthew she approaches him in public. In Mark the woman's response to Jesus' statement about throwing the children's bread to the dogs is that "even the dogs under the table eat the children's crumbs" (7:28); in Matthew the woman states "yet even the dogs eat the crumbs that fall from their *master's* table" (15:27). Finally, in Mark the woman is dismissed for her saying; in Matthew, the woman is not dismissed (7:29), but is praised for her great faith (15:28). In addition to these changes, this story stands out because it represents one of the few instances in which Matthew expands Mark's narrative. In Matthew's rendering of the narrative the woman cries out to Jesus twice (15:22, 25), employing two messianic titles (Lord and Son of David). Further, three impediments to the woman's request are added: Jesus' initial silence in the face of her request, the request by the disciples that she be sent away, and Jesus' statement that he has been sent only to the lost sheep of the house of Israel (cf. 10:5-6).

[24] Anderson, "Matthew: Gender and Reading," 13. In doing so the storyteller echoes a theme that recurs throughout the gospel: the contrast between words and deeds. However, Beare (*The Gospel According to Matthew,* 234) and Schweizer (*The Good News According to Matthew,* 229) maintain that the woman is not healed until after Jesus has spoken.

[25] The teaching on putting new wine into new wineskins follows two instances in which Jesus breaks boundaries: 9:9 (the calling of a tax collector to be a disciple) and 9:10-13 (eating with tax collectors and sinners) (Wainwright, *Towards a Feminist Critical Reading,* 213).

[26] Wainwright notes that the reference to the woman as a Canaanite echoes the earlier reference to Rahab (Matt 1:5), who was also a Canaanite and who also took initiative and crossed boundaries (*Towards a Feminist Critical Reading,* 226).

Some of these changes are consistent with those identified in the previous two stories: the alteration of the final exchange between the woman and Jesus so that a direct relationship is established between the woman and Jesus, and the emphasis on the woman's faith. Yet some of the changes run counter to those found in the other two stories: the disciples are introduced into the story, and the woman is given an increased rather than a diminished voice.[27] These changes in particular warrant consideration.

The woman's repeated and persistent request recalls the voices of the blind men in Matthew 9:27-31 and 20:29-34.[28] The same words are employed in all three pericopes: "have mercy on me, Son of David" (9:27; 15:22; 20:30).[29] Janice Capel Anderson notes that these three pericopes form a chiastic pattern (see Table A).[30] Within this chiasm the faith of the outcast supplicants (the blind men and the Gentile woman) stands in stark contrast to the lack of faith represented by the Pharisees, who seek signs, and the disciples, who lack faith to feed the multitudes.[31]

Table A[32]

A	Two Blind Men	(9:27-31)
B	Sign of Jonah	(12:38-42)
C	Feeding of 5,000	(14:13-21)
D	Canaanite Woman	(15:21-28)
C'	Feeding of 4,000	(15:29-39)
B'	Sign of Jonah	(16:1-4)
A'	Two Blind Men	(20:29-34)

[27] Joanna Dewey thinks Matthew has transformed the woman from a wit into a nag, noting that although she is more visible than the woman in Mark's narrative she is not necessarily more admirable ("Women in the Synoptic Gospels," 57).

[28] Anderson, "Matthew: Gender and Reading," 13; Wainwright, *Towards a Feminist Critical Reading*, 105.

[29] Anderson, "Matthew: Gender and Reading," 15.

[30] Ibid. 14.

[31] Ibid. 15. Wainwright notes that the woman's faith also contrasts with the disciples' "little faith" (*Towards a Feminist Critical Reading*, 114).

[32] Ibid. 14.

Further, the faith of the Canaanite woman is modified by the use of "great" (μέγα).[33] This is the only place in Matthew's gospel where "great" is attached to "faith." The only other quantitative word used in connection with faith is "little" (ὀλίγος), and this ascription is applied only to the disciples (6:30; 8:26; 14:31; 17:20).[34] The faith of the woman, therefore, is set in direct contrast to that of the disciples.[35]

The faith of the woman also stands in contrast to that of the blind men. In the first episode the blind men are healed "according to their faith" (9:29).[36] The Canaanite woman, like the woman with the flow of blood, is praised for her already demonstrated faith.[37] In the second episode the blind men must overcome the objections of the crowds. The Canaanite woman, in contrast, must overcome three obstacles, emphasizing the greatness of her faith.[38]

The introduction of the disciples into the story seems intended to add yet another obstacle that the woman must overcome in order to gain access to Jesus. Since Jesus himself initially rejects the woman's request, Jesus and the disciples are aligned in their reaction to her cry for mercy. This alignment may be significant: elsewhere in the gospel Jesus and the disciples are aligned in terms of function: both Jesus and the disciples cast out demons, heal diseases, proclaim the coming of the kingdom and, eventually, teach. The question arises, therefore, whether the storyteller has introduced the disciples at this point so that they may be instructed by Jesus' change of heart. This possibility is further suggested by the disciples' request to "send her away" (ἀπολύω). These are the words they use in 14:15 and 15:32 when they ask Jesus to send away the hungry crowds. In each case Jesus denies their request and demonstrates to the disciples their capacity to feed the people. Simi-

[33] Ibid. 242.

[34] Gundry, *Matthew,* 316; Wainwright, *Towards a Feminist Critical Reading,* 114, 242.

[35] Wainwright, *Towards a Feminist Critical Reading,* 114. In this regard Eduard Schweizer notes the similarity between the woman's cry, "Lord, help me," (15:25) and Peter's cry, "Lord, save me" (14:30) (*The Good News According to Matthew,* 330).

[36] Anderson, "Matthew: Gender and Reading," 13.

[37] Ibid. 16. The woman's "great faith" also resembles that of another Gentile, the centurion, whose faith is said to exceed that of any found in Israel (8:10) (Gundry, *Matthew,* 316; Wainwright, *Towards a Feminist Critical Reading,* 112).

[38] Wainwright sees that while the blind men are said to follow Jesus (20: 34), the woman fades from the text, and reads this as a diminishing of the role of the woman (*Towards a Feminist Critical Reading,* 116). However, following does not always indicate discipleship.

larly, in the story of the Canaanite woman Jesus comes to recognize his own capacity to feed those who do not belong to the house of Israel. Only in the feeding of the four thousand, which follows the story of the Canaanite woman, does Jesus send away (ἀπολύω) the people after they have been fed.

Although Matthew alters the narrative itself, the context for the narrative is taken over from Mark essentially unchanged. In both gospels the narrative is preceded by Jesus' teaching regarding what makes a person clean or unclean, and followed by healings. Here Matthew makes a small change from Mark, replacing the healing of the man who is blind and has a speech impediment with a summary section in which many are brought to Jesus in order to be healed. As with each of the previous two narratives involving women, the narrative of the Canaanite woman follows a pericope in which boundaries are redefined. In this particular narrative it is Jesus who redefines the boundaries of his own mission so that they extend beyond the lost sheep of the house of Israel to include the Gentile nations, represented by the Canaanite woman.[39]

Summary

This examination of narratives in which women play a central role suggests that the storyteller of the Gospel of Matthew, while operating within an androcentric worldview, has not employed a strategy to consistently limit the role of women.[40] To the contrary, the women in these narratives are shown to be examples of faith and service who experience a direct, unmediated relationship with Jesus. Further, each narrative is framed in a way that emphasizes inclusion and the breaking down of boundaries. A brief glance at other narratives involving women

[39] Beare, *The Gospel According to Matthew,* 343. Amy-Jill Levine notes that the story follows a narrative pattern in which a teacher learns from a subordinate (see especially *b. Baba Batra* 8a) ("Matthew's Advice to a Divided Readership," in David E. Aune, ed., *Matthew in Current Study* [Grand Rapids: Eerdmans, 2001] 38).

[40] So also Levine, *Social and Ethnic Dimensions,* 123. Similarly, both Celia M. Deutsch (*Lady Wisdom,* 138), and Anderson ("Matthew: Gender and Reading," 21) note that women receive a positive evaluation by the storyteller. But Claudia Setzer sees a pattern of Matthew downplaying the role of women in the Gospel ("Excellent Women: Female Witnesses to the Resurrection," *JBL* 116 [1997] 266).

reveals that these patterns persist throughout the gospel: the presence of women in the genealogy recalls the presence of women in Israel's history and suggests that salvation history must be viewed as an inclusive enterprise (1:1-17);[41] those who do the will of God include mothers and sisters (12:46-50); a woman leavening bread portrays the kingdom (13:33); the naming of "prostitutes" along with tax collectors (21:31-32) as those who will be first to enter the kingdom of God makes explicit the inclusion of women among the followers of Jesus;[42] women are among those who are properly prepared for the kingdom (25:1-13) and will be taken when the hour comes (24:41);[43] Jesus declares that a woman's prophetic action will be told in all the world (26:6-13), and women are the first to see the risen Jesus (28:9-10).

Yet this inclusive vision is fraught with tension. Although women are introduced at important points in the narrative and portrayed in exemplary roles, they are never named disciples.[44] This character group consists only of men.[45] The result is that women, by virtue of their gender, never enter into the "inner circle" around Jesus.[46] Yet only a few in the gospel do, and some who try are turned away (8:18-22). This suggests that the restrictions imposed on the role of women may be only in part related to gender.[47] It may be that the primary concern for Matthew is not gender, but group: specifically, what group has the authority to speak for Jesus.

[41] Wainwright, *Towards a Feminist Critical Reading,* 20; eadem, "The Gospel of Matthew," 642; Jane Schaberg, *The Illegitimacy of Jesus* (New York: Crossroad, 1990) 76.

[42] Kathleen Corley, *Private Women, Public Meals* (Peabody, Mass.: Hendrickson, 1993) 159. The references to the presence of women and children at the feeding of the 5,000/4,000 (14:21; 15:38) are read variously: some view these as an indication of the inclusion of women in Matthew's communities (ibid. 160; Wainwright, *Towards a Feminist Critical Reading,* 102, 251); others view them as secondary additions, reflecting Matthew's androcentrism (Levine, *Social and Ethnic Dimensions,* 92; Love, "The Place of Women in Public Settings in Matthew's Gospel," 58).

[43] J. Kopas, "Jesus and Women in Matthew," *ThTo* 47 (1990) 19; Levine, *Social and Ethnic Dimensions,* 10.

[44] Anderson, "Matthew: Gender and Reading," 21; Schaberg, *The Illegitimacy of Jesus,* 77; Wainwright, *Towards a Feminist Critical Reading,* 95.

[45] Anderson, "Matthew: Gender and Reading," 21; Wainwright, "The Gospel of Matthew," 637.

[46] Anderson, "Matthew: Gender and Reading," 16; Schaberg, *The Illegitimacy of Jesus,* 77.

[47] Although, as Anderson points out ("Matthew: Gender and Reading," 21), because the disciples are male, gender ensures that the women will always be subordinate and auxiliary.

Speaking for Jesus in the Gospel of Matthew

A number of scholars have identified evidence of leadership roles within the gospel narrative.[48] Dennis Duling observes six terms describing what he calls "functional leaders": apostles (10:2), prophets (10:40-42; 23:29-36), teachers (5:19; 28:20), scribes (13:52; 23:34), righteous (10:40-42), and *sophoi* ("wise"; 23:34).[49] Although these terms point to leadership roles, it is difficult to pinpoint exactly what functions would be associated with each role.[50] This has led some to conclude that the distinction between these "functional leaders" is fluid.[51] Prophets, for example, may also be teachers, and scribes can be *sophoi*.[52] Hence while these terms indicate that leadership roles are emerging within the Matthean communities, it appears that they have not yet attained formal status.[53]

[48] Richard S. Ascough, "Matthew and Community Formation," in David Aune, ed., *The Gospel of Matthew in Current Study* (Grand Rapids: Eerdmans, 2001) 121; Dennis Duling, "The Matthean Brotherhood and Marginal Scribal Leadership," in Philip F. Esler, ed., *Modelling Early Christianity: Social-Scientific Studies of the New Testament in its Context* (London and New York: Routledge, 1995) 179; Duling, "'Egalitarian' Ideology, Leadership, and Factional Conflict within the Matthean Group," *BTB* 27 (1997) 131; J. Andrew Overman, *Matthew's Gospel and Formative Judaism: The Social World of the Matthean Community* (Minneapolis: Fortress, 1990) 122; Wainwright, *Towards a Feminist Critical Reading,* 330.

[49] Dennis Duling, "Matthew and Marginality," *HvTSt* 57 (2001) 661; "The Matthean Brotherhood," 179; "'Egalitarian' Ideology," 128.

[50] Duling thinks these leaders were usually itinerants (5:38-39, 41; 6:29-34; 8:20; 9:6; 10:5-15; 10:17-20; 10:24-25; 11:3-8) ("'Egalitarian' Ideology," 130). However, a review of the texts cited suggests a more transparent reading than this author is willing to grant. Jack Dean Kingsbury believes that prophets in Matthew's community were itinerant missionaries to both Jews (10:41 cp. with 10:6; 17:23; 23:34 cp. with 23:29c) and Gentiles (10:41 cp. with 10:18; 24:14; 26:13; 28:19) (*Matthew as Story,* 146).

[51] Samuel Byrskog, *Jesus the Only Teacher: Didactic Authority and Transmission in Ancient Israel, Ancient Judaism and the Matthean Community* (Stockholm: Almqvist and Wiksell, 1994) 242–43; Overman, *Matthew's Gospel and Formative Judaism,* 117; Anthony Saldarini, *Matthew's Christian-Jewish Community* (Chicago: University of Chicago Press, 1994) 105.

[52] Byrskog, *Jesus the Only Teacher,* 242–43; Saldarini, *Matthew's Christian-Jewish Community,* 105; Eduard Schweizer, "Matthew's Church," in Graham Stanton, ed., *A Gospel for a New People: Studies in Matthew* (Louisville: Westminster John Knox, 1993) 140; Leland J. White, "Grid and Group in Matthew's Community: The Righteousness/Honor Code in the Sermon on the Mount," *Semeia* 35 (1986) 75.

[53] White, "Grid and Group in Matthew's Community," 75; Schweizer, *The Good News According to Matthew,* 161; Duling, "The Matthean Brotherhood," 166; Duling,

Other scholars have called attention to the notable amount of language in the gospel that seems to describe a situation in which authority is distributed equally among its members (e.g., 23:9-11: "And call no one your father on earth, for you have one Father. . . . Nor are you to be called teachers, for you have one teacher, the Messiah. The greatest among you will be your servant"). This has led some scholars to describe the Matthean communities as a fictive kinship group characterized by egalitarian relationships.[54] The ideology of this group, as expressed by the storyteller through the person of Jesus, is that God is the only father, Christ the only teacher ("you have one teacher, the Christ" [23:10]), and all others are brothers and sisters ("For whoever does the will of my Father in heaven is my brother and sister and mother" 12:50).[55] Jesus, they observe, eschews titles and roles (23:8-10), advocating instead a servant model in which the least are esteemed greatest (10:24-25; 11:11; 18:4; 20:25-27; 23:11-12).[56] Little evidence is found of formal structures.[57] Conflicts, for example, are to be resolved by members acting together rather than by administrative bodies or individual leaders (18:15-17).[58]

"'Egalitarian' Ideology," 130. Similarly Overmann, *Matthew's Gospel and Formative Judaism,* 113–14; Graham Stanton, "Revisiting Matthew's Communities," *Society of Biblical Literature 1994 Seminar Papers,* ed. Eugene H. Lovering, Jr. (Atlanta: Scholars, 1994) 20.

[54] Warren Carter, *Households and Discipleship: A Study of Matthew 19–20* (Sheffield: JSOT Press, 1994) 114; Michael Crosby, *House of Disciples: Church, Economics, and Justice in Matthew* (Maryknoll, N.Y.: Orbis, 1988) 107–108; Duling, "Matthew and Marginality," 661; idem, "The Matthean Brotherhood," 178; Edgar Krentz, "Community and Character: Matthew's Vision of the Church," 572; Levine, *Social and Ethnic Dimensions,* 257; Saldarini, *Matthew's Christian-Jewish Community,* 91; White, "Grid and Group in Matthew's Community," 75.

[55] Duling, "The Matthean Brotherhood," 178; Levine, *Social and Ethnic Dimensions,* 11. Duling ("The Matthean Brotherhood," 165) notes that in seven Matthean passages the word "brother" is used in reference to fictive kinship relationships: 5:21-26; 7:1-5; 12:46-50; 18:15-22, 35; 23:8-10; 25:40; 28:10.

[56] Crosby, *House of Disciples,* 108; Deutsch, *Lady Wisdom,* 125; Duling, "Matthew and Marginality," 661; Love, "The Household," 27; Saldarini, *Matthew's Christian-Jewish Community,* 106; White, "Grid and Group in Matthew's Community," 76.

[57] Crosby, *House of Disciples,* 97; Duling, "Matthew and Marginality," 661; Kingsbury, *Matthew as Story,* 158.

[58] Duling, "The Matthean Brotherhood," 167–69; White, "Grid and Group in Matthew's Community," 75.

The presence of language that points toward both egalitarian relationships and emerging leadership roles suggests that the Matthean communities are in a period of transition. This description of the Matthean communities is supported by the work of Duling, in his application of a sociological model based on "leaderless group" theory to the gospel.[59] According to this model, leadership emerges in three stages over a period of time.[60] During the first stage the focus is on group identity. At this stage members of the group who do not contribute to the goals or maintenance of the group are eliminated. During the second stage competition among those vying for leadership begins to occur. Factions develop and some potential leaders are eliminated. Finally, during stage three one member of the group emerges as leader. According to Duling the Gospel of Matthew is in a period of transition, moving from stage two toward stage three: i.e., from a period of competition among those vying for leadership to a period in which one group or individual emerges as leader.[61] The juxtaposition of the post-resurrection stories by the storyteller lends support to this description. Both the women and the eleven disciples to whom Jesus appears are commissioned to speak words of Jesus. However, while the women are commissioned to speak the words of the risen Jesus, the eleven are commissioned to teach all that Jesus has previously commanded (28:18-20). By juxtaposing these two stories the storyteller appears to be giving precedence to those who teach the traditions of and about Jesus as opposed to those who speak words in the spirit of the risen Jesus, and to be locating the authority to teach these traditions within a specific group. Far from being neutral, the storyteller has an interest in how the Matthean communities emerge from this period of transition.

Evidence for the Emergence of a Teaching Office

The literary analysis undertaken in the previous chapter called attention to the way in which the storyteller shaped the final chapter of the gospel so that all things pointed toward the disciples. Although a certain amount of ambiguity surrounds the term "disciple" in the Gospel of Matthew, there is clearly a circumscribed group of disciples who are

[59] Duling, "'Egalitarian' Ideology," 124–37.
[60] Ibid. 131–32.
[61] Ibid.

identified as the Twelve.[62] The Twelve are distinguished in several ways: only the Twelve are called "his" disciples (10:1; 11:1; see also 28:8, 10; 5:1);[63] it is only members of the Twelve who are named in the gospel (4:18-22; 9:9; 10:2-4; 17:1; 26:37);[64] they alone are identified as "apostles" (10:2) and sent out (10:5; 28:18-20);[65] the Twelve are given authority to judge the tribes of Israel when the Son of Man comes (19:28);[66] only the Twelve are present at the Last Supper and during the events that follow (26:20-56);[67] the final words of Jesus are addressed to the (now eleven) disciples (28:16).[68] The Twelve, therefore, form a distinct inner group among the followers of Jesus. Whether the term "disciple" should be understood to consistently refer to the Twelve is less clear.[69] However,

[62] Michael J. Wilkins, *The Concept of Disciple in Matthew's Gospel: As Reflected in the Use of the Term Μαθητής* [Leiden: Brill, 1988] 167; "Named and Unnamed Disciples in Matthew: A Literary/Theological Study," in *Society of Biblical Literature 1991 Seminar Papers*, ed. Eugene H. Lovering, Jr. [Atlanta: Scholars, 1991] 436–37) observes that the term disciple is first used in 5:1 before the Twelve are called; further, the reference to "another disciple" in 8:21 implies the existence of a larger group of disciples beyond the Twelve. However, Wire ("Gender Roles in a Scribal Community," 103 n. 57) notes that since the Twelve are not called until 10:1-16 the reference in 8:21 could conceivably be read as speaking of one who is later called among the Twelve.

[63] Wire, "Gender Roles in a Scribal Community," 103.

[64] However, Wilkins notes that Matthew tends to refer to the disciples as a generalized group, omitting references to named disciples (*The Concept of Disciple in Matthew's Gospel,* 153, 169; "Named and Unnamed Disciples," 423).

[65] Matthew uses the term "apostle" only once, and links it with both "disciples" and "the Twelve" (10:1-2) (Sean Freyne, *The Twelve: Disciples and Apostles* [London: Sheed & Ward, 1968] 168; Ulrich Luz, "The Disciples in the Gospel According to Matthew," in Graham Stanton, ed., *A Gospel for a New People: Studies in Matthew* [Edinburgh: T & T Clark, 1992] 108; Wilkins, "Named and Unnamed Disciples," 421, 439).

[66] Wilkins, "Named and Unnamed Disciples," 439.

[67] Freyne, *The Twelve,* 168.

[68] Ibid.

[69] William G. Thompson (*Matthew's Advice to a Divided Community* [Rome: Biblical Institute Press, 1970] 72 n. 5) notes that Matthew adds the modifier "disciple" to the term "twelve" at three points in Mark's text (Matt 10:1//Mark 6:7; 10:2//3:16; 20:17//10:32), but at other points uses only the term "disciple" where Mark speaks of the "twelve" (Matt 13:10//Mark 4:10; 18:1//9:35). Love ("The Place of Women in Public Settings in Matthew's Gospel," 57) and Wire ("Gender Roles in a Scribal Community," 103 n. 57) understand the term "disciple" to refer to the Twelve throughout the gospel. The ambiguity may be due in part to the fact that the author is addressing a community in which there are also disciples of the disciples.

since the Twelve are not called and given authority until 10:1-16 and references to the Twelve occur only after this point in the narrative (10:2, 5; 11:1; 19:28; 20:17; 26:14, 20, 47; 28:16), it is probable that from this point forward all references to the disciples should be heard as references to the Twelve.[70]

When Jesus commands the eleven disciples to "teach them to observe all that I have commanded you" (28:20) a new paradigm is established. Up to this point in the gospel Jesus is the only one, with the exception of his opponents, who teaches (4:23; 9:35; 11:1b; 13:54).[71] This command to the eleven disciples is particularly striking since earlier in the gospel Jesus has authorized them to carry out many of the same tasks Jesus himself performs: to proclaim that "the kingdom of heaven is at hand"(4:17; 10:7),[72] to heal diseases and cast out demons (4:23-24; 10:1),[73] and to forgive sins (6:15; 9:1-8; see also 16:19; 18:18).[74] This parallel activity establishes a strong connection between the ministry of Jesus

[70] In support of this view it can be observed that prior to ch. 10 Jesus is engaged in calling and rejecting disciples (4:18-22; 8:18-22; 9:9) while after ch. 10 and the calling of the Twelve the disciples are closely associated with Jesus and receive special teaching. This would seem to point toward a discrete group among Jesus' followers. The strongest arguments against this view can be found in 9:37 and 20:17. In 9:37 Jesus turns to his disciples and tells them that "the harvest is plentiful, but the laborers are few." In 10:1 Jesus then calls twelve disciples to send forth. This seems to suggest that the Twelve are called from a larger group of disciples. Yet it is still possible that following ch. 10 the disciples are to be understood as this specially called group of twelve. In 20:17 Jesus is said to take the twelve disciples "aside by themselves." This may suggest that Jesus is calling them apart from other disciples, but it also may simply mean apart from the crowds.

[71] Byrskog, *Jesus the Only Teacher,* 238; Robert Smith, "Were Early Christians Middle Class? A Sociological Analysis of the New Testament," in Norman K. Gottwald, ed., *The Bible and Liberation* (Maryknoll: Orbis, 1983) 65. Byrskog notes that, in each summary of Jesus' activity, teaching is always mentioned first (*Jesus the Only Teacher,* 206). Although it is only outsiders who call Jesus "teacher" in the course of the gospel narrative, Jesus does not reject the title and refers to himself as teacher four times (10:24-25; 23:8; 28:18) [Byrskog, *Jesus the Only Teacher*, 207, 212, 222; Duling, "'Egalitarian' Ideology," 130; Saldarini, *Matthew's Christian-Jewish Community,* 96, 179].

[72] Luz, "The Disciples in the Gospel According to Matthew," 100.

[73] Crosby, *House of Disciples,* 94; Luz, "The Disciples in the Gospel According to Matthew," 100.

[74] Overman, *Matthew's Gospel and Formative Judaism,* 130. Overman notes that in Mark and Luke only Jesus has the authority to forgive sins; it is never granted to the disciples.

and that of his disciples.[75] Yet it is not until after the resurrection that Jesus grants the disciples authority to teach.[76] The reason for this becomes apparent when it is observed that Jesus did not begin teaching until after he had called his first disciples (4:18-22, 23). In the same way, the disciples cannot begin teaching until they have begun to call disciples of their own and this cannot happen until Jesus is no longer physically present in the community.[77] This final command by Jesus to the disciples authorizes them to take on the activity only Jesus had the authority to carry out while he was on earth. Now that he is resurrected, the authority for these activities continues to rest with Jesus (28:18), but the responsibility for carrying them out on earth lies with the eleven disciples.[78]

Further evidence that the disciples have been singled out as those entrusted with the traditions of and about Jesus is provided by the many texts that show the disciples to be the recipients of special instruction.[79] The first time Matthew employs the word "disciples" (μαθηταί) it is in the context of Jesus' teaching (5:1).[80] Although the crowds are present (7:28), Jesus appears to direct his teaching toward his disciples (5:1-2). The disciples continue to receive special instruction throughout the gospel, far more than they do in either Mark or Luke.[81] In addition, Matthew adds the term "disciples" to several pericopes taken over from Mark, transforming them into teaching segments directed toward the disciples.[82]

[75] Gundry also notes that while many people approach (προσέρχομαι) Jesus, the only time Jesus approaches (προσέρχομαι) anyone it is the disciples (17:7; 28:18) (*Matthew*, 48). This further points to the distinctive relationship between Jesus and the disciples.

[76] Byrskog, *Jesus the Only Teacher*, 238.

[77] That there are disciples of the disciples is suggested by 10:42, where Matthew speaks of anyone who receives a little one in the name of a disciple. In Mark (9:41) the text says "in the name of Christ." (Overman, *Matthew's Gospel and Formative Judaism*, 121–22; see also Wire, "Gender Roles in a Scribal Community," 103).

[78] Duling, "The Matthean Brotherhood," 166; Kingsbury, The Verb *Akolouthein*," *JBL* 97 (1978) 74; Overman, *Matthew's Gospel and Formative Judaism*, 122, 128–30; Saldarini, *Matthew's Christian-Jewish Community*, 181.

[79] So also Love, "The Place of Women in Public Settings in Matthew's Gospel," 57.

[80] Byrskog, *Jesus the Only Teacher*, 222.

[81] Matt 9:37; 10:1-42; 11:1; 13:10-23; 13:36-52; 15:12-20; 16:13-28; 17:19-22; 18:1-35; 19:23–20:19; 21:20-22; 24:1-2 (Byrskog, *Jesus the Only Teacher*, 226–28, 234; Overman, *Matthew's Gospel and Formative Judaism*, 129; Saldarini, *Matthew's Christian-Jewish Community*, 39, 94).

[82] Matt 12:49//Mark 3:34; 13:10//4:10; 26:8//14:4; see also Matt 15:23; 19:10-12 (Wilkins, "Named and Unnamed Disciples," 423).

Concerns over false teaching (5:19) and those assuming the title of teacher (23:8-10) also are directed toward the disciples.[83] These cautions indicate that the disciples are, in fact, engaged in teaching activities.[84]

Although others may be present when Jesus teaches, only the disciples are credited with understanding Jesus' teaching (13:51; 16:12; 17:13).[85] When they lack understanding, Jesus offers them special instruction while the crowds are left to ponder in confusion (13:36-43; 15:15-20; 16:5-12; 17:1-13).[86] Yet the disciples' ability to understand does not depend, ultimately, on their ability to grasp what Jesus says.[87] They are able to understand because this "understanding" has been revealed to them (13:10-23; 16:17).[88] Thus their knowledge is rooted in divine, not human, knowing. This grants them a special authority, with the result that their words embrace not only human will, but also divine will.[89]

Matthew's several references to scribes also call attention to the storyteller's concern for teaching and tradition. The storyteller's attentiveness to right interpretation of the Law and fulfillment of the Scriptures suggests that scribal activity is a part of the Matthean communities.[90] Although the storyteller sharply criticizes "their" scribes (23:1-7, 13-15), there are positive words for scribes who, presumably, are members of the storyteller's own community (8:19; 13:52; 23:34).[91] These references, in combination with the emphasis on teaching, offer further evidence

[83] Overman, *Matthew's Gospel and Formative Judaism,* 128.

[84] Ibid.

[85] Gerhard Barth, "Matthew's Understanding of the Law," in Bornkamm, Barth, and Held, eds., *Tradition and Interpretation in Matthew,* 106; Byrskog, *Jesus the Only Teacher,* 321; Overman, *Matthew's Gospel and Formative Judaism,* 128; Wilkins, "Named and Unnamed Disciples," 422; Wire, "Gender Roles in a Scribal Community," 102.

[86] Barth, "Matthew's Understanding of the Law," 109; Byrskog, *Jesus the Only Teacher,* 233–34.

[87] Barth, "Matthew's Understanding of the Law," 110; Byrskog, *Jesus the Only Teacher,* 232.

[88] Ibid.; Overman, *Matthew's Gospel and Formative Judaism,* 129.

[89] Ibid. 131, 133.

[90] Ibid. 116; Saldarini, *Matthew's Christian-Jewish Community,* 103; Wire, "Gender Roles in a Scribal Community," 98–99.

[91] Byrskog, *Jesus the Only Teacher,* 241, 245; Duling, "The Matthean Brotherhood," 173; Overman, *Matthew's Gospel and Formative Judaism,* 115–17; Saldarini, *Matthew's Christian-Jewish Community,* 66, 178; Wilkins, *The Concept of Disciple in Matthew's Gospel,* 161; Wire, "Gender Roles in a Scribal Community," 99.

that the storyteller has a particular concern for the handing on of tradition.

The characterization of Peter underscores this concern. Among the disciples, Peter is given pride of place in the Gospel of Matthew.[92] The storyteller includes stories about Peter not found in the other gospels and on four occasions introduces Peter's name into material taken over from the Gospel of Mark.[93] Within the gospel narrative Peter is the first disciple to be called (4:18), and when the Twelve are named he is numbered "first" (πρῶτος, 10:2).[94] At the same time Peter is never portrayed as having authority over the other disciples.[95] The authority granted to Peter in 16:17-19 is granted also to the disciples in 18:18.[96] Nonetheless, he is important in the context of this discussion because it is to Peter that Jesus makes a direct transfer of authority (16:17-19). What is significant about this transfer is that it appears to refer to the authority to prohibit or permit teaching.[97] Peter is entrusted with the keys of the kingdom. In 23:13 the scribes and Pharisees are accused of locking people out of the kingdom, a charge brought forward during an invective against the teachings of the scribes and Pharisees.[98] Further, Matthew places a pericope that warns the disciples against the kind of teaching they should avoid (16:5-12) just prior to the transfer of authority in ch. 16.[99] This suggests that the charge to Peter should be read in connection with the authority to teach. This text, in combination with 28:18-20, confirms that the storyteller wants the audience to recognize

[92] Material about Peter is added to the text at 10:2; 14:28-29; 15:15; 16:17-19; 17:24-27; 18:21.

[93] Matt 4:18; 8:14; 15:15; 26:35 (Wilkins, *The Concept of Disciple in Matthew's Gospel,* 179, 176).

[94] Kingsbury, *Matthew as Story,* 132; Overman, *Matthew's Gospel and Formative Judaism,* 136. Matthew adds Peter's name to the text in 4:18, 8:14, 15:15, and 26:35.

[95] On the characterization of Peter see Kari Syreeni, "Peter as Character and Symbol in the Gospel of Matthew," in David Rhoads and Kari Syreeni, eds., *Characterization in the Gospel: Reconceiving Narrative Criticism* (Sheffield: Sheffield Academic Press, 1999) 106–52.

[96] Byrskog, *Jesus the Only Teacher,* 251; Kingsbury, *Matthew as Story,* 132; Wilkins, *The Concept of Disciple in Matthew's Gospel,* 210–11.

[97] Byrskog, *Jesus the Only Teacher,* 248; Duling, "'Egalitarian' Ideology," 130; Wilkins, *The Concept of Disciple in Matthew's Gospel,* 195.

[98] Byrskog, *Jesus the Only Teacher,* 249; Wilkins, *The Concept of Disciple in Matthew's Gospel,* 196.

[99] Byrskog, *Jesus the Only Teacher,* 248.

the group designated by the disciples as the ones who have been entrusted with the task of passing on the teachings of Jesus.

Prophets and Teachers

Not everyone to whom this gospel is addressed may share the storyteller's vision. The juxtaposition of the post-resurrection appearance stories suggests that at least one other group is a strong contender in this competition for leadership. By including the story of the post-resurrection appearance to the women, the storyteller acknowledges those who support this group's bid for leadership, but ultimately derails their claim by giving pride of place to those whose claim the storyteller favors: the "disciples." Since gender, per se, does not appear to be a concern for the storyteller, the question then arises as to what kind of group is represented in the story by the women. One possibility is that they represent prophets who rely on the spirit of Jesus.

An examination of references to "prophets" in Matthew's gospel lends support to this possibility. The importance of prophetic activity to the storyteller is evident from the numerous quotations from ancient prophets employed by the storyteller to legitimate the story of Jesus. However, not all prophetic activity belongs to the past. The storyteller also speaks of prophets who are active in the life of the Matthean communities.[100] Several references to these prophets are positive; for example, prophets are among those who are sent out by Jesus (5:12; 10:41; 23:34, 37). Yet the very first reference to prophets is a warning, alerting the audience that some of these prophets are "false" (7:15).[101] The prominence of this warning reveals the storyteller's anxiety around the activity of prophets. The source of this anxiety is never stated, although it may be hinted at in 7:22. In this verse these "false" prophets claim to be casting out demons and performing mighty works in Jesus' name. It is evident that they understand themselves to be empowered

[100] Ulrich Luz, *Matthew 1–7.* A Continental Commentary. Trans. Wilhelm Linss (Minneapolis: Augsburg, 1992) 242. Carter views the disciples as included in the group of "prophets" (*Matthew and the Margins: A Sociopolitical and Religious Reading* [Maryknoll, N.Y.: Orbis, 2000] 462).

[101] Leander Keck, "Matthew and the Spirit," in L. Michael White and O. Larry Yarbrough, eds., *The Social World of the First Christians: Essays in Honor of Wayne A. Meeks* (Minneapolis: Fortress, 1995) 150. This particular reference to false prophets is found only in Matthew.

by the spirit of Jesus (7:22).[102] This, perhaps, is the reason prophets are problematic for the storyteller of Matthew's gospel. It is difficult to distinguish the "true" prophet from the "false," particularly when both claim the spirit of Jesus at work within them. In any event, these "false" prophets are, from the perspective of the storyteller, disrupting the life of the community.[103] While the storyteller does not openly oppose prophetic activity as a whole, such activity is viewed with skepticism.[104]

A similarly cautious view is found in the storyteller's attitude toward the Spirit. In the Gospel of Matthew, the Spirit does not move about freely, but is firmly under the control of the Father (3:16; 10:20; 12:18) and the Son (3:11; 28:19).[105] At the end of the gospel it is the presence of Jesus that is promised to the community, not the presence of the Holy Spirit.[106] During the course of the gospel, the Spirit is closely aligned with Jesus: Jesus is conceived by the power of the Holy Spirit (1:18, 20), God's spirit descends on Jesus at his baptism (3:16; see also 12:18), he is led into the wilderness by the Spirit (4:1), and he casts out demons by God's spirit (12:28). On only three occasions is the Spirit spoken of in relation to the community (5:3; 10:20; 28:19). In each case the reference is directed toward the disciples. In the first reference Jesus declares: "Blessed are the poor in spirit" (5:3). The phrase "poor in spirit" occurs only here in the Second Testament. This makes any attempt at interpretation difficult, particularly since it is unclear whether "spirit" should be understood as the "Holy Spirit." While various interpretations are given to this phrase, one possible reading is as a caution against pneumatic activity.[107] Such a reading is consistent with warnings against

[102] Luz (*Matthew 1–7*, 441) observes that the reference makes sense only if it is a problem in the community. It is not clear whether the false prophets mentioned in 24:11 also are followers of Jesus. They may represent prophets from competing communities who speak against the Matthean churches.

[103] Keck, "Matthew and the Spirit," 154–55.

[104] Ibid. 152.

[105] Blaine Charette, "'I will put my Spirit upon Him': Spirit and Messiah in Matthew," in idem, *Restoring Presence: The Spirit in Matthew's Gospel* (Sheffield: Sheffield Academic Press, 2000) 21–57; Keck, "Matthew and the Spirit," 150; Luz, *Matthew 1–7*, 90; Schweizer, "Matthew's Church," 140; Smith, "Were Early Christians Middle Class?" 64, 83.

[106] Keck, "Matthew and the Spirit," 147, 148; Luz, *Matthew 1–7*, 90.

[107] Smith, "Were Early Christians Middle Class?" 63. Carter reads this phrase as a reference to the economically poor (*Matthew and the Margins*, 131); Luz sees it as a reference to humility (*Matthew 1–7*, 232–34); Harrington regards it as a reference to those who recognize God's kingdom as a gift (*The Gospel of Matthew*, 78); W. D.

pneumatic displays in Matthew's gospel (7:21-23) and the control exercised over the Spirit by the Father and the Son.[108] In the second reference, the twelve disciples are told not to be anxious about what to say when they are dragged before councils and synagogues, because the Spirit of the Father will speak through them (10:20).[109] Although the disciples will be empowered by the Spirit, the Spirit does not act on its own, but emanates from the Father.[110] The third and final reference is found in 28:19, where the disciples are instructed to baptize in the name of the Father, and the Son, and the Holy Spirit. Here again a parallel is drawn between the ministry of the disciples and the ministry of Jesus. Yet where Jesus baptizes with the Holy Spirit (3:11), the disciples are to baptize in the *name* of Father, Son, and Holy Spirit. In the Gospel of Matthew, the Spirit has no independent mission within the life of the church.[111]

Conclusion

This emphasis on the subordination of the Spirit to the Father and the Son, combined with Matthew's ambiguous attitude toward prophetic activity, suggests that the storyteller may have been engaged in a polemic against prophets who were vying for leadership within Matthean communities. In Chapter Four it was proposed that one function of the stories of the post-resurrection appearance to the women may have been to legitimate women's authority to speak as empowered by the spirit of the risen Jesus. If this "speaking for Jesus" was understood as pneumatic or prophetic activity, then the downplaying by the storyteller of the post-resurrection appearance to the women in favor of

Davies and Dale Alison (*A Critical and Exegetical Commentary on the Gospel According to Saint Matthew.* ICC [Edinburgh: T & T Clark, 1988] 1:443–44) find here a reference to the oppressed.

[108] I am not fully persuaded that this verse should be heard in relation to pneumatic activity. I am more inclined to read the expression "poor in spirit" as a reference to the human condition, in which case it is unrelated to the discussion of pneumatic activity.

[109] The phrase "spirit of the Father" is found only here in the Second Testament.

[110] Similarly, Jesus casts out demons by the Spirit of God (12:28). The parallel passage in Luke says "finger of God" (11:20).

[111] Keck, "Matthew and the Spirit," 147; Smith, "Were Early Christians Middle Class?" 83.

that to the disciples could be explained in terms of the storyteller's strategy.[112] Viewing spirit-led prophetic activity as a threat to the stability of the community, the storyteller subordinated the appearance to the women in order to legitimate the activity of those engaged in teaching the traditions of and about Jesus.[113]

The question, then, becomes: Why was the post-resurrection appearance to the women included in the gospel at all? The most persuasive answer to this question is that those women (and men) whose speech was empowered by the spirit of the risen Jesus had sufficient status within Matthean communities that they could not be simply "written out" of the tradition.[114] The several references to prophetic activity in the gospel, in combination with the juxtaposition of the two post-resurrection stories, suggest that these prophets were primary contenders with the "disciples" for leadership within Matthean communities. By subordi-

[112] Matt 10:20 may refer to such pneumatic speech. Eugene Boring thinks that prophetic activity in Matthew's group included speaking in the name of the risen Jesus (M. Eugene Boring, *The Continuing Voice of Jesus* [Louisville: Westminster John Knox, 1990] 70). Deutsch suggests that the heightening of apocalyptic motifs at the tomb may indicate that the women receive an apocalyptic vision like that ascribed to seers in Second Temple Judaism and thus reflects conversation in Matthew's group concerning the ministry of women (*Lady Wisdom,* 139–40).

[113] François Bovon views the preference given to the post-resurrection appearances to the disciples as a reaction against prophetic activity, which he notes was often displayed by women ("Le privilège pascal de Marie-Madeleine," *NTS* 30 [1984] 52). Marianne Sawicki believes that Matthew intends for resident teachers to take over from prophets but does not link this with the post-resurrection appearance to the women (*Seeing the Lord* [Minneapolis: Fortress, 1994] 86–87).

[114] Susanne Heine notes that the more pneumatic the life of the community, the greater the degree of women's participation seems to be ("Eine Person von Rang und Namen: Historische Konturen der Magdalenerin," in Dietrich-Alex Koch, Gerhard Sellin, and Andreas Lindemann, eds., *Jesu Rede von Gott und ihre Nachgeschichte im frühen Christentum: Beiträge zur Verkündigung Jesu und zum Kerygma der Kirche; Festschrift für Willi Marxsen zum 70. Geburtstag* [Gütersloh: Gütersloher Verlagshaus Gerd Mohn, 1989] 191). This thesis is supported by the work of Martin Whyte (*The Status of Women in Pre-Industrial Society* [Princeton: Princeton University Press, 1978] 182), who notes that as societies increase in complexity there is both a corresponding increase in the differentiation of social roles outside the family context and a corresponding decrease in the opportunities for women to participate in the public sphere. This reflects the situation of Matthew's group as described by Duling. In a related study, Wire ("Gender Roles in a Scribal Community," 115) writes that as the traditioning process becomes more "scribal," women are further and further removed from the traditioning process (see also Wainwright, *Towards a Feminist Critical Reading,* 257).

nating the appearance to the "prophets," represented by the women, to that of the "teachers," represented by the disciples, the storyteller endeavored to persuade the audience to recognize the claims of the "teachers" over those of the "prophets" for leadership.[115] At the same time, the way in which the storyteller narrated the two appearance stories indicates how challenging and perhaps delicate a task this was. Although the appearance to the disciples takes precedence, the disciples are dependent on the testimony of the women for their encounter with Jesus in Galilee. By maintaining this tenuous balance, the storyteller's case could be made with minimal risk of alienating a significant portion of the audience. It is also possible that the storyteller intended the post-resurrection appearance to the women as one of several cautionary words to the "disciples" against using their office to exercise an authority beyond their commission. Framed by other stories in which women display characteristics of discipleship that the disciples do not, the story of the post-resurrection appearance to the women becomes encoded, inviting those who have "ears to hear" to be attentive to this critique of the emerging leaders. This encoding also empowers these stories to witness to the lively participation of women in Matthean communities, even as at least one aspect of this participation (prophecy) is being limited.

[115] While it cannot be assumed that all women in the Matthean communities participated in prophetic activity, women may have been, proportionately, representative of this group. Conversely, the exclusion of women from the character group "disciples" may indicate that women are not participating in teaching activity. Antoinette C. Wire's analysis of Matthew's context as a scribal community suggests that they would not ("Gender Roles in a Scribal Community," 106).

Chapter Seven

Storytelling Strategies in John: The Function of the Mary Magdalene Tradition in Its Literary Context

In the appendix to the Gospel of John (21:24) the storyteller claims the identity of the "disciple whom Jesus loved," commonly known as the Beloved Disciple and later associated with John of Zebedee.[1] This verse may be building on an earlier claim by the storyteller in the main body of the gospel to be an eyewitness to the crucifixion (19:35). Both comments are intended to draw attention to the credibility of the storyteller, and on the basis of these comments we may, perhaps, presume that the audience would have recognized the storyteller. However, it also is possible that these verses are a literary device and that the storyteller was no more known to the original audiences of the gospel than to us. In the end we know no more about the teller of the story in the Gospel of John than we do about the teller of the story in the Gospel of Matthew. What we can claim is that this storyteller, too, made a self-conscious decision to include the tradition of the post-resurrection appearance to Mary Magdalene in the gospel narrative. This decision

[1] Chapter 21 is generally considered a later addition to the Gospel of John. It is noted, for example, that 20:30-31 reads like a conclusion; there are words and expressions found for the first and only time in ch. 21; the content of ch. 21 contains ideas and interests not found in chs. 1–20 (Ernst Haenchen, *A Commentary on the Gospel of John*. Hermeneia [Philadelphia: Fortress, 1984] 1:71; Francis J. Moloney, *The Gospel of John*. SP 4 [Collegeville: The Liturgical Press, 1998] 545).

reminds us, once again, that the storyteller is not neutral, but has chosen this story as a vehicle for promoting specific values and interests.

In the literary analysis that follows I will explore how the storyteller narrates the tradition of the post-resurrection appearance to Mary Magdalene in the context of the story that is the Gospel of John. Although the tradition stands on its own as a literary unit within the gospel narrative, it is woven into the larger scheme of the gospel through the use of irony, double meanings, misunderstandings, and intertextual interplay.[2] I will show how the storyteller, employing this complex patterning, shapes the Magdalene tradition so that the audience, along with Mary, becomes engaged in a movement of progression from initial perceptions to modifying experience to new perceptions.[3] Through this movement the audience journeys from confusion to insight, from despair to joyful reunion with the risen Jesus. The faithful witness who leads them there in the course of the narrative is Mary Magdalene. In this action we discover the strategy of the storyteller at work.

Weaving the Tradition into the Gospel Narrative

In the Gospel of John the storyteller combines the tradition of the post-resurrection appearance to Mary Magdalene (20:11-18) with one or possibly two other traditions (20:1; 20:2-10) to form a single narrative composed of four scenes. In the first scene Mary Magdalene comes to the tomb and sees that the stone has been removed. She then runs to Peter and the Beloved Disciple to report that the Lord has been taken away from the tomb and "we do not know where they have laid him" (v. 2). The next scene describes the two disciples running to the tomb. The Beloved Disciple arrives first. He does not enter the tomb but,

[2] Raymond E. Brown, *The Gospel according to John.* 2 vols. AB 29, 29A (Garden City, N.Y.: Doubleday, 1966–70) cxxxv–cxxxvi.

[3] Paul N. Anderson, *The Christology of the Fourth Gospel: Its Unity and Disunity in the Light of John 6* (Valley Forge, Pa.: Trinity Press International, 1996) 163. See also Paul S. Minear, "'We don't know where . . .' John 20:2," *Int* 30 (1976) 132; Sandra M. Schneiders, "The Johannine Resurrection Narrative: An Exegetical and Theological Study of John 20 as Synthesis of Johannine Spirituality" (Ph.D. diss., Pontificia Universitas Gregoriana, 1983) 274. Intertextual analysis may examine the storyteller's use of other texts as well as the playing off of one text against another within the gospel itself. For the purposes of this study I have elected to confine my observations to the storyteller's intertextual interplay within the gospel.

stooping to look in, sees the grave clothes lying there. When Peter arrives he does enter the tomb and, like the Beloved Disciple, sees the grave clothes along with the covering for the face nearby. The Beloved Disciple then enters after Peter and the storyteller reports that "he saw and believed" (v. 8). Saying nothing, the two disciples return home. As the storyteller introduces scene three, Mary is found standing near the tomb, weeping. Stooping to look into the tomb, she sees two angels. When the angels ask why she is weeping, she says to them what she said to the disciples: they have taken away her Lord and she does not know where they have laid him. Turning, she sees Jesus standing there, but does not recognize him. He, too, asks why she is weeping. She responds by telling him that if he will only tell her where he has placed the body, she will take it away. Jesus speaks her name and, turning one more time, she recognizes him. Mary reaches out and touches Jesus. Jesus stops her and commands her to go to his brothers (or brothers and sisters) and tell them that he is ascending to the Father. In the fourth and final scene Mary goes to the disciples and tells them that she has seen the Lord.[4]

Although each scene is skillfully woven into the next, this complicated narrative is held together by patterns of repetition and progression rather than coherency.[5] Verses 1-10 are shaped around references to persons coming to, going from, and entering into the tomb (vv. 1, 2, 3, 4, 6, 8, 10). Verse 11 serves as a transition, containing the final reference to the tomb and the first of four references to Mary weeping (vv. 11a, 11b, 13, 15). In the verses that follow (11-15) all coming and going ceases and the characters sit or stand (vv. 11, 12, 14) as Mary continues weeping. These two units (vv. 1-10, 11-15) are held together by the question: "Where is (the body of) Jesus?" (vv. 2, 13, 15).[6] Another transition is initiated in v. 14 with the first of two references to Mary "turning" (vv. 14, 16). In v. 16, after Mary has turned a second time, the question driving the narrative is resolved: Jesus is here. The narrative as a whole is framed by the actions of Mary Magdalene in vv. 1 and 18. In each of

[4] Mark W. G. Stibbe (*John* [Sheffield: JSOT Press, 1993] 200–201) and Charles Talbert (*Reading John* [New York: Crossroad, 1992] 248) also divide 20:1-18 into series of scenes. My outline resembles that of Talbert. However, he includes vv. 17-18 in scene four, while I include only v. 18.

[5] Paul N. Anderson (*The Christology of the Fourth Gospel,* 217) notes that John employs a linear/progressive and cyclical/repetitive style of narrative construction.

[6] Schneiders, "The Johannine Resurrection Narrative," 262, 390.

these verses she is identified by her full appellation "Mary Magdalene" (in contrast to the shorter "Mary" in vv. 11 and 16).[7] Her going to the tomb in v. 1 sets in motion the search for Jesus, and her subsequent going to the disciples in v. 18 brings the story to resolution with her words, "I have seen the Lord."

While the story of the post-resurrection appearance to Mary Magdalene in Matthew extends backwards to the crucifixion and forward to the appearance to the disciples, in the Gospel of John it is linked only tangentially to either of these events. Although Mary Magdalene is identified as one of the three women who stand by the cross (19:25), she is named third, after the mother of Jesus, and Mary, the sister of Jesus' mother and the wife of Clopas.[8] In the subsequent verses she disappears from the story altogether (19:26-27). There is no mention of women at the burial. Not until ch. 20 does Mary Magdalene appear again.[9] Following the report by Mary to the disciples in 20:18, the narrative continues, "On the evening of that day . . ." (20:19). This temporal referent tells the audience that the ensuing appearance to the disciples occurs on the same day as the appearance to Mary Magdalene, but the two narratives are otherwise unrelated. Differently from the Gospel of Matthew, the appearance to Mary Magdalene is not a prelude to other appearances.[10] It is complete in itself. The story of

[7] Schneiders notes that the reference to "Mary" in v. 11 causes the reader to refer back to v. 1 in order to identify "Mary" as "Mary Magdalene," thus linking vv. 1-11 together as a unit (ibid. 390).

[8] Mary R. Thompson suggests that since Mary Magdalene is the only non-relative among the women named at the crucifixion she must have been too important to the tradition to omit (*Mary of Magdala: Apostle and Leader* [Mahwah, N.J.: Paulist, 1995] 62).

[9] Turid Karlsen Seim ("Roles of Women in the Gospel of John," in Lars Hartman and Birger Olsson, eds., *Aspects of the Johannine Literature* [Uppsala: Almqvist and Wiksell, 1987] 64) notes that in the Gospel of John the women do not serve as a connecting link between the crucifixion, burial, and resurrection narratives. However, Robert Smith (*Easter Gospels* [Minneapolis: Augsburg, 1983] 158) sees the reference to Mary Magdalene in 19:25 and 20:1 as binding the crucifixion and resurrection together as a whole.

[10] Adeline Fehribach (*The Women in the Life of the Bridegroom: A Feminist Historical-Literary Analysis of the Female Characters in the Fourth Gospel* [Collegeville: The Liturgical Press, 1998] 165); Sandra M. Schneiders ("The Johannine Resurrection Narrative," 191; eadem, "Women in the Fourth Gospel," in Mark W. G. Stibbe, ed., *The Gospel of John as Literature* [Leiden: Brill, 1993] 141); and Charles Talbert (*Reading John*, 252) interpret 20:18 as an introduction to the next pericope through the reference to the disciples and the words of Mary Magdalene in 20:18, which are echoed

the post-resurrection appearance to Mary Magdalene, therefore, is self-contained.[11]

Storytelling Strategies: The Characterization of Mary Magdalene

The story in 20:1-18 revolves around the figure of Mary Magdalene.[12] Although Peter and the Beloved Disciple briefly assume center stage in vv. 3-10, their action is subsumed within the larger story of Mary (vv. 1-2, 11-18). This is signaled by the final reference to them in v. 10. No longer called by name, Peter and the Beloved Disciple are dissolved into the nameless group "disciples." In contrast, the repetition of Mary's name in vv. 1, 11, 16, and 18 points to the importance of her role. This is not simply any woman's story; it is Mary Magdalene's story. It is Mary's actions that initiate the narrative and bring it to conclusion. It is her character the audience is invited to identify with as they journey with her to the tomb, remain when the disciples depart, and with her they are eventually rewarded for their persistence by seeing the risen Jesus. Where the disciples slip away in v. 10, Mary ends with a startling revelation in v. 18 that draws attention to her person: "*I* [emphasis added] have seen the Lord." The audience knows her witness is credible since they, too, have seen Jesus because of Mary.

The characterization of Mary is complex. Within the narrative she moves from distress to grief to confusion to insight. She also serves as a foil for the audience, which is nudged to insight through her speech and actions, often before the storyteller allows Mary herself to see and understand. I will examine how this characterization of Mary is developed through temporal settings, actions, and dialogue.

---

in 20:25. However, the action does not carry over from one pericope to the next. The narrative of Mary Magdalene ends with v. 18.

[11] Brown, *The Gospel According to John*, 965; Schneiders, "The Johannine Resurrection Narrative," 190, 389–90; Smith, *Easter Gospels*, 156; Talbert, *Reading John*, 248.

[12] Although the Gospel of John contains fewer characters than the synoptic gospels, the characters that do appear tend to have expanded roles (Raymond E. Brown, *The Gospel According to John*, 999; Raymond F. Collins, *These Things Have Been Written: Studies on the Fourth Gospel* [Grand Rapids: Eerdmans, 1990] 151; Margaret Davies, *Rhetoric and Reference in the Fourth Gospel* [Sheffield: JSOT Press, 1992] 335).

Temporal Setting

The storyteller says that Mary came to the tomb on the first day of the week, while it was still dark (σκοτία). Although the word σκοτία ("darkness") occurs only six times in the gospel, it represents an important theme, as indicated by its use in the Prologue: "The light shines in the darkness and the darkness has not overcome it" (1:5). In four of the six verses in which σκοτία occurs it is contrasted with light (1:5; 8:12; 12:35; 12:46). In each case "light" signifies Jesus. In the remaining two verses σκοτία describes the temporal setting in narratives where faithful followers of Jesus are bereft of Jesus (6:17; 20:2). The symbolic value of these temporal uses of σκοτία is suggested by 12:35, where Jesus warns the crowds: "Walk while you have the light, lest darkness overtake you" (see also 9:4-5). In both 6:17 and 20:2, Jesus' followers find themselves in darkness because the light (Jesus) is not with them. When the audience encounter σκοτία in 20:2 they are alerted that Mary Magdalene is bereft of Jesus, both physically and spiritually. The stage is set for both the confusion that follows and the revelation that brings it to a resolution even as the darkness gives way to daylight.[13]

Actions

Although Mary speaks several times during the course of the narrative, her character is revealed to a large degree through her actions. According to the storyteller, Mary goes to the tomb and, seeing that the stone has been removed, runs to the disciples. She reappears next outside the tomb, weeping; turning, she sees Jesus, whom she mistakes for a gardener; turning a second time, she recognizes Jesus and touches him; finally, she goes to the disciples, as she has been commanded by Jesus, and announces to them that she has seen the Lord. Each of these actions is reported by the storyteller in order to define Mary's character.

In vv. 1-2 Mary is described going to the tomb and then departing from the tomb to go to the disciples. This action is repeated again in

[13] Commentators are divided on whether to attribute any significance to the use of σκοτία in this passage. Raymond E. Brown (*The Gospel According to John,* 980–81) and Rudolf Bultmann (*The Gospel of John,* trans. G. R. Beasley-Murray [Philadelphia: Westminster, 1971] 683) treat it simply as a temporal reference. Barrett (*The Gospel According to John,* 308), Koester (*Symbolism in the Fourth Gospel,* 10), Schneiders ("The Johannine Resurrection Narrative," 268), and Smith (*Easter Gospels,* 159) think there is some symbolic value to the reference.

v. 18, when she departs a second time to go to the disciples. However, the message she brings the second time is a reversal of what she reported the first time: instead of "they have taken the Lord and I do not know where they have put him" (v. 2), she proclaims, "I have seen the Lord!" (v. 18).[14] This movement is underlined by the verb "go" (ἔρχομαι), which describes each of these actions.[15] In the context of the narrative it signifies not only physical movement, but the movement in terms of understanding that has occurred between vv. 1 and 18.

It is Mary's persistence that enables her to move from confusion to insight. This persistence is revealed principally by a gap in the narrative. After Mary goes to the disciples, the audience does not hear of her again until the storyteller reports that she is standing near the tomb, weeping. However the audience chooses to fill in the gap, it is important to note that Mary is never described departing from *the tomb.* Rather, the storyteller states that she runs (τρέχω) to the disciples (v. 2) who, in turn, run (τρέχω) to the tomb (v. 4). The parallel action, signaled by the repetition of the verb "run" (τρέχω), keeps the audience focused on the tomb. In contrast, the storyteller states in v. 10 that the disciples departed (ἀπέρχομαι) and returned to their homes (20:10). The contrast between the action of the disciples and that of Mary reveals Mary Magdalene's persistence.

As Mary stands outside the tomb, she "weeps" (κλαίω). The use of this verb elsewhere in the Gospel of John suggests that the storyteller is inviting the audience to engage in intertextual interplay. The first time the audience encounters the verb is in the story of the raising of Lazarus.[16] Jesus calls for Mary, the sister of Martha (11:29). When she meets Jesus she falls at his feet (which she will anoint in ch. 12), and weeps (11:32). Jesus, seeing her tears, asks, "Where have you laid him [Lazarus]?" (11:34). The parallels between ch. 11 and ch. 20 are obvious: a woman named Mary meets Jesus because he has called her (name), she weeps, and a question is asked regarding where the one who has died can be found. In ch. 11 Jesus asks the question so that he might

[14] Schneiders, "The Johannine Resurrection Narrative," 270; Stibbe, *John,* 201.

[15] Schneiders notes an abb'a' pattern: v. 1 reads Μαρία ἡ Μαγδαληνὴ ἔρχεται, while v. 18 reads ἔρχεται Μαριάμ ἡ Μαγδαληνή ("The Johannine Resurrection Narrative," 390).

[16] Barnabas Lindars, *The Gospel According to John,* New Century Bible (London: Oliphants, 1972) 603; Ingrid R. Kitzberger, "Mary of Bethany and Mary of Magdala—Two Female Characters in the Johannine Passion Narrative," *NTS* 41 (1995) 582; Schneiders, "The Johannine Resurrection Narrative," 407; Stibbe, *John,* 205.

raise Lazarus from the dead. In ch. 20 it is Mary Magdalene who asks the question of Jesus (whom she believes to be the gardener), not yet realizing that Jesus has been raised from the dead. It is an ironic moment, for with these words she invites Jesus to reveal himself as the resurrection and the life, just as he did at the tomb of Lazarus. Although the reader knows more than Mary is able, at that moment, to understand, Mary's question reveals her to be a true follower of Jesus.[17] This is reinforced when the reader next encounters the verb "weep" in 16:19c-20a. In these verses Jesus declares: "A little while and you will not see me . . . you will weep and lament, but the world will rejoice." Here again the storyteller sets the context for Mary Magdalene's coming to the tomb and her weeping there. Her weeping shows no weakness;[18] rather, it reveals that Mary Magdalene is among the faithful followers of Jesus who weep when they do not see him, while the world rejoices. Because she is a faithful follower of Jesus, the promise in 16:16 is fulfilled in Mary's presence, "a little while, and you will no longer see me, and again a little while, and you will see me."[19]

The storyteller invites the audience to engage in intertextual interplay also with the references to Mary "turning." The first use of this verb by the storyteller is in 1:38. Here it is Jesus who turns to see two disciples of John the Baptist following him. This action is reversed in ch. 20 where Mary, the follower, turns toward Jesus. These two actions taken together—the turning of Jesus toward the disciples and the turning of Mary toward Jesus—form a complete whole. Mary's action demonstrates the appropriate response by disciples to Jesus' first turn toward them.[20]

The storyteller again uses the verb "turn" in 12:40. Here it occurs in a quotation from Isaiah 6:10, which reads: "He has blinded their eyes and hardened their heart, lest they should see with their eyes and perceive with the heart, and turn for me to heal them." Schneiders notes that the storyteller has changed the text of the LXX from "turn back" (ἐπιστρέφω) to "turn" (στρέφω), thereby establishing a direct link between 1:38, 12:40, and 20:14, 16.[21] When the audience encounter the Magdalene

[17] Kitzberger ("Mary of Bethany and Mary of Magdala," 583) hears Mary's question as legitimate since it echoes Jesus' own (11:34).

[18] Contra Moloney, *The Gospel of John*, 525; Smith, *Easter Gospels*, 161.

[19] Colleen M. Conway, *Men and Women in the Fourth Gospel* (Atlanta: Society of Biblical Literature, 1999) 193; Jane Schaberg, *The Resurrection of Mary Magdalene: Legends, Apocrypha, and the Christian Testament* (New York: Continuum, 2002) 336.

[20] Schneiders, "The Johannine Resurrection Narrative," 417. These two actions also serve as a fulfillment of Jesus' words: "Abide in me, as I abide in you" (15:4).

[21] Ibid. 418.

narrative in ch. 20 they hear first that Mary turns, and although she sees Jesus standing (ἵστημι) there, she does not know (οἶδα) him.[22] The alert audience will hear in this an echo of 1:26, where John the Baptist declares: "but among you stands (ἵστημι) one whom you do not know (οἶδα)." Only when Mary has turned a second time, after hearing Jesus call her name, does she recognize him. Paul Anderson observes that the evangelist uses disturbance and dislocation as a first step toward knowing.[23] Thus when Mary turns the first time she is like those in 12:40 who cannot see or hear.[24] Only in turning a second time does Mary reveal that she is not like those in 12:40, but a faithful follower who both sees and hears.[25]

When Jesus calls Mary by name, she reaches out and touches him (v. 17). The action itself is never described, but is suggested by Jesus' response to Mary: "do not touch me."[26] This is the only place in the Gospel of John where the storyteller employs this particular word for "touch" (ἅπτομαι); it is without parallel.[27] The audience has been prepared for this action both by the question that drives the narrative ("where is Jesus?") and by Mary's address to the "gardener" in v. 15, where she explains that if the gardener will tell her where he has put the body, she will "take it away" (αἴρω). When Mary turns and, at last, "finds" Jesus, she takes hold of him. It is a wholly human response. Jane Schaberg suggests that this action should be "read in the context of

[22] Schneiders ("The Johannine Resurrection Narrative," 430) notes other examples of "mistaken identity" in John: the good wine attributed to the "bridegroom" (2:10), Nicodemus identifying Jesus as a teacher come from God (3:2), Caiaphas proclaiming that one man must die for the people (11:50-52), the Pharisees noting that the whole world has gone after Jesus (12:19), and Pilate identifying Jesus as the "king of the Jews" (19:19-22).

[23] Anderson, *The Christology of the Fourth Gospel,* 263.

[24] Ibid. 419.

[25] Stibbe, *John,* 205. Schneiders observes, additionally, that the phrase "back" (εἰς τὰ ὀπίσω), which occurs in connection with "turn" (στρέφω) in 20:14, appears in two other locations, in John: 6:66 and 18:6. In both texts it refers to those who fall away from following Jesus. Hence the first time Mary turns she resembles those who turn away from Jesus. Turning a second time, she reverses this position and turns toward Jesus ("The Johannine Resurrection Narrative," 419).

[26] Μή with the present imperative normally signals an order to stop an action already begun, but may also be employed as a prohibition against an action that is about to occur (Herbert W. Smyth, *Greek Grammar,* rev. Gordon M. Messing [Cambridge: Harvard University Press, 1984] 410).

[27] This cautions against a too hasty comparison with the Thomas story, in which Jesus invites Thomas to "touch" him. In that story the verb employed is "place" (βάλλω). As has been shown, when the storyteller wishes the audience to make associations with other narratives within the gospel, direct verbal links are employed.

seeking to follow."[28] Four times in the gospel Jesus has said to his followers, "you will seek me . . . where I am going, you cannot come" (7:33-34; 8:21; 13:33, 36).[29] Mary has sought Jesus and found him, but where Jesus is going, she cannot come.[30] Nonetheless, it is Mary who will take Jesus back to the community and, through her witness—"I have seen the Lord"—will restore him to the disciples. The use of the perfect tense suggests that these words should be understood as "I have seen the Lord and I continue to see him." In other words, once believers have "seen" Jesus his presence continues to be experienced in their midst. Mary Magdalene, by her witness, introduces the ongoing presence of the now risen Jesus into the community. This is signified also by the clustering of titles between vv. 17 and 18:

A	πατήρ	("father")
B	ἀδελφούς	("brothers and sisters")
C	πατήρ μοῦ	("my father")
C[1]	πατήρ ὑμῶν	("your father")
D	θεός μοῦ	("my God")
D[1]	θεός ὑμῶν	("my God")
B[1]	μαθηταί	("disciples")
A[1]	κύριος	("Lord")

The physical proximity of these titles in the text manifests the relationship between those represented by the titles. The community of the faithful (brothers/sisters/disciples) is embraced by God, their Father, and Jesus, who is their Lord (13:13). The narrative concludes as Mary fulfills her commission and proclaims that she has seen the Lord. Through this action the audience recognizes Mary as a true follower of Jesus, one who keeps his commandments (14:15).

[28] Schaberg, *The Resurrection of Mary Magdalene*, 336. Schaberg develops a compelling hypothesis that the storyteller may be echoing the Elijah-Elisha story, and the audience is intended to understand Mary as a successor to Jesus (ibid. 304–19, 336).

[29] Ibid. Contra Minear, who views Mary's action as an attempt to hold Jesus back ("'We don't know where . . .' John 20:2," 130).

[30] Harold Attridge, drawing on the work of Mary Rose D'Angelo ("A Critical Note: John 20:17 and the Apocalypse of Moses 31," *JTS* 41 [1990] 529–36), posits that the prohibition against touching Jesus arises from a recognition that Jesus is in a

Dialogue

Three times in the narrative, Mary repeats the words, "they have taken away the [my] Lord and we [I] do not know where they have laid him" (20:2, 13). Their repetition demonstrates Mary's ongoing sense of loss as well as her persistence (see Table below). The audience can well believe that she will continue repeating these words until she has found Jesus again. The third time Mary speaks them they are reformulated as a request addressed to the gardener, not yet recognized as Jesus: "Sir, if you have carried him away tell me where you have laid him, and I will take him away" (20:15). The request is made of the only person who, in fact, can resolve her dilemma: Jesus himself. Hence, Mary demonstrates insight before she is even aware of her insight and her persistence is rewarded.

Patterns of Repetition

20:2	οὐκ οἴδαμεν we do not know		ποῦ ἔθηκαν αὐτόν where they have laid him
20:6		θεωρεῖ he sees	
20:9	οὐδέπω ᾔδεισαν they did not yet know		
20:12		θεωρεῖ she sees	
20:13	οὐκ οἶδα I do not know		ποῦ ἔθηκαν αὐτόν where they have laid him
20:14	οὐκ ᾔδει she did not know	θεωρεῖ she sees	
20:15			ποῦ ἔθηκας αὐτόν where you have laid him

state of transition between cross and exaltation ("'Don't Be Touching Me': Recent Feminist Scholarship on Mary Magdalene," in Amy-Jill Levine, ed., *A Feminist Companion to John* [London: Sheffield Academic Press, 2003] 163–66). Attridge's essay offers an excellent overview of approaches to this passage.

The words spoken by Mary are, not surprisingly, laden with meaning. Seeing the stone rolled away from the tomb, she runs to Simon Peter and the Beloved Disciple and exclaims, "they have taken (αἴρω) the Lord out of the tomb" (20:2). In fact, what has been taken away (αἴρω) from the tomb is the stone (20:1), but Mary is not yet able to interpret what she sees.[31] Only the audience, recalling the significance of the stone being removed (αἴρω) from the tomb of Lazarus in 11:39, 41 is able to recognize this as a prelude to resurrection. The rest of Mary's words underline this connection with the Lazarus story: "and we do not know where they have laid him" (//11:34: [Jesus] said, "where have you laid him?"). Thus the storyteller uses Mary to assist the audience in recognizing the significance of the empty tomb even before she herself is able to.

The second half of Mary's exclamation to the disciples, "and we do not know where they have laid him," reflects a theme that runs throughout the gospel: i.e., the question of where Jesus is, where he has come from, and where he is going (e.g., 1:38; 7:34; 8:14; 9:30, 33; 12:26; 13:33, 36; 14:5; 16:5, 16-19).[32] Although Jesus repeatedly states that he is going to the Father (14:28; 16:5, 10, 17, 28), the disciples continue to wonder and question (13:36; 14:5; 16:17).[33] Therefore when Mary exclaims, "we do not know where . . ." she is giving voice to the anxiety of all the disciples and bringing to a climax one of the major themes of the gospel.[34] In this way she serves both as a foil to the audience, who already know the answer, and brings to a final conclusion the question that has been on the lips of the disciples since their first encounter with Jesus: "Where are you staying?" (1:38). By coming to the tomb Mary responds faithfully to Jesus' invitation to the disciples to "come and see" (1:39).

When Mary encounters Jesus he asks her, "Whom do you seek?" (20:15). The audience knows this question, having heard it twice before. In the first instance the question is addressed by Jesus to would-be disciples (1:38).[35] In the second it is addressed by Jesus to those who have

[31] Schneiders, "The Johannine Resurrection Narrative," 277.

[32] Minear, "'We don't know where . . .' John 20:2," 130; Schneiders, "The Johannine Resurrection Narrative," 280.

[33] Minear, "'We don't know where . . .' John 20:2," 132.

[34] Ibid.; Schneiders, "The Johannine Resurrection Narrative," 281.

[35] Brown, *The Gospel According to John,* 1010; Lorraine Caza, "Disciple et apôtre à la manière de Marie de Magdala," in Michel Gourgues and Gilles-D. Mailhiot, eds., *L'Altérité, vivre ensemble différents: approches pluridisciplinaires* (Montréal: Bellarmin; Paris: Cerf, 1986) 251; Collins, *These Things Have Been Written*, 102–103; Robert Karris,

come to arrest him (18:4). R. Alan Culpepper identifies the tension that drives John's plot as the question of whether those who encounter Jesus come to recognize his identity or fail to recognize it.[36] In the second instance (18:4) those who are asked "whom do you seek?" fail to recognize Jesus' identity. This "failure" is bracketed by the storyteller with examples of persons who do recognize Jesus' identity: in the first instance Andrew, and in the second Mary Magdalene. This suggests that the storyteller assumes the audience will identify Mary with the disciples.[37]

The identification of Mary with the disciples is underlined when Jesus calls Mary by name (20:16).[38] Prior to this verse Mary has been addressed as "woman" (γύναι), first by the angels (v. 13) and then by Jesus (v. 15).[39] The use of the impersonal "woman" creates a distance between the characters, who remain anonymous to each other until Jesus calls Mary by name and she in turn recognizes Jesus as her teacher (Rabboni). The connection between 20:16 and 10:3-4 has been widely observed.[40] In 10:3-4 the shepherd calls his sheep by name and

Jesus and the Marginalized in John's Gospel (Collegeville: The Liturgical Press, 1990) 93; Kitzberger, "Mary of Bethany and Mary of Magdala," 582–83; Smith, *Easter Gospels,* 163. Stibbe (*John,* 199) thinks that ch. 20 forms an *inclusio* with ch. 1, noting in particular the repetition of the verb στρέρω and the question "What/Whom are you seeking?"

[36] R. Alan Culpepper, *Anatomy of the Fourth Gospel* (Philadelphia: Fortress, 1983) 88, 89. See also Ernst Käsemann, *The Testament of Jesus* (Philadelphia: Fortress, 1983) 35; Craig Koester, *Symbolism in the Fourth Gospel* (Minneapolis: Fortress, 1995) 37; Robert Kysar, *John: the Maverick Gospel* (Atlanta: John Knox, 1993) 149.

[37] Karris, *Jesus and the Marginalized,* 93; Kitzberger,"Mary of Bethany and Mary of Magdala," 582–83; Gail R. O'Day, "John," in Carol A. Newsom and Sharon H. Ringe, eds., *The Women's Bible Commentary* (Louisville: Westminster John Knox, 1992) 301.

[38] Conway observes that Mary is the only female character Jesus calls by her proper name (*Men and Women in the Fourth Gospel,* 194). By comparison, Jesus addresses only two of the male disciples by name: Philip (14:9) and Simon Peter (21:15-17) (ibid. n. 369).

[39] The audience will recall that Jesus also used this address when speaking to his mother at the marriage at Cana (2:4).

[40] E.g., Brown, *The Gospel According to John,* 694; C. K. Barrett, *The Gospel According to St. John* (Philadelphia: Westminster, 1978) 564; Kitzberger, "Mary of Bethany and Mary of Magdala," 583; Lindars, *The Gospel of John,* 606; Rudolf Schnackenburg, *The Gospel According to St. John* (New York: Crossroad, 1982) 3:316; Stibbe, *John,* 203; Smith, *Easter Gospels,* 163.

the sheep follow, for they know the sound of the shepherd's voice. Further, the sheep are identified as "his own," an expression used in reference to the disciples (13:1; see also 10:14). When Jesus calls Mary by name he assumes the role of the shepherd. When Mary recognizes Jesus she shows herself to be one of "his own"—i.e., a disciple.[41]

This identification is underlined again when Mary, in the moment that she recognizes Jesus, calls him "Rabboni." Throughout the gospel Jesus is addressed as "Rabbi" by his followers (1:38, 49; 3:2; 4:31; 6:25; 9:2; 11:8). However, both the first (1:38) and last time (20:16) this title is used it is accompanied by the parenthetical statement: "which means teacher."[42] This suggests that the storyteller wants the audience to hear these two verses together. Since in 1:38 it is two disciples who call Jesus "Rabbi," it is probable that Mary, also, is assumed to be speaking as a disciple when she addresses Jesus in the same way.[43] This assertion is supported by 13:13-14, where Jesus says: "You call me Teacher and Lord; and you are right, for so I am. If I then, your Lord and Teacher, have washed your feet, you also ought to wash one another's feet." These two titles are brought together again only in 20:2, 13, 16, 18 where they are spoken by Mary.[44] Since these are the titles Jesus says his followers are to use, when Mary speaks them the audience will recognize her as a disciple.[45] Mary's final statement, "I have seen the Lord" (20:18), echoes the declaration by Andrew in 1:41: "We have found the Messiah" (cf. 4:29).[46] Just as Andrew is the first of Jesus' disciples to bring faith to the others during Jesus' lifetime, Mary is the first to bring faith to the others following the resurrection.

[41] Brown, *The Gospel According to John,* 694; Ingrid R. Kitzberger, "Mary of Bethany and Mary of Magdala," 583.

[42] Brown, *The Gospel According to John,* 992; Caza, "Disciple et apôtre à la manière de Marie de Magdala," 251; Lindars, *The Gospel of John,* 607; Schnackenburg, *The Gospel According to St. John,* 317.

[43] Since only one of the disciples is identified (1:40) the question is raised as to whether the other disciple could be, either within the tradition or by literary design, Mary Magdalene.

[44] Conway also links 13:13-14 with 20:2, 16, 18 (*Men and Women in the Fourth Gospel,* 187).

[45] Contra Davies, *Rhetoric and Reference,* 180; Smith, *Easter Gospels,* 163.

[46] Lorraine Caza, "Disciple et apôtre à la manière de Marie de Magdala," 251.

Storytelling Strategies: Mary Magdalene and the Disciples

Whereas the inclusion of Mary Magdalene and the other Mary in the Gospel of Matthew created narrative difficulties for the storyteller, it is the inclusion of Simon Peter and the Beloved Disciple that creates narrative difficulties for the storyteller of the Gospel of John. Their presence is unnecessary to the story and difficult to explain. Indeed, were vv. 2-10 to be removed, the audience would perceive no gap in the text or sense their omission. Their inclusion, then, is cause for notice. What difference does the inclusion of Simon Peter and the Beloved Disciple make and what impact does it have on how the audience views Mary Magdalene?

One question invited by their inclusion is whether or not Mary Magdalene belongs to the character group "disciples." It is evident from the analysis above that the storyteller *characterizes* Mary as a disciple, but does the storyteller view Mary as a member of the character group "disciples"? To put it another way, is the storyteller creating a contrast between Mary and the disciples, or among disciples of Jesus?

"Disciple" is by far the most common term used for followers of Jesus in the Gospel of John.[47] However, only five persons are specifically identified as "disciples" in the main body of the gospel (excluding the appendix, ch. 21): Andrew (6:8), Judas Iscariot (12:4), the Beloved Disciple (13:23), Joseph of Arimathea (19:38), and Simon Peter (20:10).[48] Others who can be counted among the disciples include Philip—the only person who is called to "follow" Jesus (1:43)—as well as Nathanael, Judas, and Thomas, each of whom is named in a context that identifies him as a disciple of Jesus.[49] Far more often the storyteller simply refers to the "disciples" as a whole, without further specification.[50] In addition, several verses suggest that the "disciples" should be understood broadly,

[47] Raymond E. Brown, *The Community of the Beloved Disciple* (New York: Paulist, 1979) 86; Schnackenburg, *The Gospel According to St. John,* 205.

[48] If ch. 21 is included, the sons of Zebedee (who are mentioned nowhere else in the gospel) would be included in this number, along with Thomas and Nathanael, who are identified as disciples in chs. 1–20 by implication.

[49] Nathanael (1:45-51; [21:2]); Judas (14:22); Thomas (11:16; 20:24-29; [21:2]).

[50] 2:2, 11, 12, 17, 22; 3:22, 25; 4:2, 8, 27, 31, 33; 6:3, 12, 16, 22, 24, 60, 61, 66; 7:3; 8:31; 9:2; 11:7, 8, 12, 54; 12:16; 13:5, 22, 35; 15:8; 16:17, 29; 18:1, 2, 19, 25; 20:18, 19, 20, 25, 26, 30; [21:1, 2, 4, 7, 8, 12, 14].

as a group inclusive of all followers of Jesus (6:60, 66; 7:3; 8:31).[51] The "disciples," then, appear to be a largely nameless group of indeterminate number.[52]

At the same time, the text hints at boundaries to this group on the basis of gender. No women are explicitly identified as disciples, while one verse appears to specifically exclude women from the disciples (4:27). In this verse Jesus' disciples are astonished to find him speaking with a woman. If there are women among the disciples, why would the disciples be astonished to find Jesus speaking with a woman? This seems to argue strongly against the presence of female disciples.[53] However, the disciples' astonishment may be intended to echo the objection raised by the woman herself earlier in the narrative: "How is it that you, a Jew, ask a drink from me, being a Samaritan woman (γυναικὸς Σαμαρίτιδος)?" Such a reading is, at least, plausible since the conversation between Jesus and the woman focuses on the relationship between Jews and Samaritans, not men and women.[54] Hence the disciples' astonishment would be heard as a reaction to Jesus speaking to a woman of Samaria, not a person of the female gender. Yet even if such a reading is rejected, it is difficult to argue on the basis of a single verse in the first twenty chapters that women are excluded from the character group "disciples." The very lack of specificity with regard to the disciples suggests that who is in and who is out in terms of gender is not of great concern to the storyteller.

[51] Adela Yarbro Collins, "Crisis and Community in the Gospel of John," *CurTM* 7/4 (1980) 203; Käsemann, *The Testament of Jesus,* 21; Kysar, *John: the Maverick Gospel,* 152–53; Adele Reinhartz, *Befriending the Beloved Disciple* (New York: Continuum, 2001) 120.

[52] Brown, *The Community of the Beloved Disciple,* 86; Bultmann, *The Gospel According to John,* 693; Moloney, *The Gospel of John,* 231; Carolyn Osiek and David Balch, *Families in the New Testament World* (Louisville: Westminster John Knox, 1997) 144; Schnackenburg, *The Gospel According to St. John,* 208, 324; Schneiders, "The Johannine Resurrection Narrative," 494; D. Moody Smith, *John* (Philadelphia: Fortress, 1981) 22; Smith, *Easter Gospels,* 167. But cf. Barrett (*The Gospel According to St. John,* 306) and Lindars, *The Gospel of John,* 275, who assume that readers would have recognized the Twelve as an inner circle from the synoptics. Sjef van Tilborg (*Imaginative Love in John* [Leiden: Brill, 1993] 111) believes there is a core group of disciples but also a larger, vague group.

[53] Reinhartz, *Befriending the Beloved Disciple,* 121.

[54] This is not to ignore the clear sexual dynamic that underlies this text, but to suggest that this sexual dynamic is employed as a means to describe the relationship between Jews and Samaritans and, more specifically, the relationship between the Jewish Jesus and the Samaritan woman.

This changes when ch. 21, the "appendix" to the gospel, is included. In 21:14 the storyteller makes reference to a third appearance by the risen Jesus to the disciples. Counting backwards from the appearance by the Sea of Tiberias recorded in ch. 21, the two appearances to the disciples behind closed doors are included (20:19-23, 26-29), but the appearance to Mary Magdalene is not (20:1-18). This suggests that from the perspective of that storyteller Mary Magdalene is not a disciple.[55] Here, then, is the strongest evidence that women are not numbered among the disciples in John. However, since ch. 21 is often viewed as a later addition to the gospel, it may reflect a shift in perspective. Taking the first twenty chapters alone, it is unclear whether Mary would be recognized as a disciple or not. Both Peter and the Beloved Disciple are explicitly called "disciples" within the narrative while Mary is not, yet her action signals to the audience that she both knows and is known by these two disciples.[56] It is on the basis of her word that they come to the tomb. While this does not necessarily point to her inclusion among the disciples, it does indicate that she is granted some status among them. From v. 2 onward the storyteller consistently refers to the Beloved Disciple as the "other disciple" (vv. 2, 3, 4, 8), describing that disciple in relationship to Peter. In contrast, no mention is made of Mary going to the "other disciples" in v. 18 (cf. 20:25). However, little weight can be ascribed to what is *not* said.

This ambiguity suggests that what may be important for the narrative is not so much whether Mary is or is not a member of the character group "disciples," but the inclusion in the narrative of these two particular disciples. This is signaled in v. 2 when Mary is described going not to "the disciples" but to Simon Peter and the Beloved Disciple, who are consistently referred to by name until they depart in v. 10.[57] These two disciples whom Mary approaches have prominent roles in the gospel beyond that of other disciples.[58] In having Mary seek them out in her distress the storyteller continues to highlight their prominence.

[55] Reinhartz does not include Mary Magdalene among the disciples (*Befriending the Beloved Disciple*, 122).

[56] Tilborg, *Imaginative Love in John*, 173.

[57] With the exception of 20:4, where it is said that the "two disciples" ran to the tomb. The Beloved Disciple is referred to throughout the narrative as "the other disciple," a shorthand for the longer designation "the other disciple—the one whom Jesus loved."

[58] Whereas most of the disciples are singled out by virtue of speaking in one or two places in the gospel, Simon Peter and the Beloved Disciple are the focus of more

As the narrative unfolds, it becomes clear that the storyteller is playing each of these characters off one another. At Mary's behest they come to the tomb. The Beloved Disciple outruns Peter and arrives at the tomb first. He does not enter the tomb but, looking in, he sees the grave clothes lying there. When Peter arrives he does enter the tomb ahead of the Beloved Disciple and, like the Beloved Disciple, sees the grave clothes. Only then does the Beloved Disciple also enter the tomb (after the storyteller reminds the audience that it was the Beloved Disciple who arrived at the tomb first). The storyteller says that "he saw and believed" (v. 8). If the audience is not utterly confused at this point, it is because they understand that the storyteller is carefully juggling the status of these two disciples. The Beloved Disciple arrives first, but Peter is the first to enter the tomb. Both see the grave clothes, but the Beloved Disciple "saw and believed." A similar juggling for status between these two disciples is found in 21:15-23 (see also 13:21-27).

It is possible that this juggling act extends beyond the two disciples to include a third person, Mary Magdalene. Mary comes to the tomb first, but then she summons two prominent disciples. The storyteller says that the Beloved Disciple, after entering the tomb and seeing the grave clothes, "believed." Exactly what the Beloved Disciple "believed" remains enigmatic in light of the following verse, where the storyteller reports that the disciples "did not understand the Scripture that he [Jesus] must rise from the dead" (20:9).[59] The presence of the grave clothes evokes, for the audience, the raising of Lazarus who emerged from the tomb wrapped in grave clothes (11:44).[60] Whether it evokes the same image for the Beloved Disciple is unclear.[61] Characters in the gospel often understand far less than the audience. He may simply

than one episode within the narrative: Simon Peter (1:40-42; 13:6-11; 18:10-11, 15-27; 20:2-10 [21:1-23]); Beloved Disciple (13:23-26; 19:26-27; 20:2-10; 21:20-24).

[59] Schneiders ("The Johannine Resurrection Narrative," 309–10) proposes that what the disciple whom Jesus loved "believes" is a sign represented by the σουδάριον, which signifies that Jesus is no longer in the world but has gone to the Father (cf. Exod 24:16-17; 34:29-35).

[60] The care taken here to describe the presence of the grave clothes in the tomb suggests that something different has occurred (Smith, *Easter Gospels,* 160; Talbert, *Reading John,* 250).

[61] Many maintain that the disciple comes to some understanding of faith (Barrett, *The Gospel According to St. John,* 561; Brown, *The Gospel According to John,* 987; Lindars, *The Gospel of John,* 602; Willi Marxsen, *The Resurrection of Jesus of Nazareth* (Philadelphia: Fortress, 1970) 58; John Rena, "Women in the Gospel of John," *EgT*

have believed what Mary told him, that "they have taken away our Lord" (v. 2).[62] Since the Beloved Disciple does not share what it is he believes with other characters in the story, it is up to the audience to decide. However, the silence of the storyteller on this point suggests that perhaps it is not what the Beloved Disciple *believes* that is important, but what the Beloved Disciple *does.* What he does, along with Peter, is to return to where he came from—as silent as the grave.

As the disciples depart from the scene, Mary Magdalene suddenly reappears, alone at the tomb. Sandra Schneiders suggests that Mary has remained at the tomb because the disciples have not provided an answer to her question.[63] Like the disciples, she stoops to look into the tomb. No one is prepared for what she sees: two angels. Why do the disciples see grave clothes, while Mary sees angels? The only other reference to angels in the Gospel of John is in 1:51, where Jesus tells Nathanael, "you will see heaven opened and the angels of God ascending and descending upon the son of man."[64] Jane Schaberg wonders whether Mary's "seeing in John 20:12 may fulfill in some way the promise to Nathanael in 1:51," noting that the "you" in that verse is plural.[65] Perhaps Mary sees angels because she remains at the tomb while the disciples do not. Whatever the reason, the angels signify a major shift in the narrative. The space previously defined by grave clothes has given way to the presence of the divine realm, to which Jesus is now ascending. This is a space in which the two other disciples have no part, but Mary does.

The angels ask Mary why she is weeping. She tells them what she told the disciples: "they have taken away my Lord and I do not know where they have laid him" (20:13). She then turns away from the tomb and the angels, neither of which is mentioned again.[66] This marks

17 [1986] 143; Schnackenburg, *The Gospel According to St. John,* 312; Schneiders, "The Johannine Resurrection Narrative," 264; Smith, *Easter Gospels,* 157; Stibbe, *John,* 203–204; Charles Talbert, *Reading John,* 249, 259. Rudolf Bultmann (*The Gospel of John,* 684) thinks that both the disciple whom Jesus loved and Peter come to faith.

[62] Colleen Conway, *Men and Women in the Fourth Gospel,* 191–92; Paul S. Minear, "'We don't know where . . .' John 20:2," 127; Martin Scott, *Sophia and the Johannine Jesus* (Sheffield: Sheffield Academic Press, 1992) 227.

[63] Sandra Schneiders, "The Johannine Resurrection Narrative," 263.

[64] Some manuscripts add a verse to the pericope in 5:1-9 that describes an angel of the Lord stirring the waters of the pool.

[65] Jane Schaberg, *The Resurrection of Mary Magdalene,* 336.

[66] It is beyond the scope of this book to consider, but an interesting question to pursue would be the relationship of Jesus to angels in early Christian thought and

another major shift in the story and brings to a conclusion all dealings with the tomb. If the story of Mary were to parallel that of the disciples, Mary would, at this point, return home. She has looked into the tomb and seen a sign she is not yet able to understand. The disciples, having had a similar experience, turn from the tomb and silently slip away. Yet the story of Mary is not over. When Mary turns her back to the tomb she sees Jesus, whom she mistakes for the gardener (v. 15).[67] When Jesus speaks Mary's name, she turns again and immediately recognizes him. Jesus tells Mary to go to the disciples with the words, "I am ascending to my Father and your Father, to my God and your God" (20:17). Mary does go, and she announces to them, "I have seen the Lord." In anticipation of this movement, the final reference to Simon Peter and the Beloved Disciple in v. 10 identifies them as "the disciples." Prior to v. 10 they have been referred to by name (vv. 2-8). The reference to them as "disciples" locates them among those to whom Mary proclaims her news. The device of locating Peter and the Beloved Disciple in this group leaves to Mary alone the bearing of testimony that Jesus has been raised from the dead. It is her testimony that will enable the disciples to properly interpret what they previously could not understand.

It is Mary's action in v. 18 that prompts the question whether the storyteller is less interested in what the Beloved Disciple believes than in what he does. The storyteller says that the Beloved Disciple entered the tomb, saw the grave clothes, and "believed." What he believed is unclear. Yet even if the Beloved Disciple believed that Jesus has been raised from the dead, he keeps this revelation to himself. At no point does he speak to Simon Peter or Mary Magdalene, nor is there any indication in the narrative that he shares what he "believed" with anyone after he returns from the tomb. Whatever he believes, he does not make it known. In contrast, Mary remains at the tomb until she experiences an unambiguous moment of revelation. She then carries this revelation to the disciples, among whom she witnesses to what she has seen and heard. By her actions she exemplifies what it means to be a true follower of Jesus, demonstrating the way believers are to respond

---

the possibility that the storyteller is wanting to establish that Jesus is something more than the angels, signified by Mary's turning from the angels, knowing that Jesus is not among them.

[67] The reader is reminded, then, that the tomb is located in a garden (19:41). In that moment the empty tomb gives way to new creation (Smith, *Easter Gospels*, 163). While it is tempting to see the garden as the Garden of Eden, it must be noted that in Gen 2:15 (LXX) the word for "garden" is παράδεισος, not κῆπος.

to the revelation of Jesus.[68] She does this in a way that the two disciples do not.

For a brief moment Mary appears to assume status over the two disciples. If the audience does not recognize her as a member of the character group "disciples" the contrast may be even greater. On the other hand, if the audience assumes that the Beloved Disciple recognized the grave clothes as a sign of the resurrection, then Mary Magdalene's role as the first witness to the resurrection is undercut and her status diminished.[69] It is diminished further if it is assumed that Mary seeks out the two disciples in the first place because her testimony to the empty tomb, of itself, is inadequate. Yet then the audience is left with the tension created by the silence of Simon Peter and the Beloved Disciple in contrast to Mary's final witness to the resurrection. It is she who shares that news with the other disciples. Regardless of how the audience chooses to resolve these issues, it is evident that the storyteller has created a narrative in which three figures—Simon Peter, the Beloved Disciple, and Mary Magdalene—are each given prominence at the same time that their prominence is challenged by the presence of the others.

Conclusion

The Mary Magdalene narrative in the Gospel of John is confined to vv. 1-18 of ch. 20. The narrative is divided into four scenes. The first two are dominated by Simon Peter and the Beloved Disciple while the final two are dominated by Mary Magdalene. The division of the narrative into these two parts is represented not only by the characters, but also by the verbal action and spatial settings. Although the scenes with the two disciples take up half the narrative space (vv. 2-10), it is the character of Mary Magdalene who holds the two parts of the narrative together: She introduces the question that drives the narrative to its conclusion ("Where is Jesus?"); it is her report to the disciples that motivates them to come to the tomb; she remains at the tomb when they depart; it is she to whom Jesus reveals himself; it is she who testifies to the disciples that she has seen the Lord. Her role in holding the

[68] Anderson, *The Christology of the Fourth Gospel,* 221; Culpepper, *Anatomy of the Fourth Gospel,* 88, 145; Käsemann, *The Testament of Jesus,* 35; Craig Koester, *Symbolism in the Fourth Gospel,* 37; Kysar, *John: the Maverick Gospel,* 149.

[69] So Fehribach, *The Women in the Life of the Bridegroom,* 164.

narrative together is further emphasized by the repetition of her full appellation in vv. 1 and 18.

The importance of her role is reinforced by the complexity of her character, which is revealed through intertextual interplay within the gospel. Coming to the tomb while it is yet dark, she is unable to find Jesus (12:35). She weeps because she cannot see him (16:20), yet is persistent in her search (1:38; 13:36). When Jesus first appears, she continues to be blinded by her confusion (1:26; 12:40). Only when she hears his voice, the voice of the good shepherd, calling the name of "his own" (10:3-4), does she turn toward Jesus in recognition (1:38) with the cry, "Rabboni!" (1:38; 13:13-14). She does what Jesus commands (14:15) and goes to the disciples, carrying the words of Jesus and proclaims (20:12//20:18), "I have seen the Lord!" (1:41; 20:25). Although the storyteller also reports that the Beloved Disciple "believes," his moment of recognition is a private affair and remains ambiguous. It is Mary who captures the attention of the audience and invites them to participate in her journey from confusion to faith. It is Mary Magdalene who, at the last, pulls together many of the threads woven through the gospel and demonstrates the journey of the faithful disciple from beginning to end.

Yet the text is not without tension. This tension is created by the introduction into the narrative of Simon Peter, but most especially of the Beloved Disciple. Their presence prompts questions concerning Mary's status, both in terms of gender and her role as a revelatory witness. This suggests that, in addition to the storytelling strategy at work within the narrative, there may be another persuasive strategy at work, one that is directed toward John's historical audience and addresses concerns around gender and status in relation to the risen Jesus. It is these concerns that I will take up in the next chapter.

Chapter Eight

The Mary Magdalene Tradition and Johannine Communities: The Function of the Tradition in Response to Historical Circumstances

Like the teller of the story in the Gospel of Matthew, the teller of the story in the Gospel of John has shaped and framed the narrative of the post-resurrection appearance to Mary Magdalene for a purpose. A part of that purpose is literary. The storyteller uses the Magdalene narrative to draw together several themes introduced in the gospel, and through the Magdalene, to guide the audience from empty tomb to risen Jesus. Another part of that purpose is persuasion. In the previous chapter I suggested that the storyteller creates tensions in the Magdalene narrative by the introduction of Simon Peter and the Beloved Disciple. Although these two do not interact directly with Mary Magdalene, their presence invites questions about the status of Mary and her reliability as a witness. In turn, her actions raise questions concerning the witness of these two disciples, who come to the tomb but return home again silent, even though the storyteller says that the Beloved Disciple "believes." These tensions raise the possibility that the storyteller has engaged a polemic within Johannine communities concerning witness, status, and leadership. What is not immediately clear is whether this polemic is driven by concerns around gender, the status of one group or individual over another within the community, or some combination of these two.

To sort out the storyteller's interests in this polemic, I will undertake a two-part investigation. First I will examine how the storyteller has constructed and framed narratives in which women are primary characters in order to determine what, if any, boundaries are imposed on the roles of women in the Gospel of John. Second, I will explore the question of status among followers of Jesus within the gospel. Specifically, I will seek to determine whether the storyteller describes an egalitarian community, as some have suggested, or whether there is evidence of emerging roles described either by person or group.

Women in the Gospel of John

The narratives in the Gospel of John that involve women stand out for a number of reasons. Nearly all are unique to John.[1] The narratives represent crucial points in the gospel: i.e., (2:1-11) Jesus' mother is present when he performs his first sign; (4:46) Jesus reveals his true identity for the first time to a woman; (11:27) at the raising of Lazarus, a woman confesses Jesus' true identity; (12:1-8) a woman anoints Jesus' feet, anticipating Jesus' own washing of the disciples' feet; (20:1-18) a woman is the first to see the risen Jesus.[2] The women relate directly to Jesus. Their interaction is never through the mediation of men.[3] They are never assigned a role by a male party.[4] They function in the public sphere.[5] They are depicted engaging in complex theological discussions.[6] Women in John consistently take initiative and act indepen-

[1] Martin Scott, *Sophia and the Johannine Jesus* (Sheffield: Sheffield Academic Press, 1992) 174. The only narrative that has a parallel in the synoptic gospels is that of Mary Magdalene (John 20:1-18//Matt 28:9-10). The characters Mary and Martha also appear in the Gospel of Luke (10:38-42).

[2] Ibid. 174–75. See also Robert Kysar, *John: the Maverick Gospel* (Atlanta: John Knox, 1993) 148; Gail R. O'Day, "John," in Carol A. Newsom and Sharon H. Ringe, eds., *The Women's Bible Commentary* (Louisville: Westminster John Knox, 1992) 294.

[3] Sandra M. Schneiders, "Women in the Fourth Gospel," in Mark W. G. Stibbe, ed., *The Gospel of John as Literature* (Leiden: Brill, 1993) 131. The story of the woman caught in adultery, which would present an exception to this pattern, is not regarded as original to John's text (Ernst Haenchen, *A Commentary on the Gospel of John.* Hermeneia [Philadelphia: Fortress, 1983] 1:22).

[4] Adele Reinhartz, "The Gospel of John," in Elisabeth Schüssler Fiorenza, ed., *Searching the Scriptures: A Feminist Commentary* (New York: Crossroad, 1994) 594, 595; Schneiders, "Women in the Fourth Gospel," 131.

[5] Ingrid R. Kitzberger, "Mary of Bethany and Mary of Magdala—Two Female Characters in the Johannine Passion Narrative," *NTS* 41 (1995) 575.

[6] Scott, *Sophia and the Johannine Jesus,* 201.

dently.[7] Thus in general the portrayal of women in the Gospel of John is notably positive.[8]

Yet the Gospel of John also reflects an androcentric worldview. The gospel is dominated by Father-Son language.[9] There is a tension between the masculine and feminine elements present in Jesus as Logos/Sophia: It is unclear whether the storyteller is intimating that the feminine is part of the divine or is attempting to undercut the feminine by replacing it.[10] Jesus is identified as the son of Joseph rather than the son of Mary (1:45; 6:42).[11] Further, in 2:1-11 Jesus' mother must give way to the will of the Father, and willingly submits.[12] In 12:1-8 Mary becomes the object of discussion by men. Most of the passages involving women contain the address γύναι ("woman") (2:4; 4:21; 19:26; 20:13, 15), while men are never addressed in a corresponding way.[13] In the scenes between Jesus and the disciples, those who speak are always identified as men. In some narratives the independence of women is undercut by their function within the gospel of waiting on men (e.g., the Samaritan woman is asked to serve Jesus water [4:7]; Martha serves a meal [12:2]; Mary of Bethany anoints Jesus' feet [12:3]).[14]

[7] Schneiders, "Women in the Fourth Gospel," 131; Turid Karlsen Seim, "Roles of Women in the Gospel of John," in Lars Hartman and Birger Olsson, eds., *Aspects on the Johannine Literature* (Uppsala: Almqvist and Wiksel, 1987) 58; Sjef van Tilborg, *Imaginative Love* (Leiden: Brill, 1993) 171.

[8] Colleen M. Conway, *Men and Women in the Fourth Gospel* (Atlanta: Society of Biblical Literature, 1999) 201; Kysar, *John: the Maverick Gospel*, 149; Schneiders, "Women in the Fourth Gospel," 129. Adeline Fehribach finds the portrayal of women "inherently androcentric and patriarchal," although they function as "positive paradigms" (*The Women in the Life of the Bridegroom* [Collegeville: The Liturgical Press, 1998] 169).

[9] Carolyn Osiek and David Balch, *Families in the New Testament World* (Louisville: Westminster John Knox, 1997) 143. But Gail R. O'Day sees the Father-Son language as primarily relational, not patriarchal ("John," 304).

[10] Adela Yarbro Collins, "New Testament Perspectives: the Gospel of John," *JSOT* 22 (1982) 50, 51.

[11] Osiek and Balch, *Families in the New Testament World*, 143.

[12] Turid Karlsen Seim, "Roles of Women," 62. But Osiek and Balch note that, contrary to the synoptic tradition, Jesus' mother is an active participant in his ministry and is present at the cross (*Families in the New Testament World*, 144).

[13] Seim, "Roles of Women," 59. However, Seim also notes that the common use of γύναι emphasizes the presence of the women (ibid. 60).

[14] Margaret Davies, *Rhetoric and Reference in the Fourth Gospel* (Sheffield: JSOT Press, 1992) 227.

Yet, like the storyteller of the Gospel of Matthew, the storyteller of the Gospel of John reflects the world in which the audience lived—a world they would recognize and with which they could identify. In examining narratives in the Gospel of John in which women are primary characters I will consider to what degree the storyteller reinforces this worldview and to what degree the storyteller challenges it. In addition, I will consider ways in which the storyteller may characterize women as disciples.[15] My investigation will focus on three narratives in which women play a central role: the Samaritan Woman, Martha and the Raising of Lazarus, and Mary and the Anointing of Jesus.[16]

The Samaritan Woman (4:1-42)

Moving from Judea to Galilee, Jesus passes through the region of Samaria. Stopping by a well, he asks a woman who has come to draw water to give him a drink. The woman remains nameless throughout the narrative. While this may appear to diminish her status, it reflects a device employed by the storyteller to signal that a character represents a group or collective.[17] The opening verses of the encounter identify the woman twice as "a woman of Samaria" (vv. 7, 9). This would seem to underscore two points of potential conflict (ethnic relations and gender), yet the woman specifies the primary issue: Jews do not interact with Samaritans (v. 9). This polemic, the relationship between Jews and Samaritans, becomes the focus of the dialogue between Jesus and the woman.

[15] R. Alan Culpepper (*Anatomy of the Fourth Gospel* [Philadelphia: Fortress, 1983] 106) does distinguish between the disciples as a character group and what he calls minor characters. However, he also identifies some of the minor characters as "disciples" (ibid. 137, 141).

[16] References to women in the Gospel of John fall into four categories: (1) women as protagonists (4:1-42; 11:1-44; 20:1-18); (2) women as secondary characters (2:1-11; 19:25-27); (3) women as objects of discussion (12:1-8); (4) women as exemplars (16:21-22); there are also (5) passing references (2:12). With the exception of 20:1-18 and possibly 12:1-8, all of these references are unique to John. In addition, mention should be made of the depiction of Jesus as Logos/Sophia. However, as the comments in the text indicate, there is some ambiguity with respect to how gender is to be understood in relation to this image.

[17] Sandra M. Schneiders, *Written That You May Believe* (New York: Crossroad, 1999) 137.

This dialogue has been variously interpreted. Schneiders argues persuasively that the apparent twists and turns in the conversation are driven by points of Samaritan theology and history: the Samaritans' emphasis on Jacob and the Mosaic tradition rather than the Davidic tradition, their seeking after the gods of five foreign tribes (2 Kgs 17:13-34), their worship on Mount Gerizim rather than in Jerusalem, and their expectation of a prophetic Messiah.[18] This conversation reveals the woman to be theologically informed and able to engage Jesus in lively debate.[19] As the conversation evolves, so does the woman's insight into Jesus' identity as well as Jesus' own self-revelation. When the Samaritan woman declares, "I know Messiah is coming . . . and when he comes, he will show us all things (ἅπαντα [v. 25]), Jesus responds, "I who speak to you am he" (v. 26). This is the first time in the gospel that Jesus reveals himself using the "I am" (ἐγώ εἰμι) formula.[20] At this point in the narrative the disciples return and the storyteller reports that they are astonished to discover Jesus speaking with the woman (v. 27). Their reaction underlines the enormity of what has just taken place. The woman, however, is undeterred. Leaving her water jar (no longer needed since she has discovered "living water"), she returns to the city, proclaiming that she has met a man who has told her everything (πάντα) she has ever done—which affirms that he is the prophet Messiah (v. 25)—then adds, "This one is not (μήτι) the Christ, is he?" Although her words reveal some ambivalence,[21] they are sufficient to draw the people out of the city to Jesus.[22] Meanwhile, the storyteller

[18] Schneiders, *Written That You May Believe,* 137–41. (See also Sandra M. Schneiders, *The Revelatory Text* [2nd ed. Collegeville: The Liturgical Press, 1999] 189–91).

[19] Fehribach views this conversation in a negative light, noting that the woman continually misunderstands Jesus (*The Women in the Life of the Bridegroom,* 63). Yet the same is true of Nicodemus in his conversation with Jesus. It is difficult for me to see this as a specifically gender-related issue.

[20] Barnabas Lindars, *The Gospel of John.* New Century Bible (London: Oliphants, 1972) 191; Scott, *Sophia and the Johannine Jesus,* 191; Reinhartz, "The Gospel of John," 573; Schneiders, "Women in the Fourth Gospel," 132. Contra C. K. Barrett, *The Gospel According to John* (Philadelphia: Westminster, 1978) 239.

[21] Gail R. O'Day, *Revelation in the Fourth Gospel* (Philadelphia: Fortress, 1986) 76.

[22] The woman's insight and actions resulting from her conversation with Jesus stand in sharp contrast to Jesus' earlier conversation with Nicodemus, a Jewish man who is a leader of his people, which ends in obfuscation (3:1-10) (Adela Yarbro Collins, "Crisis and Community in the Gospel of John," *CurTM* 7/4 [1980] 203; Culpepper, *The Anatomy of the Fourth Gospel,* 136; Craig Koester, *Symbolism in the Fourth Gospel* [Minneapolis: Fortress, 1995] 48).

again turns to the disciples, who wonder whether Jesus is hungry (v. 31). When Jesus responds that he has food to eat, they misunderstand him—just as the woman did earlier in the narrative when Jesus offered her water [v. 11]. However, while the disciples sit idly by, the woman brings the city—from which the disciples have just returned—to see Jesus, fulfilling Jesus' words to the disciples, "Others have been laboring, and you have entered into their labor" (v. 37).[23] Many believe initially because of the woman's testimony, but when they hear the testimony of Jesus they believe because "we have heard for ourselves, and we know that this is indeed the Savior of the world" (v. 42). Like John the Baptist who has announced just prior to this pericope that "[Jesus] must increase, but I must decrease" (3:30), the Samaritan woman steps aside so that those who have come out to see may enter into a direct relationship with Jesus.[24]

In this narrative the storyteller underlines the characterization of the Samaritan woman as a disciple in several ways.[25] Like Andrew and Philip, she announces what she has seen and heard, and she encourages others to come see for themselves (cf. 1:40-41, 44-45).[26] Adeline Fehribach notes that while Andrew and Philip both state positively that they have found the Messiah (1:41, 42), the woman asks tentatively, "This one is not the Christ, is he?"[27] This undercuts the power of her words, yet within the narrative she does what the disciples do not: she brings the people of the city to Jesus. In witnessing to Jesus she anticipates Jesus' prayer in 17:20 for "those who believe in me through their [the disciples'] word."[28] She also begins the process of gathering "into one the children of God who are scattered abroad" (11:52; see also

[23] Raymond E. Brown, "Roles of Women in the Fourth Gospel," *TS* 36 (1975) 692; Tilborg, *Imaginative Love*, 188.

[24] John Rena, "Women in the Gospel of John," *EgT* 17 (1986) 140; Schneiders, "Women in the Fourth Gospel," 133; Scott, *Sophia and the Johannine Jesus*, 194–95.

[25] Those who view the Samaritan woman as a disciple include Brown ("Roles of Women," 691), Raymond F. Collins (*These Things Have Been Written* [Grand Rapids: Eerdmans, 1990] 17, 111), Culpepper (*Anatomy of the Fourth Gospel*, 137), O'Day ("John," 296), Rena ("Women in the Gospel of John," 140), Schneiders ("Women in the Fourth Gospel," 133), and Scott (*Sophia and the Johannine Jesus*, 192).

[26] Jerome Neyrey, *An Ideology of Revolt* (Philadelphia: Fortress, 1988) 122; O'Day, "John," 296; Reinhartz, "The Gospel of John," 573; Schneiders, *The Revelatory Text*, 193; Scott, *Sophia and the Johannine Jesus*, 194–95.

[27] Fehribach, *The Women in the Life of the Bridegroom*, 77.

[28] Brown, "Roles of Women in the Fourth Gospel," 691.

10:16).[29] At the same time it is clear that, within the scope of the narrative, the Samaritan woman is not a member of the character group "disciples." Rather, her behavior points to deficiencies in the behavior and understanding of the disciples.

This positive portrayal of the Samaritan woman is embedded in two images that underscore the androcentric world of the text. The first involves the use of the "betrothal" type scene to structure the narrative, with the result that the woman is cast as the "bride" of Jesus.[30] The second is the prophetic marriage metaphor, which describes God as a husband whose wayward bride is Israel, in this case the "bride" being Samaria, represented by the woman.[31] Both these images highlight the male-female dynamic of the narrative, and most particularly the subordinate role of women in androcentric relationships. Yet within this androcentric worldview the Samaritan woman does not utterly conform to type. She challenges Jesus, engaging him in debate (while the disciples are afraid to speak [v. 27]), and she serves as an evangelist. While her behavior may not wholly redeem the narrative from its androcentric world, it does create tension within it.

This tension is highlighted by the reaction of the disciples to Jesus speaking with a woman (v. 27). As I suggested in the previous chapter, it is possible that the storyteller intends the audience to hear "a woman" as a reference, specifically, to a *Samaritan* woman, thus keeping the focus on the relationship between Samaritans and Jews. It may also reflect a moment of irony: The Samaritans are about to be brought into the fold, and all the disciples can worry about is Jesus is speaking with a woman.[32] The androcentric context of the narrative, however, may lend some weight to the dominant reading of this verse as an objection to Jesus' interaction with a female. Some have suggested that the reaction of the disciples may reflect doubt on the part of some members of Johannine communities about women's suitability for leadership,

[29] Seim, "Roles of Women," 69.

[30] Fehribach, *The Women in the Life of the Bridegroom,* 69. For other examples of the betrothal type-scene see Gen 24:10-61; 29:1-20; Exod 2:16-22 (Schneiders, *Written That You May Believe,* 133).

[31] Schneiders, *Written That You May Believe,* 145.

[32] From a post-colonialist perspective an important dynamic in this text is the cultural eradication of the Samaritans, whose messianic expectations are displaced by those of the Jews. However, this conversation goes beyond the scope of the present study.

witnessing, or teaching.[33] The response of the storyteller is by way of example. The woman becomes a better evangelist than the disciples, demonstrating the essential role of women in the work of discipleship.[34]

Martha and the Raising of Lazarus (11:1-44)

The story of the raising of Lazarus unfolds in four scenes: Jesus learns of Lazarus' illness (vv. 1-16); Jesus has an exchange with Martha (vv. 17-27); Jesus has an exchange with Mary (vv. 28-37); Jesus comes to the tomb and raises Lazarus (vv. 38-44). Although many characters people this narrative, Martha alone (in addition to Jesus) appears in all four scenes. As a result she provides a thread of continuity running through the narrative (vv. 1, 5, 19-27, 28, 39). Her prominence is signaled in other ways as well. Although the first reference to Martha is as Mary's sister (v. 1), her name appears first when the storyteller relates that "Jesus loved Martha and her sister and Lazarus" (v. 5). When Martha is next mentioned, her name again appears first (v. 19), followed by Mary's. She is the first to greet Jesus (v. 20); then she calls her sister to him (v. 28). Thus she is characterized as the one who initiates action. In the final scene (vv. 38-44) Martha is the only one, in addition to Jesus, who speaks. These several points demonstrate that, in the course of the narrative, Martha enjoys an expanded role beyond that of other characters.

In addition to Martha's prominence within the narrative, there are indications that Martha and her sister Mary were prominent among the followers of Jesus. By identifying Bethany as "the village of Mary and her sister Martha" the storyteller assumes that Mary and Martha are known to the audience, whereas Lazarus (identified only as "a certain man") is not.[35] Further, it is Martha and Mary who send word to Jesus that Lazarus is ill (v. 3).[36] While this is not remarkable from the perspective of social custom, it reinforces the impression that Martha and her

[33] Mary Rose D'Angelo, "(Re)Presentations of Women in the Gospels: John and Mark," in Ross S. Kraemer and Mary Rose D'Angelo, eds., *Women & Christian Origins* (New York: Oxford University Press, 1999) 141, 216; Schneiders, *The Revelatory Text,* 192; eadem, *Written That You May Believe,* 141, 216; Scott, *Sophia and the Johannine Jesus,* 198.

[34] Brown, "Roles of Women," 692; Seim, "Roles of Women," 70.

[35] Kitzberger, "Mary of Bethany and Mary of Magdala," 571.

[36] Ibid. 573; Tilborg, *Imaginative Love,* 172.

sister Mary know Jesus since, in 10:39-40, the storyteller states that Jesus has gone into hiding (see also 11:16). Only those closest to him, presumably, would know where to find him.[37]

This image of Martha as among Jesus' followers is reinforced when Jesus arrives and Martha goes out to meet him. She greets him with the words: "Lord, if you had been here, my brother would not have died" (v. 21). Whether these words are heard as a reproach or a plea, they assume Martha's already established relationship with Jesus and express her confidence in his capacity to heal. This confidence is underlined by what she says next: "But even now I know (οἶδα) that whatever you ask God, God will give to you" (v. 22). When Jesus responds by stating that her brother will rise again (v. 23), Martha again answers that she "knows (οἶδα) he will rise in the resurrection on the last day" (v. 24). Despite her two confident assertions that she "knows," Martha still does not fully grasp what Jesus is saying to her. Like every character who enters into dialogue with Jesus, Martha must be led through a progression from perception to modifying experience to new perception.[38] As in the narrative of the Samaritan woman, the moment of new perception arrives with Jesus' self-revelatory statement employing the "I am" (ἐγώ εἰμι) formula (v. 25):[39] "I am the resurrection and the life." In both narratives, observes Colleen Conway, Jesus takes what each woman understands "as a future reality and moves it decisively into the present in the form of the revelation of his identity."[40]

When Jesus asks Martha, "do you believe this?" she replies, "Yes, Lord; I believe that you are the Christ, the Son of God, who is coming into the world" (v. 27). Martha's confession represents the most complete statement of faith in the entire gospel, bringing together three significant titles for Jesus: Christ (1:41), Son of God (1:49), and "the one coming into the world" (1:9). By placing the verb "believe" in the perfect tense the storyteller underscores the constative aspect of Martha's words: I have believed and I continue to believe. No other confession expresses so thoroughly the perspective of the storyteller (cf. 1:41, 45; 6:68-69; 20:28).[41] It echoes, in reverse order, the words of ch. 1 (1:41; 1:18;

[37] Kitzberger, "Mary of Bethany and Mary of Magdala," 573.

[38] Paul Anderson, *Christology in the Fourth Gospel* (Valley Forge, Pa.: Trinity Press International, 1996) 163.

[39] Reinhartz, "The Gospel of John," 581.

[40] Conway, *Men and Women in the Fourth Gospel,* 141.

[41] Robert Karris, *Jesus and the Marginalized* (Collegeville: The Liturgical Press, 1990) 87.

1:9) and anticipates the closing verse of ch. 20 (v. 31).[42] Where the honor falls to Peter in the synoptic gospels, in the Gospel of John it is Martha who articulates for the readers and hearers of the story the full nature of Jesus and his significance for humankind.[43]

Martha's confession of faith in Jesus comes before Jesus raises Lazarus.[44] This makes her statement in v. 39 something of a puzzle. When Jesus commands that the stone be rolled away from the tomb, Martha objects that there will be a stench. Some hear in Jesus' response ("Did I not say to you that if you believe you will see the glory of God?" [v. 40]) a rebuke, casting a shadow on Martha's previously declared faith.[45] Sandra Schneiders proposes that Jesus' statement is not a rebuke, but signals that something even greater is about to happen: Lazarus will be resuscitated from the dead.[46] Since the raising of Lazarus follows not on Martha's confession (vv. 20-27), but on Mary's display of grief (which prompts Jesus to go to the tomb [vv. 32-37]), there is a narrative break between the two episodes. There is no reason for Martha to expect that Jesus is about to resuscitate Lazarus. Hence Martha's conviction remains intact. Yet there may be a hint that Martha's elevated status is on the decline. In v. 39 she is described as "the sister of the dead man." Where previously Lazarus' identity has been embedded in his sisters', Martha's identity is now embedded in Lazarus.

Although gender *per se* is not an issue in the narrative, it comes to the fore in the verses where characters are identified in relation to one another. The narrative begins with the statement "a man was ill, Lazarus of Bethany," then goes on to identify Bethany as "the village of Mary and her sister Martha" (v. 1). This identification of Bethany makes

[42] Lindars, *The Gospel of John,* 397; Karris, *Jesus and the Marginalized,* 86; Scott, *Sophia and the Johannine Jesus,* 204.

[43] Schneiders, "Women in the Fourth Gospel," 135; Elisabeth Schüssler Fiorenza, *In Memory of Her* (New York: Crossroad, 1984) 329; Scott, *Sophia and the Johannine Jesus,* 203.

[44] Adele Reinhartz, "Gospel of John," 581.

[45] Fehribach, *The Women in the Life of the Bridegroom,* 110; Ingrid R. Kitzberger, "'How Can This Be?' (John 3:9): A Feminist-Theological Re-reading of the Gospel of John," in Fernando Segovia, ed.,*"What is John?" Volume II: Literary and Social Readings of the Fourth Gospel* (Atlanta: Scholars, 1998) 34. Conway states that although v. 39 does not "negate the strength of her conviction . . . it does create ambiguity regarding Martha's characterization" (*Men and Women in the Fourth Gospel,* 149). Robert Fortna thinks that Martha "fails" at the last (*The Fourth Gospel and its Predecessor* [Philadelphia: Fortress, 1988] 250 n. 45).

[46] Schneiders, *Written That You May Believe,* 159.

it clear that it enjoys prominence because of Mary and Martha, not Lazarus. Hence Lazarus' identity is embedded in that of his sisters, marking a contrast with common practice.[47] A few verses later, when the storyteller states, "Now Jesus loved Martha and her sister and Lazarus" (v. 5), Lazarus again is subordinated to his sisters, who are named first. This pattern shifts in 11:39, where Martha is identified as "the sister of the dead man," and again in ch. 12, when Jesus dines at the "home of Lazarus." Once he is restored to human society, Lazarus again assumes his role as head of the household, while Martha remains in the background and "serves." This undercuts, to a degree, the status Martha has enjoyed earlier in ch. 11.[48] The storyteller does not overthrow the androcentric world altogether, yet Martha's role in ch. 11 presents some challenges to it: She is the character who takes initiative, who interacts with Jesus at every point of the narrative, and who gives voice to Jesus' true identity in its most complete representation in the gospel.

The storyteller also appears to signal to the audience that Martha should be recognized as a disciple.[49] In v. 5, the storyteller says that Jesus loved Martha. This is language that is used explicitly to describe Jesus' relationship to his disciples.[50] In 13:1, for example, the storyteller says that Jesus, "having loved his own who were in the world, . . . loved them to the end" (see also 13:34; 15:9, 12). Whether Martha belongs to the character group "disciples" is less clear. In 11:7 the storyteller relates, "Then after this he [Jesus] said to his disciples, 'Let us go into Judea again.'" Since the disciples are accompanying Jesus, Martha (and Mary) would appear to be excluded from this group.

Mary and the Anointing of Jesus (12:1-8)[51]

Mary is first introduced in 11:1-2. After describing Bethany as "the village of Mary and her sister Martha," the storyteller goes on to identify

[47] Brown, "Roles of Women," 694 n. 19; Kitzberger, "Mary of Bethany and Mary of Magdala," 572; Seim, "Roles of Women," 70.

[48] Fehribach, *The Women in the Life of the Bridegroom,* 111.

[49] Culpepper, *The Anatomy of the Fourth Gospel,* 141; Kitzberger, "Mary of Bethany and Mary of Magdala," 575.

[50] D'Angelo, "(Re)Presentations of Women in the Gospels: John and Mark," 131; Koester, *Symbolism in the Fourth Gospel,* 66.

[51] The relationship between this text and the anointing narratives in the synoptic gospels is a subject of debate (see Matt 26:6-13; Mark 14:3-9; Luke 7:36-50). There is

Mary as "the one who anointed the Lord with oil and dried his feet with her hair." Since the anointing does not take place until ch. 12, this description is "out of place" within the chronological sequence of the gospel. By introducing it here the storyteller signals the importance of the story and Mary's role in it.[52] Her status is underlined when the storyteller names Mary prior to Martha in v. 1. Although Martha has moved to the fore of ch. 11 by v. 5, Mary is named along with Martha and Lazarus as one whom Jesus loved (v. 5).

Mary reappears briefly in 11:28-37. Having been informed by Martha that "the Teacher is here and is calling you" (v. 28; cf. 10:3), Mary runs to Jesus and kneels at his feet, repeating the words of her sister, "Lord if you had been here, my brother would not have died" (v. 32; cf. v. 21). Her action anticipates ch. 12, where she will again kneel at Jesus' feet to anoint them (12:3). These two actions are linked by the theme of death: in 11:32 Mary protests her brother's death to Jesus while in 12:7 she anticipates Jesus' own death by anointing him.[53] Hence by the time the storyteller arrives at ch. 12 the audience already knows the story they are about to hear. That the storyteller has chosen to anticipate the events of 12:1-8 in ch. 11 underscores the importance of Mary's action and her prominence within the narrative.

In the opening verse of ch. 12 the storyteller describes the scene as the home of Lazarus. This establishes that Lazarus has, indeed, been resuscitated and is again integrated into the community of believers. However, this description also has the impact of embedding Mary in Lazarus' identity, as a member of his household. Nonetheless, R. Alan Culpepper notes that in neither this pericope nor the preceding one does Lazarus speak.[54] Although he is the object of the defining miracle in the gospel, only Mary and Martha take initiative and interact with Jesus. The two women, in this way, are granted far greater visibility than the head of the household.

---

little evidence of direct literary dependence (Francis J. Moloney, *The Gospel of John.* SP 4 [Collegeville: The Liturgical Press, 1998] 357).

[52] The reference to the story of the anointing of Jesus by Mary in 11:2 also suggests that the story was known outside the context of the gospel narrative.

[53] Mary's anointing of Jesus' feet also anticipates the preparation of Jesus' body for burial by Nicodemus and Joseph of Arimathea (19:38-42), but whereas they anoint Jesus in secret, Mary anoints him openly (O'Day, "John," 299; Mark W. G. Stibbe, *John* [Sheffield: JSOT Press, 1993] 132).

[54] Culpepper, *The Anatomy of the Fourth Gospel*, 140.

The anointing is described in a single verse (v. 3). In an extravagant gesture, Mary takes a pound of pure nard, very costly, and, after anointing Jesus' feet, wipes them with her hair. Calling attention to the expansiveness of this gesture, the storyteller adds that "the house was filled with the fragrance of the oil." Mary's gesture echoes the evocative imagery of the Song of Songs, with its descriptions of the lover and her beloved.[55] Within the context of the Gospel of John this language is translated into the love shown between Jesus and his disciples (11:5; 13:34-35). When Mary anoints Jesus' feet and wipes them with her hair she anticipates Jesus' own demonstration of this love when he washes the feet of the disciples and wipes them with a towel (13:1-11).[56] Jesus' action is presented to the disciples as a paradigm of how they ought to serve one another. Mary, in "washing" the feet of Jesus, shows herself to have already embraced this model of discipleship.[57]

In the remaining verses of the story (vv. 4-8) the focus shifts from Mary to Jesus and Judas Iscariot, who engage in a debate concerning the cost of the oil. It is striking that no objection is raised to Mary's action on the basis of gender or propriety. The argument surrounds her use of money (thereby indicating that she has control over a considerable sum—enough, at least, to purchase the nard). One effect of the debate is to objectify Mary and render her use of the money subject to the approval of men, thereby highlighting the androcentric perspective of the storyteller. However, it also becomes a means by which the storyteller invites the audience to draw comparisons between Mary and Judas, and, in the end, to vindicate Mary as Jesus does. Judas objects to Mary's use of the nard, claiming that it could be sold and the money given to the poor (v. 5). The storyteller carefully frames Judas' comments, warning the audience that Judas is the one who is going to betray Jesus (v. 4) and observing that Judas, in fact, does not care at all for the needs of the poor, but is a thief who steals from the community funds (v. 6).[58] The

[55] Ann Roberts Winsor, *A King is Bound in the Tresses: Allusions to the Song of Songs in the Fourth Gospel* [New York: Peter Lang, 1999] 17–27).

[56] Ibid.; Schneiders, "Women in the Fourth Gospel," 138; Schüssler Fiorenza, *In Memory of Her,* 330; Seim, "Roles of Women," 73. Lending support to this view is the use of the verb ἐκμάσσω in both narratives (12:3; 13:5).

[57] Reinhartz, "The Gospel of John," 583; Schüssler Fiorenza, *In Memory of Her,* 330; Seim, "Roles of Women," 73.

[58] Only in the Gospel of John is Judas identified as the one who objects. This change and the interjections that follow are evidently from the hand of the author. They find no parallel in the synoptic gospels.

disingenuousness of Judas' comments stands in sharp contrast to the utter genuineness of Mary's actions. Jesus' response to Judas, that Mary should be allowed to keep the nard for his day of burial (v. 7), draws even more attention to Judas' deceit, since it is Judas who will hand Jesus over to death. This calls the audience's attention to yet another point of comparison: In 11:57 it is reported that the chief priests and the Pharisees have given orders that if anyone knows where Jesus is, they are to let them know in order that they might arrest him. When Jesus appears in Bethany at the home of Mary, Martha, and Lazarus, they know where he is and they do not betray him.[59] Judas is only waiting for the right moment to arrive.

Summary

This examination of three major narratives focusing on women in the Gospel of John suggests that the storyteller has employed a strategy that challenges, to a limited degree, androcentric assumptions about the role of women. In addition, the storyteller consistently characterizes the women in the narrative as disciples. The Samaritan woman, after coming to belief in Jesus as the Messiah, brings others to him and then steps aside so that they might enter into a direct relationship with Jesus. Martha is portrayed as an intimate of Jesus, one whom he loves—the language used of disciples—and is given the central confession of faith within the gospel. Mary of Bethany stands as a model of faithfulness while all around are those who are seeking Jesus' death, and in her anointing of Jesus she anticipates the paradigm that he himself will offer for discipleship. Thus the storyteller does not appear to limit the role of women, but rather gives women significant scope within the gospel narrative.

That gender is *not* an issue within Johannine communities is less readily apparent. The objection raised by the "disciples" to Jesus' speaking with a woman (4:27) may signal discomfort on the part of some surrounding women's roles as followers of Jesus. In this case Jesus vindicates the woman, suggesting that the objection by the disciples does not correspond to the ideology of the storyteller. However, ambiguity is introduced again when the storyteller has Jesus speak to the disciples about his intended visit to Bethany (11:7). This passing comment implies that Mary and Martha are not numbered among the

[59] Kitzberger, "Mary of Bethany and Mary of Magdala," 578, 579–80.

disciples although, like the disciples, they are said to be "loved" by Jesus. What makes this reference ambiguous is the observation, noted in the previous chapter and developed below, that the character group "disciples" has no clear boundaries. It is difficult to say with certainty who is included and who is not. Nonetheless, these references cast a shadow over the prominent role granted women by the storyteller, raising the possibility that tension exists within the text, and possibly within Johannine communities, surrounding the role of women. To gain clarity on this issue it is necessary to examine more closely the character group "disciples" and their role in the Gospel of John.

The Disciples in the Gospel of John

In the synoptic gospels three terms are employed in association with followers of Jesus: μαθηταί (disciples), ἀπόστολοι (apostles), and ὁ δώδεκα (the twelve). In the Gospel of John only one term is consistently employed: μαθηταί (disciples). The word "apostle" appears only once in the gospel and then in a non-technical sense (13:16: "Truly, truly I say to you that a slave is not greater than his master nor a messenger ["apostle"] greater than the one who sends him").[60] References to "the twelve" occur twice. In the first (6:67-71), the storyteller says that when many of Jesus' disciples pull back he asks the twelve, "Do you also wish to go away?" (6:67). Simon Peter replies, ". . . we have believed and have come to know that you are the Holy One of God." Jesus responds in the next verse, "Did I not choose you, the twelve, and one of you is a devil?" (6:70).[61] This fleeting reference identifies the twelve as "chosen" and names Simon Peter and Judas Iscariot among their number. In the second reference (20:24), Thomas is described as "one of the twelve." This reference can be read in two ways: (1) The twelve are those to whom Jesus appears in 20:19-23 and Thomas, one of that number, was not present; or (2) Thomas, one of the twelve, was not present when Jesus appeared to the disciples (a larger group).[62] Three things

[60] Raymond E. Brown, *The Community of the Beloved Disciple* (New York: Paulist, 1979) 81 n. 150.

[61] Collins, *These Things Have Been Written,* 84; Sandra M. Schneiders, "The Johannine Resurrection Narrative: An Exegetical and Theological Study of John 20 as Synthesis of Johannine Spirituality" (Ph.D. diss., Pontificia Universitas Gregoriana, 1983) 494.

[62] Eduard Schweizer, *Church Order in the New Testament* (London: SCM, 1959) 124.

suggest that the latter reading is to be preferred: (1) "disciples" continues to be the dominant word used to identify followers of Jesus after 6:67; (2) there are references to what appears to be a larger group of disciples following the reference to "the twelve" in 6:67 (7:3; 8:31; 9:27, 28; 19:38); (3) in John "the twelve" serve no apparent function:[63] they are not called, named, sent out, or commissioned.[64] This suggests that this one reference to "the twelve" following 6:67 merely identifies Thomas as one of "the twelve" rather than designating the gathered disciples as "the twelve." Sandra Schneiders observes that individuals "are not identified as members of the Twelve except when they are in trouble because of their doubt, betrayal, or denial of Jesus."[65]

In contrast to "the twelve," the disciples figure prominently in the gospel and are described in largely positive terms. Disciples are those who seek Jesus out (1:35-39), who believe in him (2:11), who hear his voice (10:3, 27), who remember and keep his words (2:17, 22; 8:51; 12:16; 14:23, 26; 16:4; 17:6), who abide in Jesus and bear fruit (15:5), who imitate Jesus by showing their love for one another (13:34-35; 15:9-10, 12, 17), and who bring people to Jesus so that they might have a direct encounter with him (1:40-42, 45; 6:8-9; 12:21-22).[66] All these characteristics firmly root the disciples in the person and revelation of Jesus. The only reference to any independent activity on the part of the disciples is found in 4:2, where the storyteller specifies that it is the disciples, not Jesus, who are baptizing.

Yet the disciples are not so wholly identified with Jesus that they are inseparable. Although the disciples frequently accompany Jesus, there are numerous occasions when Jesus appears to go off on his own (2:13-

[63] Rudolf Bultmann (*The Gospel of John,* trans. G. R. Beasley-Murray [Philadelphia: Westminster, 1971] 115 n. 5) and Margaret Davies (*Rhetoric and Reference,* 321) read all occurrences of the term "disciples" following 6:67 as references to the twelve.

[64] Bultmann, *The Gospel of John,* 444; Collins, *These Things Have Been Written,* 81; Rudolf Schnackenburg, *The Gospel According to St. John* (New York: Crossroad, 1982) 3:206.

[65] Schneiders, *Written That You May Believe,* 54.

[66] Anderson, *Christology in the Fourth Gospel,* 174, 175; Collins, *These Things Have Been Written,* 49; Culpepper, *The Anatomy of the Fourth Gospel,* 115; idem, *The Johannine School* (Missoula: Scholars, 1975) 271; Werner Kelber, "The Authority of the Word in St. John's Gospel," *Oral Tradition* 2/1 (1987) 111; Garrett C. Kenney, *Leadership in John: An Analysis of the Situation and Strategy of the Gospel and the Epistles of John* (Lanham, Md.: University Press of America, 2000) 67; Koester, *Symbolism in the Fourth Gospel,* 68; Kysar, *John: the Maverick Gospel,* 114–16; Davies, *Rhetoric and Reference,* 137.

21; 4:43-54; 5:1-47; 7:1–10:39).[67] Jesus also reminds the disciples that they will not always be able to follow where he goes (13:33; see also 11:16; 13:36-38). This distance between Jesus and the disciples is signified in other ways. Despite their many positive characteristics, the disciples often misunderstand Jesus (4:27, 31; 6:7; 12:4, 16; 13:6-11; 14:5, 8; 16:17).[68] Some turn back from Jesus because they find his teaching difficult (6:66). After the crucifixion the remaining disciples hide behind locked doors. The disciples are in no way ideal.

Notably lacking in this description of the disciples are narratives in which Jesus calls a discrete group of disciples to himself, sends out the disciples while Jesus himself is in the world, or instructs the disciples to teach, preach, or heal. Disciples, in the Gospel of John, are those who "abide in Jesus."[69] This description is underscored in ch. 20 when the risen and glorified Jesus appears to the disciples. The appearance is to the group. No disciple is singled out by name, nor is any one disciple or group of disciples given a separate charge that would set them apart from the others. Jesus sends this group of "disciples" [into the world] just as he was sent [into the world] (20:21; see also 4:38; 13:20; 17:18).[70] The mission of the Son thus becomes the mission of the disciples.[71] Next, Jesus breathes on them the Holy Spirit (20:22; see also 1:33).[72] This "baptism" with the Spirit not only empowers the disciples to carry out their mission, but becomes a guarantor of Jesus' continued presence with them (14:16-17, 26; 15:26; 16:7).[73] Finally, Jesus tells the disciples

[67] Tilborg, *Imaginative Love*, 121.

[68] Brown, *The Community of the Beloved Disciple*, 84; Culpepper, *The Anatomy of the Fourth Gospel*, 118–19; Davies, *Rhetoric and Reference*, 322; Koester, *Symbolism in the Fourth Gospel*, 255.

[69] Collins, "Crisis and Community," 203; Ernst Käsemann, *The Testament of Jesus* (Philadelphia: Fortress, 1983) 21; Kysar, *John: the Maverick Gospel*, 152–53.

[70] Barrett, *The Gospel According to St. John*, 569; Davies, *Rhetoric and Reference*, 137; Kysar, *John: the Maverick Gospel*, 120.

[71] Anderson, *Christology of the Fourth Gospel*, 266; Davies, *Rhetoric and Reference*, 14; Schnackenburg, *The Gospel According to St. John*, 3:324.

[72] The comment in 4:2 that "Jesus himself did not baptize, but only his disciples" now is clarified: the baptism Jesus gives is of the Holy Spirit. This baptism cannot be given until Jesus has fulfilled his mission (but see 3:22).

[73] Anderson, *Christology of the Fourth Gospel*, 266; Barrett, *The Gospel According to St. John*, 88–89; Raymond E. Brown, *The Gospel According to John*. AB 29, 29A (Garden City, N.Y.: Doubleday, 1966–70) 1140–41, 1143; Davies, *Rhetoric and Reference*, 14; Kysar, *John: The Maverick Gospel*, 110; Schnackenburg, *The Gospel According to St. John*, 149, 324; D. Moody Smith, *Theology of the Gospel of John* (Cambridge: Cambridge

that if they forgive the sins of any, they are forgiven; if they retain the sins of any, they will be retained (20:23).[74] While this invests the disciples with tremendous power, it is a shared power in which the disciples, together, have authority over one another.[75] No one disciple can claim more authority than another (7:18). All are empowered by and subject to the Spirit/Paraclete who teaches the disciples (14:26), guides them in the truth (16:12), declares the things of Jesus to them (16:14), and reminds them of what Jesus told them (14:26).[76]

This description of the disciples drawn from chs. 1–20 suggests that the ideological perspective of the storyteller supports a discipleship of equals (17:21). There is little evidence of hierarchy or office within these chapters.[77] The images used to describe the disciples emphasize their common identity in and dependence upon Jesus (e.g., 10:2-4, 7-16; 15:1-10, 13-15),[78] while the relationship between the disciples is described in terms of kinship (1:12; 20:17-18; see also 19:25-27), friendship (13:34-35; 15:12-17), and servanthood (13:12-16).[79] These chapters also contain

University Press, 1994) 140, 142; D. Bruce Woll, *Johannine Christianity in Conflict: Authority, Rank, and Succession in the Farewell Discourse* (Chico: Scholars, 1981) 88. Not everyone thinks that the Holy Spirit and the Paraclete are the same (see Eugene Boring, "Influence of Christian Prophecy on the Johannine Portrayal of the Paraclete and Jesus," *NTS* 25 [1978] 114). Contra Brown (*The Gospel According to John,* 1135), who cites 14:26 in support of the thesis that they are.

[74] This verse has a close parallel in Matthew (Matt 16:19; 18:18). But while in Matthew this power is granted first to Peter and then to the disciples, in John it is given to the gathered disciples only.

[75] Bultmann, *The Gospel of John,* 693; Collins, *These Things Have Been Written,* 202; Schweizer, *Church Order,* 124.

[76] Brown, *The Gospel According to John,* 1135; Käsemann, *The Testament of Jesus,* 31, 45; Kenney, *Leadership in John,* 67.

[77] Anderson, *Christology in the Fourth Gospel,* 249, 256; Brown, *The Community of the Beloved Disciple,* 87–88; Collins, "Crisis and Community," 201, 202; eadem, "New Testament Perspectives: the Gospel of John," 52; Culpepper, *The Johannine School,* 270; D'Angelo, "Reconstructing 'Real' Women in the Gospel Literature: The Case of Mary Magdalene," 111; Schnackenburg, *The Gospel According to St. John,* 325; Schneiders, "The Johannine Resurrection Narrative," 497.

[78] Collins, "Crisis and Community," 202; eadem, "New Testament Perspectives," 52; O'Day, "John," 303.

[79] Anderson, *Christology in the Fourth Gospel,* 249, 256; Collins, "Crisis and Community," 201; Culpepper, *The Johannine School,* 270; idem, *Anatomy of the Fourth Gospel,* 96; Karris, *Jesus and the Marginalized,* 80; Paul S. Minear, "'We don't know where . . .' John 20:2," *Int* 30 (1976) 137; O'Day, "John," 300; Osiek and Balch, *Families in the New Testament World,* 144; Seim, "Roles of Women," 65–66.

warnings against seeking status or rank (7:18; 13:16; 15:20; cf. 14:12; see also the earlier discussion of "the twelve").[80] In downplaying the role and significance of any one individual the storyteller engages a rhetorical strategy that emphasizes the authority of the group over the authority of the individual. Within the group, restraint is effected by Jesus' command to the disciples to be known for their love of one another and through the model of servanthood he offers them by washing their feet.

Despite the prominence of this ideological perspective within chs. 1-20, there is evidence that it is being challenged. While the disciples, for the most part, remain a nameless mass whose identity is defined purely in terms of their orientation toward Jesus, seven individuals stand out by virtue of speaking at some point in the text: Andrew, Simon Peter, Philip, Nathanael, Judas Iscariot, Judas (not Iscariot), and Thomas.[81] It is possible that these disciples represent an "inner group" among Jesus' followers, although they are never named as such. The two references to "the twelve" underline movement in this direction. In both cases the members of the group are male, underscoring divisions along gender lines.

In addition to those mentioned above, two disciples play roles in the gospel that set them apart from the other disciples: Simon Peter and the Beloved Disciple.[82] Of the two, Simon Peter has the more pronounced role. His name appears more often in chs. 1–20 than that of any other disciple;[83] he is distinguished from the other disciples when Jesus renames him (1:42); on one occasion he speaks on behalf of the disciples (6:67-69);[84] he correctly identifies Jesus as the "Holy One of God" (6:68); and he is one of the two disciples who are called to the tomb (20:2-10). Nonetheless, Peter's role is not wholly flattering. He misunderstands when Jesus washes his feet (13:3-11); he draws a sword to protect Jesus, unable to recognize that Jesus willingly gives over his life (18:11); and he claims he will lay down his life for Jesus (13:37) only to deny that he

[80] Kelber, "The Authority of the Word in St. John's Gospel," 117.

[81] Andrew: 1:41; Simon Peter: 6:68; 13:6, 8, 9, 24, 36, 37; 18:17, 25; Philip: 1:45, 46; 6:7; 14:8; Nathanael: 1:48, 49; Judas Iscariot: 12:5; Judas: 14:22; Thomas: 11:16; 14:5; 20:25, 28. In addition, Joseph of Arimathea, who claims the body of Jesus from Pilate, is described as a "secret disciple" (19:38).

[82] Although Thomas also enjoys an expanded role because of his actions in ch. 20, it is not of the same quality as that of Simon Peter and the Beloved Disciple.

[83] John 1:40, 42, 44; 6:8, 68; 13:6, 8, 9, 24, 36, 37; 18:10, 11, 15, 16, 17, 18, 25, 26, 27; 20:2, 3, 4, 6.

[84] Reinhartz, *Befriending the Beloved Disciple,* 127.

knows him (18:15-17; 25-27). Hence Simon Peter's prominence results, for the most part, from visibility within the narrative rather than positive attributes or actions.

In contrast to Simon Peter, the Beloved Disciple appears only three times in chs. 1–20 (13:23; 19:26; 20:2-10), yet within these few verses he is characterized in a way that clearly sets him apart from the other disciples.[85] In 13:21-30, during the Last Supper, the Beloved Disciple is described lying close to Jesus' breast (κόλπος). This word appears elsewhere only in 1:18, where it is said that the Son is in the κόλπος of the Father. Thus the relationship of the Beloved Disciple to Jesus is described with language used for the relationship of Jesus to God.[86] In the same narrative Simon Peter prompts the Beloved Disciple to ask Jesus the question no one else dares ask: who it is that will betray Jesus (13:24). At the crucifixion the Beloved Disciple is present with the women, and during his last moments it is to the Beloved Disciple that Jesus entrusts the care of his mother (19:25-27). Finally, it is the Beloved Disciple who runs with Peter to the empty tomb and who the storyteller says "believed" (20:8). Only this one disciple is singled out in such a way.

The prominent roles of Simon Peter and the Beloved Disciple are intensified with the inclusion of ch. 21. In this chapter Jesus once again appears to the disciples, but it is to a discrete group of disciples, among whom is Simon Peter (21:2). As the narrative unfolds, Jesus addresses Simon Peter directly, asking him three times, "do you love me?" With each affirmative answer Jesus instructs Peter to "feed my sheep" (21:15-17). Here, for the first time, a commission is given to an individual who is charged with assuming the role carried out by Jesus while he was alive on earth (10:11-18). Whatever ambiguity surrounded the role of Peter prior to this chapter is swept away. With these words of Jesus, Peter assumes a role and a status that clearly distinguish him from the other disciples. But he is not alone in this elevation of status. The final word belongs to the Beloved Disciple.[87] It is this disciple who,

[85] Brown, *The Community of the Beloved Disciple,* 31; Bultmann, *The Gospel of John,* 485; Davies, *Rhetoric and Reference,* 232; Collins, *These Things Have Been Written,* 43, 45; Lindars, *The Gospel of John,* 579. But not all agree regarding whether the disciple whom Jesus loved represents a historical person or a symbol.

[86] Culpepper, *The Johannine School,* 75; idem, *The Anatomy of the Fourth Gospel,* 121.

[87] The shift between chs. 1–20 and ch. 21 is underscored by the way in which each is brought to conclusion: In 20:20 the focus is on the signs performed by Jesus in the presence of the "disciples"; in 20:24 the focus shifts to the testimony of the one disciple.

in the words of Jesus, is destined to remain until Jesus comes again (21:20-23), and whose testimony forms the basis of the gospel narrative (21:24).[88] Ultimately, then, both of these disciples are assigned roles that stand in stark contrast to the ideology of a "discipleship of equals" promoted by the description of the character group "disciples" in chs. 1–20.

However, these roles introduce another layer of tension into the text. Simon Peter is present throughout the gospel, a follower of Jesus from the beginning, while the Beloved Disciple appears only at the last, to be given the final word (21:24). At the Last Supper the Beloved Disciple rests at the breast of Jesus, yet he follows Peter's prompting and asks Jesus who it is that will betray him (13:23-24). At the tomb the Beloved Disciple arrives first, but enters only after Simon Peter has arrived and entered the tomb. The Beloved Disciple is entrusted with the care of Jesus' mother while Simon Peter is given care over all Jesus' "sheep." The contrasts between the two disciples suggest that no one individual or group can yet claim leadership without challenge.

Chapter 21 also alters the characterization of Mary Magdalene. While there is ambiguity surrounding her status as a disciple within chs. 1–20, the addition of ch. 21 eliminates the ambiguity, making it clear that she is not. Further, ch. 21 excludes the possibility that Mary Magdalene was among the gathered disciples when Jesus breathes on them the Holy Spirit (20:19-23).[89] Consequently, she is not among those "sent into the world"; rather, she is sent to the disciples who, for the storyteller of ch. 21, consist only of "brothers." The ideological shift between chs. 1–20 and ch. 21 points not only to the emergence of competition among individuals (or groups represented by those individuals) for leadership within the Johannine communities, but also to tension surrounding the role of women, as intimated in the narratives discussed earlier.[90] It is possible that this tension surrounds not only the role of women in general but also the role of one woman in particular: Mary Magdalene. She alone is brought into proximity with Simon

[88] Kenney sees the storyteller enhancing the authority of the Beloved Disciple over against that of Peter, and understands the gospel as "an attempt to inhibit further developments in authority structures for the Johannine community" (*Leadership in John*, 78, 87).

[89] D'Angelo suggests that the appearance in 20:19-23 may have been added in order to undercut the appearance to Mary Magdalene in 20:1-18 ("Reconstructing "Real" Women in Gospel Literature: The Case of Mary Magdalene," 112).

[90] Reinhartz, *Befriending the Beloved Disciple*, 124.

Peter and the Beloved Disciple and in a way that is suggestive of a competition for status among these three individuals. Her exclusion from the group "disciples" by the storyteller of ch. 21 may represent a deliberate attempt to undermine her authority (she is the only individual prior to ch. 21 to whom Jesus appears) and that of her followers, while giving precedence to the male disciples and those who promoted their legacy in early Christian communities.[91]

Conclusion

The post-resurrection appearance to Mary Magdalene serves not only the literary strategy of the storyteller, but a persuasive strategy as well. If this description of the Johannine communities is considered in relation to the "leaderless group" model employed by Dennis Duling in his study of the Gospel of Matthew it is evident that the communities described by John's gospel are at a different stage from the communities described by Matthew. The model identifies three stages in the development of leadership within groups. In stage one, the focus is on group identity.[92] In stage two, competition begins to occur among those vying for leadership.[93] In stage three, one member of the group emerges as leader.[94] As described by the gospel narrative, the Johannine communities appear to be in stage one (with its emphasis on group identity), moving toward stage two (with competition emerging among those vying for leadership). This may explain, in part, the ambiguous role of women within the gospel. In a study on the status of women in preindustrial society Martin K. Whyte observes that women's participation in the public sphere is greatest in those societies where there is a minimum of differentiation in social roles outside the family.[95] The lack of role differentiation in the description of the disciples in chs. 1–20 suggests that women were active participants in the communal life of

[91] Jane Schaberg offers an interesting proposal concerning "Magdalene Christianity" in her book *The Resurrection of Mary Magdalene* (New York: Continuum, 2002) 300–56.

[92] Dennis Duling, "'Egalitarian' Ideology, Leadership, and Factional Conflict within the Matthean Group," *BTB* 27 (1997) 131.

[93] Ibid. 132.

[94] Ibid.

[95] Martin K. Whyte, *The Status of Women in Preindustrial Society* (Princeton: Princeton University Press, 1978) 182.

the Johannine communities. However, as status differentiation began to occur (most evident in ch. 21), the roles of women became problematic, leading ultimately to restrictions. Additional support for this view comes from the work of Susanne Heine, who notes that the greater the pneumatic life of the community, the greater the degree of women's participation.[96] Within chs. 1–20, where the authority and guidance of the Spirit hold sway, women are indeed prominent and critical to the narrative.[97] Nonetheless, tensions are beginning to emerge. With the addition of ch. 21, where the role of the Spirit is supplanted by the shepherd (Peter) and written witness (the Beloved Disciple), the status of women is finally compromised. These events are anticipated in the Magdalene narrative, where the presence of Simon Peter and the Beloved Disciple fractures the text and alerts the audience that the community of disciples is beginning to fragment as first one and then another vies for leadership. Among the emerging leaders are Simon Peter and the Beloved Disciple, both of whom are known and remembered. In their midst stands another, also known, but often forgotten: Mary Magdalene. Her presence in the Gospel of John invokes the memory of communities of believers who have long since been displaced but who, through her story, continue faithfully to witness to disciples everywhere, "We have seen the Lord."

[96] Susanne Heine, "Eine Person von Rang und Namen: Historische Konturen der Magdalenerin," in Dietrich-Alex Koch, Gerhard Sellin, and Andreas Lindemann, eds., *Jesu Rede von Gott und ihre Nachgeschichte im frühen Christentum* (Gütersloh: Gerd Mohn, 1989) 191. See also François Bovon, "Le privilège pascal de Marie-Madeleine," *NTS* 30 (1984) 52; Ross S. Kraemer, *Her Share of the Blessings* (Oxford: Oxford University Press, 1992) 124.

[97] Eugene Boring observes a chain of revelation in the Gospel of John that is similar to that found in the book of Revelation. In Revelation the revelatory word passes from God to Jesus Christ to the angel to the servant, who passes the word on to the churches (Rev 1:1-14). In the Gospel of John the revelatory word takes the form of the Paraclete, who is sent from God the Father (14:26) and from Jesus (14:26) to the disciples (14:16) and to the world (16:8). ("The Influence of Christian Prophecy," 115–16).

Chapter Nine

Conclusion

What we remember, and why, is important for understanding who we are. This study of stories of a post-resurrection appearance to Mary Magdalene has been an effort to explore different ways in which the Magdalene stories were remembered by early Christian communities in order to give meaning to their present and reimagine their future. The stories were examined in three rhetorical contexts: the oral, storytelling environment of the world of antiquity, the Gospel of Matthew, and the Gospel of John. In each of these contexts, ways in which the storyteller gave shape to the story were analyzed, uncovering persuasive strategies by which the storyteller sought to influence the life and direction of particular communities. On the basis of this study, I conclude with the following observations and proposals:

1. Although we have inherited the Magdalene stories as written texts, it is probable that in the oral storytelling environment of the first century C.E. the tradition of a post-resurrection appearance to Mary Magdalene was more often heard as story than read as text. The written texts we have inherited (Matt 28:9-10; John 20:1-18; Mark 16:9-11) represent only three versions of a story that would take new shape as each storyteller introduced characters and dialogue into the narrative and engaged the audience through the reactions of the characters. While this oral storytelling environment, with the many versions of the Magdalene tradition it produced, is lost to us, it invites us to hear the versions we have inherited apart from their written contexts: to envisage different ways in which they might be framed, developed, and

encoded, and to imagine various ways in which they may have been heard. While such an undertaking must remain heuristic at best, it challenges us to hear the stories in relation to living communities of diverse persons.[1] This, in turn, may assist us in hearing the stories in relation to living communities of diverse persons today and remind us that the stories can never serve only one purpose or represent one set of interests. Even when we are in the position of storyteller, the stories may be heard and received in ways we could not begin to imagine.

2. The Magdalene stories were told in polemical contexts.[2] This is most apparent in the written texts we have inherited. In the Gospel of John the narration of the Magdalene story reveals competition between emerging leaders and those who supported them within Johannine communities. This competition may have reflected different commitments to how the risen Jesus was understood to be present in the community: i.e., through visionary and prophetic experiences (represented by Mary Magdalene), pastoral oversight (represented by Simon Peter), or written testimony (represented by the Beloved Disciple). It is evident from the addition of ch. 21 (the "appendix" to the gospel) that gender was introduced as one means of undermining those who aligned themselves with Mary Magdalene. In the Gospel of Matthew the narration of the Magdalene story engaged competition between prophets and teachers for the authority to "speak for Jesus." While gender appears to have been less obviously an issue here, women are not numbered among the "disciples" who, within the gospel narrative, receive the commission to teach. These polemical contexts remind us that, in each instance, the Magdalene stories were narrated as a means of persuasion. This invites us to consider why these stories were persuasively effective. In what ways did the storyteller give voice to the experience and interests of the audience through the stories? The polemical contexts also caution us to remember that in each instance the polemics engaged by the storyteller through the Magdalene stories remained unresolved. The storyteller's narrative was never more than a proposal an audience could accept or reject. We, who have the benefit

[1] John Miles Foley observes that the "audience has been written out of existence by decades of exclusively textual discourse" ("Words in Tradition, Words in Text: A Response," *Semeia* 64 [1994)] 172).

[2] This is not to imply that the Magdalene stories were told *only* in polemical contexts; however, these are the contexts I have chosen to focus on in this study, as indicated in the Introduction.

of hindsight, may point to later texts and trends and, with caution, find their beginnings in the gospel narratives, but the storytellers of the gospels could not see so far ahead. The written texts, therefore, offer us an opportunity to enter the moment of engagement and reflect upon whose interests are represented by the voice of the storyteller as well as whose interests are not, to weigh the arguments that are presented in the rhetorical structure of the narrative, to consider the historical contingencies that led the early church, ultimately, to favor one narrative over another, and to consider the consequences that have been played out in history by subsequent readings of the texts.

3. This analysis of the Magdalene stories in both their oral and literary contexts, and of the historical polemics toward which these contexts point, underlines the central role of women in Christian origins. The reconstruction of the oral storytelling environment in particular provides significant evidence that women were active in giving voice to and shaping the narratives of early Christian communities. This role needs to be more thoroughly investigated, as does the process by which "tradition" was shaped and molded by communities. Such an investigation may help us to restore women to their roles as agents, rather than subjects, in the narratives of early Christian communities and to understand the active role that women played in the formation and function of those communities. The present study has been an effort in that direction by demonstrating that, although the Magdalene stories can never be completely divorced from issues of gender, neither should they be limited to issues of gender in terms of their storytelling capacity.

In both the Gospel of Matthew and the Gospel of John, Mary Magdalene exhibits characteristics that each storyteller associates with discipleship. In both, she is a character against whom other characters are judged and whose behavior the audience is invited to emulate. These are not stories directed exclusively to women or addressing only the concerns of women. They are stories for the whole community. Among the concerns they engage are competition between named leaders and the groups that supported them, the emergence of roles such as prophet and teacher, distinctions between ways of experiencing the risen Jesus (such as visionary or scribal) and disputes surrounding who has the authority to "speak" for the risen Jesus. Recognizing that women were active participants in these concerns may help us to both see and hear women in texts and stories where we had not previously expected to find them. It should, unquestionably, challenge us to reconstruct our narratives of Christian origins so that the women are seen and their voices heard at the very heart of the struggle to be faithful in life and practice.

We are all storytellers to one degree or another, whether we are writing a story of Christian origins, reframing a story in a sermon, or weaving the text into the story of our lives. Although we may not always recognize them as such, our stories are acts of persuasion as we struggle to see our way through the polemics that define the path before us. Our stories are also acts of power, whether written or oral. Jonathan Draper observes, "There is always a power dynamic to [the written] text, since it freezes the Word and places it in the hands of interpretive experts."[3] On the other hand, Werner Kelber notes that in oral story the speaker is in charge of the text, setting the interpretive frame and shaping the story to his or her own ends.[4] Women, in times past and present, have often gravitated toward oral storytelling, sometimes because they could not read the written text, but perhaps more often because oral stories have allowed us to "give the silenced women of the Bible a voice, and . . . to claim [our] identity within [our] understanding of the message."[5] The result is sometimes a story in which characters act in new and different

[3] Jonathan Draper, "Confessional Western Text-Centered Biblical Interpretation and an Oral or Residual-Oral Context," *Semeia* 73 (1996) 75. In contrast, Paulo Fernando Carneiro de Andrade notes that in ecclesial base communities the shift from oral to written text has allowed for a plurality of interpretations, whereas the interpretation of the oral text remained in the control of a single person ("Reading the Bible in the Ecclesial Base Communities of Latin America: The Meaning of Social Context," in Fernando Segovia and Mary Ann Tolbert, eds., *Reading from this Place* [Minneapolis: Fortress, 1995] 2:239).

[4] Werner Kelber, *The Oral and the Written Gospel* (Bloomington: Indiana University Press, 1983) 93. While this often results in empowering women when they assume the role of storyteller, we should not assume that an "oral" environment always favors women. As Martin S. Jaffee reminds us, in a rabbinic setting oral texts represent "male elites' texts" ("Figuring Early Rabbinic Literary Culture: Thoughts Occasioned by Boomershine and J. Dewey," *Semeia* 64 [1994] 72).

[5] Ranjini Rebera, "Polarity or Partnership? Retelling the Story of Martha and Mary from Asian Women's Perspective," *Semeia* 78 (1997) 97. Kwok Pui-lan also describes how, in Asia, women are engaging the Bible through storytelling, dance, music, prayer, and testimony (*Discovering the Bible in the Non-Biblical World* [Maryknoll, N.Y.: Orbis, 1995] 52–53). Jonathan Draper, in his field work on interpretive processes among illiterate and semi-literate peoples in South Africa, observes that "the Bible does not operate primarily as printed text, but as a starting point for oral performance in the Christian community" ("Confessional Western Text-Centered Biblical Interpretation," 72–75).

ways.[6] For those of us who rely on the written text for our interpretive framework this oral storytelling environment may introduce a frightening "prospect of hermeneutical instabilities,"[7] and "rival interpretations."[8] Yet if this study of the Magdalene narratives has revealed anything at all, it is just this: that such hermeneutical instabilities and rival interpretations are precisely at the heart of our gospel narratives.[9] It may be that in the midst of this witness and counterwitness we may discern the voice of the gospel most clearly.

[6] Kwok, *Discovering the Bible in the Non-Biblical World,* 53.

[7] Kelber, *The Oral and the Written Gospel,* 93.

[8] Werner Kelber, "Jesus and Tradition: Words in Time, Words in Space," *Semeia* 65 (1994) 161.

[9] Ingrid Kitzberger observes: "Theology can no longer be considered in terms of 'content,' pre-existent and abstracted from the text, but should be more adequately conceived as part of the form, the rhetoric of the Gospel" ("'How Can This Be?' [John 3:9]: A Feminist-Theological Re-Reading of the Gospel of John," in Fernando Segovia, ed., *"What is John?" Volume II: Literary and Social Readings of the Fourth Gospel* [Atlanta: Scholars, 1998] 39).

Appendix A

Storytelling by Women in Greco-Roman Texts

Source and Storyteller	Audience	Setting	Story
Achilles Tatius *Leucippe and Clitophon* (8.15) Leucippe	men (her father, her beloved, a priest)	meal (in Temple)	not given
(8.16) Leucippe	men (her father, her beloved, a priest)	meal (in Temple)	personal narrative: story of prostitute who is disguised as Leucippe
Apuleius *Metamorphosis* (IV.27–VI.24) old woman	a young woman	countryside (camp of thieves)	story of Cupid and Psyche
(IX.17-22) old woman (a "gossip")	baker's wife	home	story about a local Senator and his unfaithful wife
Ovid *Metamorphoses* (IV.32–167) woman	women (sisters)	home, while spinning and weaving	story of Pyramus and Thisbe
(IV.168–273) woman	women (sisters)	home, while spinning and weaving	stories of the Sun's loves
(IV.274–388) woman	women (sisters)	home, while spinning and weaving	story of how Hermaphroditus came to have the body of both man and woman
(IX.285–325) woman	woman	home?	story of how she gave birth to Hercules
(IX.325–91) woman	woman	home?	story of her sister
(X.559–736) woman	her male lover	countryside	story of a woman who can marry only the one who can defeat her in a foot race
(XIII.738–898) nymph	woman	realm of the sea nymphs	story of how she was forced to accept the advances of Cyclops

Source and Storyteller	Audience	Setting	Story
(XIV.130–154) sibyl	man	journey	story of how she was denied eternal life because she spurned Phoebus' love
Plato *Laws* (X.887.D) mothers, nurses	children	home	not given, but described as stories about the gods
Plato *Republic* (II.377C) mothers, nurses	children	home	not given
Plutarch *On Educating Children* (5) nurses	children	home	not given, but it is said that they should be "tales of noble deeds"
Theseus (23.3) mothers	children	home	not given, but said to be told for purpose of comforting and encouraging
Xenophon *An Ephesian Tale* (3.9) old woman	men	inn	story about the untimely death of a young woman

Appendix B
Storytelling by Men in Greco-Roman Texts

Source and Storyteller	Audience	Setting	Story
Achilles Tatius *Leucippe and Clitophon* (1.2–8.18) young man (a stranger)	narrator (a man)	shrine (votive painting); narrator arrives at Sidon after a sea journey and is touring the city	story of Leucippe and Clitophon
(2.33-34) young man (a stranger and fellow traveler)	two men on a journey	a boat story told over breakfast	personal story of his ill-fated love for a young man
(2.34) man	fellow traveler	a boat story told over breakfast	not given
(8.5) narrator (a man)	men and one woman (his beloved)	Temple of Artemis narrative told over supper	summary story of personal adventures involving shipwreck and kidnapping
(8.15) man (a priest)	men and one woman (followed by stories told to one another)	Temple of Artemis narrative told over supper "as had become the customary manner"	not given
(8.17) man (father)	men and one woman	Temple of Artemis narrative told over supper	story of daughter's suitor
Apuleius *Metamorphosis* (I.5-19) man (a traveler)	man (a fellow traveler)	walking on the road	a "true" story of ill-fortune "circulating on everyone's lips" about death of a friend
(II.20-29) man (a dinner guest)	men and women	private residence banquet hosted by one of the town's leading women	personal story of how he came to lose his ears and nose
(IV.9-11) man (a thief)	men (fellow thieves); women within hearing distance	hideaway in country	personal story about robbing a householder

Source and Storyteller	Audience	Setting	Story
(IV.12) man (a thief)	men (fellow thieves); women within hearing distance	hideaway in country	personal story about robbing an old woman who outwits the robber
(IV.13-21) man (a thief)	men (fellow thieves); women within hearing distance	hideaway in country	personal story about three failed robberies resulting in the death of three comrades
(X.24) man (a baker)	woman (his wife)	home	story about the fuller and his wife
Dio Chrysostom *Oration* (20.10) entertainer (male)	general populace	marketplace	not given
Longus *Daphnis and Chloe* (2.32) old men	one another	drinking together	not given, described as stories of their youth
(2.33-34) man	men and women	over supper in open countryside	story of the god Pan
(3.9) men (and women; specifically a mother, father, daughter, and her beloved)	one another	private residence over supper	not given
Ovid *Metamorphoses* (III.582–691) man	man		personal story of how he came to be a follower of Bacchus
(IV.772–786) man	Ethiopian chiefs	banquet	personal story relating how he won the Gorgon's head
(IV.787) man	Ethiopian chiefs	banquet	not given, but described as personal narrative
(VII.517–660) man	man	house	personal story of how his kingdom was ravaged, then restored
(VII.675–862) man	man	banquet	personal story of how his marriage was destroyed

Source and Storyteller	Audience	Setting	Story
(VIII.617–726) man	comrades	house of the river god	story of how an old man and woman welcomed the gods in disguise
(X.793–803) man	Ethiopian chiefs	banquet	story of Medusa
(XII.169–535) man	men	banquet	story of Caeneus
(XII.536–579) man (a hero)	men	banquet	story of how Hercules slew the sons of Neleus
(XIII.635–74) man	man	banquet	personal story of how his daughters were turned into doves by Bacchus
(XIV.223–441) man	man		personal story about Ulysses
Suetonius *Augustus* (74) professional storytellers	men and women	banquets	not given
(78) professional storytellers	man (Emperor Augustus)	bedside	not given
Xenophon *Anabasis* (VII.iii.33) professional entertainers	general populace	marketplace	not given
An Ephesian Tale (5.1) two men	to one another	fisherman's hut	personal story about his deceased lover (female)

Appendix C

Storytelling in Jewish Texts

Source and Storyteller	Audience	Setting	Story
***b. B. Bat.* 133a-134b** "A tale is told . . ."	interaction between Rabbis within narrative		story of a man whose sons did not behave properly
***b. Bek.* 36a**	interaction between Rabbis within narrative	house of study *(setting within narrative)*	story of dispute over an answer given by R. Joshua
***b. Ber.* 16a-b** "A vignette about Rabban Gamaliel . . ."	interaction between Rabbi and his disciples within narrative	home (setting within narrative)	story of when Rabban Gamaliel got married
***b. Ber.* 16b** "A tale is told . . ."	interaction between Rabbi and his disciples within narrative	home (setting within narrative)	story of how the disciples of R. Eliezer visit him when his bondwoman dies
***b. Ber.* 27a-28a (= *y. Ber.* 4:1, 7c-d)** "Our masters taught . . ."	interaction between Rabbis, and between a husband and wife within narrative		story of how R. Gamaliel is removed and then reinstated in office
***b. Ber.* 28b**	interaction between Rabbi and his disciples within narrative	home (setting within narrative)	story of how the disciples of R. Yohanan ben Zakkai visit him when he is ill
***b. Ber.* 33a** "Our masters taught . . ."	interaction between Rabbi and people of the community within narrative		story about R. Hanina ben Dosa and a lizard
***b. Ber.* 34b** "It is said of R. Hanina ben Dosa . . ."			story about when he knew his prayer would be answered
***b. Ber.* 34b** "A story is told . . ."	interaction between Rabbi and two scholars within narrative		story about when the son of Rabban Gamaliel fell ill
***b. Ber.* 48a (= *y. Ber.* 7:2, 11b)** R. Simeon Ben Shetach	court of King Yannai	banquet	not given

Source and Storyteller	Audience	Setting	Story
***b. Ber.* 61b** "Our master taught . . ."			story about when the Romans forbade study and practice of Torah
***y. Beṣah* 3:8, 62b (= t. *Besa* 3:8)** "It is said . . ."			story of R. Eleazar bar Zadok and of Abba Saul ben Batnit
***b. Beṣah* 15b** "Our masters taught . . ."			story about R. Eliezer lecturing on the festival laws
***b. ʿErub.* 64b**	interaction between two Rabbis	journey (setting within narrative)	story of how R. Gamaliel and R. Ilai encounter a heathen while on a journey
***y. Giṭ.* 1:2, 43c** "A story is told . . ."	interaction between Rabbi and his wife within narrative		story of a certain disciple who gave a decision in front of his master
***b. Giṭ.* 58b** "Our masters taught . . ."			story about when R. Joshua ben Hananiah ransomed a child from prison
***b. Ḥag.* 14b** "Our masters taught . . ."	interaction between Rabbi and his disciple within narrative	journey (setting within narrative)	story of a Rabbi and his disciple on a journey
***b. Ḥag.* 14b**	interaction between two Rabbis within narrative	journey (setting within narrative)	story of R. Yohanan ben Zakkai and a disciple having a discussion while on a journey
***b. Hor.* 10a-b**	interaction between two Rabbis within narrative	journey (setting within narrative)	R. Gamaliel and R. Joshua meet on a ship
***b. Ketub.* 67a** "It is related of Hillel . . ."			story of how Hillel hired a horse for a poor man
***b. Ned.* 5:7, 39b**	interaction between Rabbi and disciples within narrative	home (setting within narrative)	story of how the disciples of Hillel visit him while he is ill

Source and Storyteller	Audience	Setting	Story
***b. Ned.* 50a**			story of the daughter of Kalba Shebuʿa, who married R. Akiba
b. *Ned.* 62a (= *y. Šebu.* 4:2, 35b) "It is related of R. Tarfon"	interaction between Rabbi and tenant within narrative		story of how he was accused of stealing grapes
***y. Peʾah* 1:1, 15c**	interaction between a woman and Rabbis within narrative	home (setting within narrative)	story of R. Tarfon's mother when disciples come to visit her son who is ill
***b. Pesaḥ.* 72b-73a** "It once happened . . ."	interaction between Rabbis within narrative		story about how R. Tarfon missed a meeting in the house of study
***b. Pesaḥ.* 112a**	interaction between father and son within narrative		story of how a father gives seven charges to his son
***b. Qidd.* 32b**	interaction between Rabbis within narrative	banquet (setting within narrative)	story of how the Rabbis discuss who is greatest
***b. Sanh.* 11a** "Our masters taught . . ."		upper room (setting within narrative)	story of the departure of the Holy Spirit from Israel
***b. Sanh.* 11a**		banquet in upper room (setting within narrative)	story about Samuel the Little
***b. Sanh.* 24b**	interaction between father and son, and between Rabbi and student within narrative	house of study (setting within narrative)	story of R. Eliezer ben Hyrcanus' desire to study Torah
***b. Sanh.* 101a-b** "Our masters taught . . ."	interaction between Rabbis within narrative	home (setting within narrative)	story of when four elders came to visit R. Eliezer while he was sick
***y. Šabb.* 6:1, 4d** "A story is told . . ."	interaction between husband and wife within narrative		story about the wife of R. Akiva and the wife of R. Gamaliel
***b. Šabb.* 30b-31a** "Our masters taught . . ."			story of two men who made a wager

Source and Storyteller	Audience	Setting	Story
***b. Šabb.* 134a** "R. Simeon ben Eleazar later related . . ."	interaction between Rabbis within narrative		story of when R. Meir was ill
***y. Soṭah* 1:4, 16d** "R. Zechariah the son-in-law of R. Levi would tell this story . . ."	interaction between husband and wife, and between Rabbi and woman within narrative	synagogue (setting within narrative) home (setting within narrative)	story of a woman who came to listen to R. Meir in the synagogue
***b. Sukkah* 27b** "Our masters taught . . ."	interaction between two Rabbis within narrative		story of how R. Eliezer was questioned on laws of Sukkah while in Galilee
***b. Sukkah* 28a** "Our masters taught . . ."	interaction between Rabbis within narrative	house of study (setting within narrative)	story of how R. Eliezer questioned on laws of Sukkah while in Galilee
***b. Taᶜan.* 19a, 23a** "Our masters taught . . ."			story of Honi the Circle Maker praying for rain
***b. Taᶜan.* 23a** "R. Yohanan said . . ."			story about Honi the Circle Maker
***b. Taᶜan.* 23a-b**	interaction between husband and wife within narrative		story of Abba Hilkiah, Honi the Circle Maker's grandson
***b. Taᶜan.* 24b-25a**	interaction between husband and wife within narrative	home (setting within narrative)	story of a miracle performed for R. Hanina ben Dosa's wife
***b. Taᶜan.* 25a** "Pelimo said: 'I saw that house and its beams projected about a cubit on each side'; and I was told: 'This is the house that through his prayer, R. Hanina ben Dosa framed with beams.'"	interaction between Rabbi and woman, and between neighbors within narrative		story of how Hanina ben Dosa framed a house through prayer
***b. Taᶜan.* 25a** "R. Phinehas said . . ."	interaction between husband and wife within narrative		a story about how R. Hanina ben Dosa came to have goats

Source and Storyteller	Audience	Setting	Story
***b. Ta*ʿ*an.* 25a**	interaction between father and daughter within narrative		story of when the daughter of R. Hanina ben Dosa mistook vinegar for oil
***b. Ta*ʿ*an.* 25b** "[Samuel the Little] said, 'I will tell you the parable of a servant . . .'"	people in the community		a servant who asks his master for a gratuity
***b. Yebam.* 16a** "It is taught . . ."	interaction between Rabbis within narrative	house of study (setting within narrative)	story of an encounter between Jonathan and R. Akiva
***b. Yebam.* 121b** "Our masters taught . . ."	interaction between father and daughter, and neighbors and Rabbi within narrative		story of a woman who falls into a pit
***b. Yoma* 35b**		house of study (setting within narrative)	story of how Hillel the Elder listened through skylight in order to study Torah
4 Macc 16:18-24 Mother	her sons		stories about Abraham and Daniel
4 Macc 18:6-19 Mother	her sons		stories about the father of her children

Appendix D

Storytelling in the Second Testament

Source and Storyteller	Audience	Setting	Story
Gospel of Mark (1:40 // Matt 8:2, Luke 5:12) unknown	leper	Galilee	not given, but implied: stories about Jesus' capacity to heal
(1:45 // Luke 5:15) man (a leper)	local community	Galilee	not given, but described as personal story about how Jesus healed him
(2:3 // Matt 9:2, Luke 5:18) unknown	friends of paralytic	Capernaum home (setting within narrative)	not given, but implied: stories about Jesus' capacity to heal
(2:15 // Matt 9:10, Luke 5:29) unknown	tax collectors and sinners	meal at home (setting within narrative)	not given, but implied: stories about Jesus
(4:2-8 // Matt 13:3-8, Luke 8:4-8) Jesus	crowds	shores of Sea of Galilee	parable of sower
(5:16 // Luke 8:36) those who saw demoniac healed	local community of Gerasenes	country of the Gerasenes	not given, but described as story about healing of demoniac
(5:20 // Luke 8:39) man (demoniac)	local community	region of the Decapolis	not given, but described as story about how Jesus healed him
(5:22 // Matt 9:18, Luke 8:41) unknown	ruler of synagogue	local community	not given, but implied: stories about Jesus' capacity to heal
(5:27 // Matt 9:20, Luke 8:43) (unknown)	woman with hemorrhage	local community	not given, but implied: stories about Jesus' capacity to heal
(6:14 // Matt 14:1, Luke 9:7) (unknown)	Herod	court of Herod	not given, but implied: stories about Jesus
(6:29 // Matt 14:12) unknown	disciples of John		not given, but described as story about death of John the Baptist

Source and Storyteller	Audience	Setting	Story
Gospel of Mark (7:25 // Matt 15:22) unknown	woman with daughter who is possessed	a house (setting within narrative)	not given, but implied: stories about Jesus' capacity to heal
(7:32) unknown	those who bring man who is deaf and dumb to be healed	region of the Decapolis	not given, but implied: stories about Jesus' capacity to heal
(8:22) unknown	those who bring blind man to be healed	Bethsaida	not given, but implied: stories about Jesus' capacity to heal
(8:27 // Matt 16:13, Luke 9:18) unknown	crowds ("who do people say that I am")	traveling to villages of Caesarea Philippi (setting within narrative)	not given, but implied: stories about Jesus
(9:17 // Matt 17:15, Luke 9:38) unknown	father of epileptic son	local community	not given, but implied: stories about Jesus' capacity to heal
(9:38 // Luke 9:49) unknown	man casting out demons in Jesus' name	home in Capernaum	not given, but implied: stories about Jesus capacity to heal
(10:17 // Matt 19:16, Luke 10:25; 18:18) unknown	man who desires to inherit eternal life	as Jesus sets out on journey (setting narrative)	not given, but implied: stories about Jesus as a wise teacher
(10:47 // Matt 9:27; 20:30, Luke 18:35) unknown	Blind Bartimaeus	Jericho	not given, but implied: stories about Jesus capacity to heal
(12:1-11 // Matt 21:33-42, Luke 20:9-19) Jesus	disciples	Jerusalem	parable of the vineyard
(14:3 // Matt 26:7) unknown	woman with alabaster jar	Jerusalem/meal	not given, but implied: stories about Jesus
(14:67 // Matt 26:69, Luke 22:56, John 18:25) unknown	serving girl in courtyard	Jerusalem	not given, but implied: stories about Jesus
(15:40 // Matt 27:55, Luke 23:49) unknown	women who follow Jesus	Galilee	not given, but implied: stories about Jesus
(15:43 // Matt 27:57, Luke 23:50, John 19:38) unknown	Joseph of Arimathea		not given, but implied: stories about Jesus

Source and Storyteller	Audience	Setting	Story
Gospel of Matthew (6:19–7:27 // Luke 6:39-49) Jesus	crowds	open space	parables
(8:5 // Luke 7:2, John 8:46) unknown	centurion	Capernaum	not given, but implied: stories about Jesus' capacity to heal
(8:19 // Luke 9:57) unknown	scribe	shore of Sea of Galilee	not given, but implied: stories about Jesus' capacity to heal
(9:32; 12:22) unknown	dumb demoniac	local community	not given, but implied: stories about Jesus' capacity to heal
(11:2 // Luke 7:18) unknown	John the Baptist	prison (setting within narrative)	not given, but implied: stories about Jesus
(12:24) unknown	Pharisees	local community	not given, but implied: stories about Jesus' casting out demons
(13:24-30, 36-50) Jesus	disciples	house	parables
(13:33 // Luke 13:20-21) Jesus	disciples	house	parable of leaven
(14:13) unknown	Jesus		not given, but described as story about death of John the Baptist
(21:28-32) Jesus	religious leaders	Temple	parable of two sons
(22:1-14 // Luke 14:15-24) Jesus	religious leaders	Temple	parable of banquet
(22:34) unknown	Pharisees	local community	not given, but described as stories about Jesus silencing the Sadducees
(28:12-14) unknown	populace	Jerusalem	stories about Jesus' disciples

Source and Storyteller	Audience	Setting	Story
Gospel of Luke (1:58, 65) (unknown)	neighbors and kinsfolk	local community	not given, but implied: story of John's birth
(7:40-42) Jesus	Simon (a Pharisee)	banquet in a home	riddle story
(8:2-3) unknown	Mary Magdalene, Joanna, Susanna, and other women		not given, but implied: stories about Jesus
(10:38) unknown	Martha	home (setting within narrative)	not given, but implied: stories about Jesus
(11:37) unknown	Pharisee who invites Jesus to dine with him	meal at home (setting within narrative)	not given, but implied: stories about Jesus
(14:1) unknown	ruler who is a Pharisee	meal at home (setting within narrative)	not given, but implied: stories about Jesus
(15:1-32) Jesus	Pharisees and scribes		parables
(16:1-9) Jesus	disciples		parable of dishonest manager
(17:13) unknown	ten lepers	journey to Jerusalem (setting within narrative)	not given, but implied: stories about Jesus
(18:1-8) Jesus	disciples		parable of the widow and the unjust judge
(18:9-14) Jesus	"some who trusted in themselves that they were righteous"		parable of the Pharisee and tax collector
(19:2-4) unknown	Zacchaeus	meal at home (setting within narrative)	not given, but implied: stories about Jesus
(24:13-24) two disciples who are traveling	to one another to Jesus	walking on the road	stories about Jesus' last days
(24:22-23) women	disciples	Jerusalem	not given, but implied: as a story about what happened when they went to the tomb
(24:35) two disciples	disciples	Jerusalem	not given, but described as a story about their encounter with Jesus on the road to Emmaus

Source and Storyteller	Audience	Setting	Story
Gospel of John (1:19) unknown	priests and Levites	Jerusalem	not given, but implied: stories about John the Baptist
(1:40-42) Andrew	Peter, his brother	local community	not given, but implied: story about Jesus
(1:45) Philip	Nathanael	local community	not given, but implied: story about Jesus
(3:1-2) unknown	Nicodemus	Jerusalem	not given, but implied: story about Jesus
(4:1) unknown	Pharisees		not given, but described as stories about Jesus baptizing
(4:39) Samaritan woman	local community	local community	not given, but described as story about her encounter with Jesus
(5:10-15) man healed by Jesus	local community	Jerusalem	story of his encounter with Jesus
(9:11, 15) man born blind	local community	Jerusalem	story of his encounter with Jesus
(12:20-26) unknown	Greeks		not given, but implied: stories about Jesus
(12:46) unknown	Pharisees	Jerusalem	not given, but implied: stories about Jesus
Acts of the Apostles (11:1-17) Peter	circumcised believers	Jerusalem	personal story of the conversion of the house of Cornelius
(21:19) Paul	Council of Jerusalem	gathering of the elders in Jerusalem	personal story about his travels and ministry
1 Corinthians (1:11) Chloe's people	Paul		not given, but implied as stories about people in Corinth
1 Timothy (5:13) women (widows)	(other women)	house	not given

Appendix E

Appearance Stories in Greco-Roman Texts

Source and Temporal Setting	Spatial Setting	Persons	Reaction	Words Spoken	Expansions
Dionysius *Roman Antiquities* (II.63.3)	Traveling on a road—coming from country to Rome	Julius Romulus		Spoken by Romulus: I am conducted to gods, having finished mortal life; my name is Quirinius.	Julius described as a husband, a man of blameless life, a descendent of Ascanius; Romulus described as fully armed
Livy *History of Rome* (I.16.5-7) Morning		Julius Proculus Romulus	Julius is confused; he prays	Spoken by Romulus: I declare that Rome shall be my capital; let them practice the art of war in order to teach that no one can defeat Rome.	Romulus descends and ascends
Ovid *Fasti* (II.500-508) Night (moon is shining)	Traveling on a road—coming from Alba Longa	Julius Proculus Romulus	Julius recoils; his hair bristles	Spoken by Romulus: forbid the Quintes to mourn; bid them worship me and cultivate art of war.	Romulus described wearing a fine robe; Romulus vanishes

Source and Temporal Setting	Spatial Setting	Persons	Reaction	Words Spoken	Expansions
Plutarch Romulus (XXVIII.1-3)	Traveling on a road	Julius Proculus Romulus	Julius is frightened	Spoken by Julius: Why have you left us? Spoken by Romulus: I was mortal only long enough to establish Rome; tell Romans to practice restraint so they can attain power; I will be your deity Quirinius.	Julius described as patrician of noble birth and blameless reputation; a colonist of Alba; Romulus described as arrayed in armor; expanded dialogue
Plutarch *Romulus* (XXVIII.4)	Traveling on a road	Travelers Aristeas of Proconnesus			

Appendix F

Appearance Stories in the Talmud

Source and Temporal Setting	Spatial Setting	Persons	Reaction	Words Spoken	Expansions
***b. Ber.* 39**	Traveling on a road	R. Yose Elijah		Dialogue on prayer and the exile of the Jews	Expanded dialogue
***b. B. Meṣiʿa* 83b-84a**		R. Ishmael Elijah		Dialogue on behavior of R. Ishmael	Expanded dialogue
***b. B. Meṣiʿa* 85b**	House of Study	R. Judah Elijah		Dialogue on those whose prayer is powerful enough to bring the Messiah	Expanded dialogue; Elijah is punished for revealing a secret.
***b. Ḥag.* 15b**		Rabbah bar R. Shila Elijah		Dialogue on the Holy One's recitation of the law in the name of R. Meir	Expanded dialogue
***b. Ketub.* 105b-106a**		R. Anan Elijah			A story of R. Anan's behavior as a judge leads to observation that Elijah was a frequent visitor up to that point; only after R. Anan prayed and fasted did Elijah return to him.

Source and Temporal Setting	Spatial Setting	Persons	Reaction	Words Spoken	Expansions
***b. Sanh.* 98a**	A cave entrance	R. Joshua ben Levi Elijah		Dialogue on entering the world to come	Expanded dialogue; Second scene interrupts dialogue in which R. Joshua visits Messiah.
***b. Soṭah.* 49a-b**	House of R. Joshua Prison Cave	R. Joshua Elijah		Elijah announces death of R. Akiva to R. Joshua	Non-recognition motif; Expanded dialogue; Scenes added in which R. Joshua and Elijah tend to burial of R. Akiva.
***b. Ter.* 8:4, 46b**		R. Joshua Elijah		Dialogue on why Elijah stopped visiting R. Joshua	A story of R. Joshua's urging Ulla to give himself up to Romans leads to second scene where Elijah appears only after R. Joshua has fasted; Elijah then chastises R. Joshua for his behavior.

Appendix G

Appearance Stories in the Second Testament

Source and Temporal Setting	Spatial Setting	Persons	Reaction	Words Spoken	Expansions
Gospel of Matthew (28:9-10) First day of the week	Traveling on a road	Mary Magdalene the other Mary Jesus	Women worship Jesus	Spoken by Jesus: God to my brothers; tell them they will see me in Galilee.	
(28:16-20) unspecified; sometime after the discovery of the empty tomb	Mountain in Galilee	eleven disciples Jesus	Some worship; some doubt	Spoken by Jesus: all authority given to me; you are to baptize all nations and teach all my commandments; I am with you always.	
Gospel of Luke (24:13-35) First day of the week	Traveling on a road Meal at Emmaus	Cleopas and an unnamed disciple Jesus Eleven disciples and those with them	Afterward the disciples report the their hearts "burned within us" while they were speaking with Jesus	Dialogue about events of recent days. Spoken by disciples: the Lord has risen and appeared to Simon.	Expanded dialogue; Non-recognition motif; Two additional scenes.
(24:36-53) First day of the week	Gathering of disciples in Jerusalem Bethany	Eleven disciples and those with them Jesus	Those gathered are startled and frightened	Spoken by Jesus: Why are you frightened? See my wounds; places events in the context of scripture; disciples are to be witnesses; Jesus will send power from on high.	Proofs are offered of Jesus' corporeality Additional scene.

Source and Temporal Setting	Spatial Setting	Persons	Reaction	Words Spoken	Expansions
Gospel of John (20:1-18) First day of the week	Garden Unspecified location where disciples are gathered	Mary Magdalene Jesus Disciples	Mary attempts to hold on to Jesus	Dialogue about Mary's distress over missing body; Spoken by Jesus: Go tell my brothers I am ascending; Spoken by Mary: I have seen the Lord.	Non-recognition motif; Expanded dialogue; Additional scene.
(20:19-23) First day of the week	Locked room in Jerusalem	Disciples Jesus	Disciples are glad	Spoken by Jesus: Jesus gives Holy Spirit and authority to forgive sins.	Proof of Jesus' corporeality
(20:26-29) Eight days after the discovery of the empty tomb	Locked room in Jerusalem	Disciples Thomas Jesus	Thomas confesses faith: "My Lord and my God."	Spoken by Jesus: invites Thomas to touch his wounds; "Blessed are those who do not see, yet believe."	Proof of Jesus' corporeality
(21:1-23) "After these things"	Sea of Tiberias	Peter, Thomas, Nathanael, sons of Zebedee, two other disciples; Jesus	Beloved Disciple immediately recognizes Jesus; Peter dives into the water and swims to shore.	Dialogue on fishing; Dialogue between Jesus and Peter: "Feed my sheep."	Expanded dialogue; Non-recognition motif; Demonstration of Jesus' power.
Longer Ending of Mark (16:9-11) First day of the week		Mary Magdalene Jesus Disciples			Description of Mary Magdalene Additional scene.

Index of Biblical and Ancient Sources

First Testament

Second Testament

Apocrypha and Pseudepigrapha

Josephus

Early Christian Apocrypha and Pseudepigrapha

Greek and Latin Texts

Inscriptions and Papyri